MORALITY & CONTEMPORARY WARFARE

MORALITY & CONTEMPORARY WARFARE

James Turner Johnson

Yale University Press New Haven and London

Published with assistance from The Mary Cady Tew Memorial Fund.

Designed by Gregg Chase. Set in Minion and Trade Gothic type by Keystone
Typesetting, Inc., Orwigsburg, Pennsylvania.
Printed in the United States of America by Vail-Ballou Press, Binghamton, New York.

Library of Congress Cataloging-in-Publication Data

Johnson, James Turner.
    Morality and contemporary warfare / James Turner Johnson.
      p.   cm.
    Includes bibliographical references and index.
    ISBN 0-300-07837-4 (alk. paper)
     1. War—Moral and ethical aspects.   2. Low-intensity conflicts
    (Military science)   I. Title.
    U21.2.J6324   1999
    172′.42—dc21   98-54952

A catalogue record for this book is available from the British Library.

10 9 8 7 6 5 4 3 2 1

CONTENTS

Acknowledgments   vii

Introduction   1

1 Politics, Power, and the International Order   8

2 Conditions for Just Resort to Armed Force: Just
   Cause, Competent Authority, and Right Intention
   in Historical and Contemporary Context   41

3 The Question of Intervention   71

4 War Against Noncombatants   119

5 Conflicts Inflamed by Cultural Difference   159

6 War Crimes and Reconciliation after Conflict   191

7 Conclusion:
   Reshaping and Affirming a Consensus on the
   Purposes and Limits of War   219

   Notes   229

   Select Bibliography   249

   Index   257

Acknowledgements

While this book, like *Can Modern War Be Just?* (published by Yale University Press in 1984) before it, seeks to explore present-day implications of a moral perspective on war grounded broadly in my historical work on just war tradition, the immediate antecedents of the present study are a number of invited lectures I have given over the past several years. These include "Just War Tradition and Low-Intensity Conflict" for a conference held at the United States Naval War College in April 1992; "Religion as a Source of Cohesion and Conflict" at a conference sponsored by the United States Institute of Peace in July 1993; "Ethical Issues in the International Use of Force in Support of Humanitarian Relief Efforts," given at a session of the Program on Humanitarian Assistance of the World Conference on Religion and Peace in September 1993; "The Just War Idea and the Ethics of Intervention," the Sixth Annual Joseph A. Reich Distinguished Lecture on War, Morality, and the Military Profession, given at the United States Air Force Academy in November 1993; two lectures, "Just War Tradition and the International Use of Force" and "Islamic Tradition on War, Peace, and Statecraft," given in the National Endowment for the Humanities Summer Institute on Ethics and International Affairs at the University of Virginia in June 1994; "Humanitarian Intervention: An Ethical Analysis" at the Calvin College Conference on International Morality in September 1994; and "The Concept of Just Cause in Contemporary Armed Conflict," given at a conference on Just War and the Cold War sponsored by the Ethics and Public Policy Center held in Washington in December 1996. While none of these lectures is reproduced in the present book, my analyses and arguments below build on lines of thought I first began to develop on these various occasions, and I am grateful to all the sponsoring organizations and to my debate partners on those occasions for leading me to reflect in a directed way on important moral issues related to contemporary armed conflict.

The actual writing of a full draft of the book was completed during the spring, summer, and fall of 1997. I am especially grateful for a grant from Earhart Foundation of Ann Arbor, Michigan, which facilitated the greater part of this writing during the summer of 1997.

In preparing this book I drew on the resources of two research libraries, Rutgers University's Alexander Library and Princeton University's Firestone Library.

In February 1998, I presented portions of earlier versions of chapters 3 and 6 at the University of Delaware, in lectures sponsored by the University and by the Wilmington World Affairs Council. In August 1998, while I was in the process of final revision, I presented parts of these same chapters and of chapter 4 in Oslo, Norway, in a series of lectures sponsored by the International Peace Research Institute of Oslo and the Ethics

Program of the Norwegian Research Council. I am thankful for these opportunities to test the thinking advanced in these chapters and appreciate the responses I received.

This book has also benefited greatly from a close reading and comments by Professor G. Scott Davis of the University of Richmond. I deeply appreciate the care he brought to this task.

Whatever faults readers may find in the analyses and arguments below, though, are my own, not those of any of my partners in dialogue on the occasions mentioned or in other contexts.

As always, I am deeply grateful to my wife, Pamela, for her support in this project and in life.

James Turner Johnson

August, 1998

MORALITY & CONTEMPORARY WARFARE

The nature of war changes continually, and the moral questions posed by one form of war often turn out to be less pressing in another, which in turn introduces its own particular quandaries. The shape of war may vary because of many factors, but among the most important of these are the kinds and amounts of weapons employed, the overall political context within which hostilities occur, and the character of the political communities that are drawn into belligerency—their wealth, their type of government, the presence or absence of links of commonality with the adversary, their relation to the goals of international order, and so on.

Since World War II, in American society, analysis of the moral issues involved in using military force has moved through three main stages, reflecting shifts in the nature of war as empirically perceived. The first stage, from the 1950s through the 1960s, focused principally on nuclear weapons, the possibility of their use in a World War II–like conflict between the United States and the Soviet Union, and deterrence aimed at avoiding such a war. The second phase, beginning in the late 1960s and continuing through the period of United States involvement in the war in Vietnam, centered on moral issues particular to that conflict, including the morality of intervention, the morality of methods of insurgency and counterinsurgency war, and (a question internal to the logic of moral analysis of war) whether the use of unjust means in fighting a war renders the war itself unjust. The rise of a vigorous anti-war movement during this conflict raised another issue to a position of primacy which it had not earlier held in moral debate: whether war as such is inherently immoral.[1] The overall political context surrounding this stage in American moral discussion of war remained that of United States–Soviet rivalry. While nuclear weapons and delivery systems continued to be developed, updated, and deployed, and the theory of deterrence continued to develop in policy circles, nevertheless, the focus of moral analysis was the experience of the war in Vietnam. During the 1980s, by contrast, a third stage in moral debate came into being, in which the priorities of moral analysis shifted back to the questions surrounding nuclear weapons, deterrence, and the possibility of nuclear war. While this debate in the main picked up on issues and lines of analysis and argument established where moral reasoning had left them at the end of the 1960s, an important new element was provided by the opposition to all war that had emerged as a major force in moral judgment on war during the Vietnam era.[2]

Such were the three main stages in American moral attention to the problems of warfare. To be sure, there were, during this period from the immediate aftermath of World War II to the end of the 1980s, other matters involving the use of armed force to which moral analysis occasionally turned an eye. In particular, during the 1970s and 1980s these included two connected phenomena: the growth of terrorist activity as a form of war directed against the United States and other Western countries and the rise of militant Islam as a destabilizing force in the Middle East. But the main focus of moral analysis never shifted to these or other issues in what came during the 1980s to be called "low-intensity conflict." The type of war that held its place at the center of moral analysis and debate in this latter period remained nuclear exchange between the United States and its NATO allies and the Soviet Union and its Warsaw Pact allies, a form of war routinely described as a "global nuclear holocaust."

Though nuclear weapons and other weapons of mass-destructive capability, including chemical and biological agents, continue to cast their shadow on future warfare, the characteristic shape that warfare has actually taken since the end of the cold war is quite different from that envisioned by the prophets of global holocaust. Contemporary warfare has in fact taken the form of local conflicts, more often than not civil wars, in which no great alliances of nations are involved; these have been wars fought for reasons based in local rivalries, typically inflamed by historical animosities, ethnic disparity, or religious difference, rather than for reasons of global *Realpolitik;* they have been fought not with nuclear weapons (or, indeed, other types of weapons of mass-destructive capability) or the latest in military technology, but instead with conventional weaponry, often of old design, and often limited to the rifles, knives, grenades, and light, crew-served weapons which individual soldiers can carry on their persons. A further feature of empirical contemporary warfare is that it involves face-to-face uses of military power by the participants against one another, not the remote destruction of distant, unseen, and often abstract targets.

This type of war brings to the fore its own moral problems, and the purpose of this book is to focus upon what I believe to be the principal moral issues connected with this form of war. Moral analysis has been slow to react to this changed empirical face of war, and when it has reacted, it has done so on the basis of dominant assumptions from the moral debate of the 1980s. Yet that debate, shaped by the threat of superpower nuclear conflict, led to forms of analysis and conclusions that are both inadequate and misleading as a guide to moral judgments about contemporary warfare. In this book I work from a more fundamental understanding of moral issues in the use of military force within the context of statecraft, seeking to address the particular problems posed by contemporary warfare from the perspective of just war tradition.

As compared to the two world wars of this century or a possible global nuclear war, contemporary armed conflicts are limited, low-level affairs; yet the moral problems they pose are both serious and distinctive. A major issue is that because these conflicts are often inflamed by ancient hostilities involving ethnic or religious differences, they commonly have involved the direction of armed force against the entire enemy population by one or both belligerents. Not only has this directly and intentionally caused great loss of life, but it has created much deprivation and fear among those who have remained alive; sometimes they have been left to starve in their homes, while at other times massive numbers of refugees have been created as noncombatants have been driven from place to place in search of food, shelter, and safety. The larger context of such conflict includes changes in the shape of the international order, an increased consciousness of divisions among peoples across major cultural fault-lines, and the erosion of limits on war established in moral tradition and international law.

The emergence of contemporary war as a form of war that does not involve large states and alliances or, at least up to the present, weapons with massively destructive capability returns the practice of war to a scale very much below that of the world wars and the global holocaust which many expected would result from the cold war. At the same time, some of the worst features of these earlier twentieth-century conflicts lie at the heart of contemporary warfare: the understanding of war as an all-or-nothing conflict that can end only when one side is entirely victorious and the other entirely vanquished or driven into unconditional submission; the conception of the enemy as including all members of the opposing society, making a distinction between combatants and noncombatants irrelevant; the use of atrocity as a means of war; the use of ethnic, religious, or other cultural differences in much the same way as ideology was earlier employed to make the enemy appear less than fully human and, in any case, totally in the wrong. In these respects, contemporary conflicts are total wars, though their scale is far below that of the great conflicts—actual and imagined—of the twentieth century.

Yet the past hundred years, it must not be forgotten, has also been the era in which international consensus coalesced into formal agreements limiting the resort to war, banning certain weapons and uses of otherwise accepted weapons, seeking to protect from the ravages of war whole classes of people not directly involved in the prosecution of war, and the institution of war crimes proceedings to punish persons guilty of egregious violations of these restraints. Indeed, the growth of formal efforts to restrain the incidence and destructiveness of war has directly paralleled the realization of war's increasingly devastating capabilities and the use of armed power during war to attack civilian noncombatants. To emphasize only cases in which these efforts at restraint have broken down, as the modern-war pacifist critique of war does,[3] is to tell only part of the story and to forget that the standard represented by the internationally agreed limits has in fact been widely honored. This is especially important for moral argument from the perspective of just war tradition, since, historically and thematically, these restraints deeply reflect the moral requirements set forth in that tradition. But it should be understood as important for other moral traditions from around the world as well, since the international agreements establishing the limits in question have been accepted globally.

The challenge to these limits on war posed by contemporary warfare should be met and turned back. There is nothing about the character of these wars that places them beyond the possibility of restraint. Indeed, some features of these conflicts, such as their limited scope and the relatively basic weapons used in them, fit standard definitions of limited war.[4] One of the major challenges posed by contemporary warfare is to deny or ignore the distinction between noncombatants and combatants and to attack noncombatants directly. This kind of assault on noncombatants is characteristically direct and intentional, and it is very clearly wrong, both morally and in international law. Ending it is, at root, a matter of a decision not to target noncombatants and the enforcement of this decision through command discipline and control. Lacking such a decision, there is strong reason for enforcement of noncombatant protection by war crimes proceedings, as initiated at the end of World War II and now under way for the conflicts in former Yugoslavia and Rwanda. As the elimination of the enemy population may itself be a war aim in conflicts driven by ethnic, religious, or other cultural difference, the idea that such differences can ever justify war must be attacked directly and rejected, as in the lesson which has guided main-line moral and political thought about war since the beginning of the seventeenth century: religious and other such differences provide no justification for war. Examining contemporary warfare from a perspective in just war tradition and drawing attention to the historical, thematic, and substantive connection between this tradition and international law relating to armed conflicts, I argue the importance of just war tradition for the practice of national and international statecraft and the goal of international order. In treating contemporary warfare, I focus on four distinct types of moral problems: those associated with military intervention as a response to great humanitarian need caused by local conflict, those arising from warfare systematically directed against noncombatants, those having to do with the role of major cultural differences between warring parties, and those encountered in the tension between efforts to punish war criminals and efforts to reintegrate societies torn apart by armed conflict. I argue throughout for a reaffirmation of the moral consensus as to the proper limits on war defined in just war tradition and stress the importance of international law on armed conflicts and on human rights as deeply consistent with the moral requirements of just war.

The problems posed by contemporary war are both particular to it and similar to problems already experienced and addressed in moral reflection on other wars. The overall task of the discussions that follow, then, is to bring the moral tradition of just war to bear on contemporary war so as to identify its particular injustices and to advance an argument as to how to respond to them and seek to remedy them.

1

The Need for a Renewed Moral Debate
The Legacies of Vietnam and Fear of Nuclear Holocaust

It is generally accepted that the end of the cold war found policymakers ill prepared to deal with the conflicts and associated problems that have since erupted. Less widely remarked upon, but equally striking, has been a perhaps even greater lack of readiness for this new era in applied moral reasoning related to politics, power, and the international order. The reason in both cases is the same: the legacy of preoccupation by policymakers and moral analysts alike with the United States–Soviet rivalry, and in particular with how to manage this relationship so as to limit the threat of catastrophic nuclear war between these superpowers and their allies. The face of contemporary war, though, has proven to be not a superpower nuclear exchange, but civil wars, conflicts between regional powers, and criminal activity across international boundaries involving organized use of violent force. The task of limiting and terminating such armed strife and alleviating its consequences is not illuminated by political and moral doctrine on nuclear deterrence, however sophisticated such doctrine might be. Nor can ad hoc efforts of policymakers and ethical theorists to address particular crises substitute for more broadly gauged reflection and public debate on the implications of this changed reality for an understanding of politics, power, and the international order.

For Americans, to embark on such reflection and debate will inevitably recall the last major public discussion over morality and nonnuclear uses of power, that occasioned by the Vietnam War. As argued in the Introduction above, the moral debate over this war represents one of three discrete stages in recent moral analysis and argument over war. While the legacy of Vietnam, with all the pain attached to it, continues to cast a shadow over efforts to think about military involvement in low-level conflicts, the Vietnam debate produced only limited, and often problematical, moral guidance for dealing with the conflicts of the post–cold war age. That debate was cast in a very different sociopolitical context, that of United States–Soviet rivalry, and was accordingly heavily shaped by a dominant conception of the war in strongly bipolar terms, both by the policy community and by the majority of those who sought to apply moral wisdom to it. In addition, both these groups were themselves sharply divided into two camps in their approaches to the war, one committed to opposing it and finding arguments against it, the other committed to prosecuting the war and finding justifications for doing so.

Nonetheless, the debate over the Vietnam War raised to view certain issues of central importance for reflection on the use of military force in the present context. These important issues include the role of third-party states, alliances, and the international community in regional conflicts, including civil wars; the question of when and under what conditions military intervention in such conflicts may be justified; whether it is possible in such warfare to fight according to the established international laws of armed conflict; and how to define international responsibility for protection of the victims of such conflicts. These are in fact central themes treated in this book, and in treating them I will make use of the thought of two major ethical writers who contributed to the debate over the Vietnam War, Paul Ramsey and Michael Walzer. Neither was a captive of the bipolar conception of international politics that then ruled in the political arena and much of the moral debate, and thus what they argued has much broader application than to the Vietnam conflict alone. Also important is that both worked out of a moral framework shaped by the just war idea, as I do in this book, though they differed significantly in how they understood this idea and drew out its implications.

With the end of American involvement in the war in Vietnam, the specific kinds of ethical reflection it had occasioned on force, politics, and international relations quickly diminished along with other forms of the public debate over the war. By the early 1980s policy analysis on the possibility of war had developed so as to address five kinds of circumstances that might lead the United States to use military force: war between the superpowers involving use of strategic nuclear weapons, armed conflicts (in particular a war in Western Europe between NATO and Warsaw Pact forces) involving tactical/theater nuclear weapons, a conventional armed conflict between established powers in which the superpowers might become involved, insurgency or revolutionary conflict employing conventional weapons but outside the normal rules of war between nations, and international terrorist activity that might evoke a military response.[1] As I have already noted in the Introduction, ethical analysis and argument in the post-Vietnam era focused chiefly, if not entirely, on the questions of nuclear deterrence and the use of nuclear weapons, tactical or strategic, in a possible armed conflict.

Though developed in the context of the superpower rivalry, the debates within the policy and military communities during this period were often broadly oriented and multi-textured, with the military community in particular treating ethical questions with deep interest and sophistication. While the central focus in both policy and military circles continued to be on potential nuclear conflict between the United States and the Soviet Union, during this period civilian and military analysts paid considerable attention to conflicts at the other end of the spectrum and how to deal with them under the "nuclear umbrella" without precipitating superpower nuclear war. Thus, throughout the 1980s and into the decade of the 1990s, Department of Defense analysts paid considerable attention to developing policies and procedures for low-intensity conflict, a rather broad concept that included support for non-Communist forces in Central America, the Grenada and Panama incursions, and use of military assets against the traffic in drugs.[2]

During this same period, though, the central concern of religious and philosophical ethical analysis was clearly nuclear weapons and the possibility of nuclear war, a concern epitomized in official statements by the bishops of two of the largest American religious bodies: first, in early 1983, the American Catholic bishops' pastoral letter, *The Challenge of Peace,* and three years later the United Methodist Church bishops' *In Defense of Creation.*[3] Both statements focused on ethical problems posed by nuclear weapons and the superpower relationship: deterrence, the arms race, and "the global threat of nuclear war."[4] Indeed, both these documents, as well as much other moral opinion in what turned out to be the last decade of the

*attends only
to bi-polar
war*

cold war, understood the nature of modern war unidimension-
ally as indiscriminately destructive nuclear war, so reprehensible
and so necessary to avoid that the Catholic document begins by
declaring a "presumption against war" and rules out "offensive
war of any kind" as ever morally justifiable.[5] The analysis of
these pastoral letters, as well as most of the response they generated, paid no attention to the empirical reality that other sorts of
conflict, not involving nuclear weapons and not directly involving the superpowers, had in fact become the characteristic form
of "modern war." Thus the two pastoral letters, along with much
other ethical analysis during the 1980s, turned away from the
particularly difficult problems posed by insurgency, covert activity, civil war, and ideologically charged conflict that held central place in policy planning for low-intensity conflict.

Reading and Responding to the Contemporary Context

In a very short span of time, the end of the cold war, the
collapse of the Warsaw Pact, and the breakup of the Soviet
Union revealed the limitations of ethical and policy positions on
military force that dealt mainly or exclusively with the threat
of superpower nuclear war. While the nuclear arsenals of the
United States and the former Soviet Union still remain capable
of creating global catastrophe, and despite the threat posed by
the proliferation of nuclear weapons to nations with unproven
records of nuclear responsibility, the superpower rivalry is no
more, and former enemies now embrace, in the name of peace,
democracy, cooperation, and economic growth. The shape of
ethical analysis has changed as well. In a sequel to *The Challenge
of Peace* published ten years after the original, the American
Catholic bishops, while reiterating their concern over the threat
of nuclear weapons, gave new emphasis to "the illusion and
moral danger of isolationism" and called for greater United

States involvement in a range of activities aiming, among other things, at "securing human rights," "assuring sustainable and equitable development," and "restraining nationalism and eliminating religious violence."[6] In an even more striking change from the earlier document's pervasively negative judgment regarding a role for resort to military force in the contemporary world,[7] the new statement explicitly accepted the possibility of justified intervention by military force in ongoing conflicts to achieve "humanitarian objectives" and establish "conditions necessary for a just and stable peace."[8] Other voices as well, previously raised in opposition to the use of military force in international affairs, now call instead for interventionary military involvement in the name of high moral causes such as those named by the Catholic bishops, particularly the causes of providing humanitarian relief and securing human rights.

Responding to external and internal pressures, the United Nations has expanded the nature and role of its involvement in conflicts and its peacekeeping operations to meet such concerns. While United Nations peacekeeping has traditionally been limited to conflicts in which the warring parties have reached a cease-fire and invited the United Nations forces in, various recent developments have represented an attempt to do much more.[9] UNPROFOR (the United Nations Protective Force) in Bosnia labored in the middle of an ongoing war and was given missions earlier not thought to be the responsibility of United Nations peacekeeping forces, including protection of relief convoys and interventionary action to rescue victims of firefights. UNOSOM (the acronym means United Nations Operation in Somalia), inserted in Somalia without formal invitation from a recognized government because the government had fallen apart, never focused on traditional peacekeeping but from the first was involved in protecting and convoying humanitarian

13

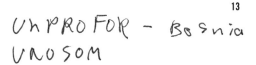

Bosnia
Somalia

relief efforts. After the arrival of American troops, elements of UNOSOM took on the task of the rebuilding of civil society, and for a time in 1993 the United Nations also attempted to take on the role of a criminal justice system, using UNOSOM (or more precisely, US troops in the capital city of Mogadishu) in an effort to hunt down and arrest General Farah Aidid, head of one of the chief warring clans. Finally, the United Nations has also utilized regional defense alliances, notably NATO in the former Yugoslavia and the alliance of Gulf States at the time of the Iraqi invasion of Kuwait, for purposes of military enforcement aimed at repairing breaches of international order—tasks well outside the core mandate of such organizations.[10]

Viewed in the most positive light, such developments may be regarded as welcome signs of a greater willingness among the nations of the world and their leaders to cooperate to create a genuine international order, bring an end to violent conflicts, increase protection of human rights, and stimulate the growth of new civil societies based on the democratically expressed will of the people in place of despotic or anarchic societies marked by violence and oppression. From this perspective, the United Nations is precisely the agency that should take the lead in mobilizing efforts toward these ends. Regional defense alliances like NATO, as well as national military establishments, are properly to be redirected to such worthy ends, rather than serving purely national interests.[11] On this view, decisions for military and other forms of intervention to bring an end to armed conflicts, provide humanitarian relief, protect human rights, and establish peaceful civil societies should not have to depend on the expressed willingness of the conflicting parties to welcome arbitrators or peacekeeping forces and to exercise self-restraint in pursuing their own ends in the conflict in question. Rather, international, or even national, third parties may intervene proactively, even by means of military force, to compel the conflicting parties to end their warfare and to reach a peaceful settlement of their dispute. This somewhat too rosy view of recent historical developments leads to a vision of the world as one in which military force operates rather like a domestic police force, and nations, far from being locked in a Hobbesian state of "war of all against all," can work together to resolve their differences like good citizens of a growing global order.

The same recent developments can, however, be viewed in terms of a less idealistic and more chastened view of international politics in the contemporary world. While I will argue below that the recently changing (and not yet settled) roles of the United Nations, regional security organizations, and individual states can be examined and assessed in the context of thinking in just war terms about politics, the use of force, and international order today, it is important not to confuse the goals of good politics (including international cooperation, restraining unjust violence, protecting human rights, and establishing just civil order) with the instrumentalities that might be used to serve these goals (for example, a stronger UN, use of regional defense establishments or even national military forces as proactive police forces), which may be ethically appropriate or not depending on the specific context. No particular instrumentality is inherently good in itself, and all must be tested continually against the goals of good politics.

When particular historical means are assimilated to ideal goals, the result is a form of utopianism in politics. This is the problem in contemporary concepts of world order that deprecate individual states and the state system, view an increased role for the United Nations as a sign of historical progress, and at the extreme envision the strengthening of the United Nations into a form of centralized world order as an end in itself. The classical

international institution or instrument

vs Kant

model for such world-order utopianism is that of the "perpetual peace" movement which developed in Western Europe during the Enlightenment era. While the theorists of this movement differed among themselves on many details, they shared a suspicion of the state and a positive conception of international government as the means to eradicate the evils of politics, which they identified as inherent in the state system.[12] The perpetual peace movement was, in turn, a secularized expression of a Christian theology of history that can be traced back through the Middle Ages to the fourth-century *City of God* of St. Augustine of Hippo. The secular utopianism of the perpetual peace movement and its contemporary successors, however, embodies a view of the forces of history very much at odds with that of the Augustinian tradition and far closer to the spirit of the romantic ideal of progress. From the standpoint of Augustinian theology, world-order utopianism is a form of idolatry. It is also profoundly unrealistic. At the very least, it is necessary to say, against world-order utopianism, that there is a real and lasting void between the ideal goal of a peaceful, secure, just, and stable world order and the present institutions and means that are embraced as furthering that goal. The most fundamental divide, in terms of moral analysis, is the great difference between the Augustinian theology of history, according to which God's grace is understood as invisibly and inexorably transforming a fallen world into the City of God, and the secularized philosophies of history that undergird the utopian vision of world order found in the perpetual peace movement and in present-day idealism about the possibilities of international cooperation in the wake of the cold war.

Indeed, while an Enlightenment-era conception of perpetual peace such as Kant's had a coherent philosophy of history as its base, contemporary post–cold war support for the goals of an ideal international order is less well thought through. If God is not the motive force for transforming the world (as Augustine thought), then a contemporary secular entity such as the United Nations, NATO, or even the United States acting alone must take God's place as the motive force in history; this is a tall order indeed! Moreover, while Augustine, writing in faith that a transformation was happening though it could not be seen, could accept historical reversals like the fall of Rome to the Vandals, the secular utopian expects to see positive results, even if only incremental ones, from actions taken. Things *must* get better in the here and now; it is not enough to have faith that all will work out at the end of history, in God's own good time. This places a heavy burden on institutions like the United Nations, NATO, or the government of the United States, and on means like peacekeeping, conflict resolution, humanitarian relief initiatives, police actions, and interventionary efforts to build civil societies, which may be invoked even when too much is being asked of them.

Another problematical element in the recent upsurge of approval of international activism in support of high values is that the moral backing for the kinds of actions indicated seems often to go no further than an expression of outrage at the evils that are to be combated. When the outrage disappears or gets redirected, the moral support quickly fades. Recent history is full of examples. Strong public opinion, fueled in no small degree by moral outrage, propelled the United States into military action against Iraq in the Gulf War and then, almost equally rapidly, evaporated, leaving new expressions of moral sentiment against the harm the war (and especially American military action) had done. Similarly, strong public feeling, fueled by moral outrage at television and newspaper pictures of starving children, fed the political decision to insert American military units in Somalia in order to protect humanitarian relief efforts and thus succor the

17

victims of that conflict; yet, very quickly, the tide of public opinion and moral outrage turned against the Somalia operation, so that it became politically untenable for American troops to remain even in this humanitarian role. Likewise, public opinion and moral outrage, focused by reports of atrocities in the name of ethnic cleansing and by pictures of children and adults who lost limbs or lives in the siege of Sarajevo, fueled the call for American military intervention there to end the fighting and undergirded the decision to insert NATO troops, including a large American force, as peacekeepers after the Dayton Accords. Yet there is nothing to keep public opinion and moral outrage from reversing course yet again should circumstances change, in particular if American military personnel should begin to suffer casualties or lose their lives.

While alone it is not sufficient, moral outrage may be a proper component of ethical judgment. Throughout *Just and Unjust Wars* Michael Walzer consistently relies on examples illustrating that the judgments underlying moral restraints on war are rooted in experiences of repulsion, outrage, and rejection in the face of particular horrors of war. Yet, as *Just and Unjust Wars* also makes clear, moral outrage at a particular horror is by itself not enough; this has to be integrated into a larger system of moral judgment including such fundamental ideals as justice and fairness. The horrible events and actions confronted in war must be divided between those evil in all respects and those that can be set into a relationship of priorities along with other relative evils. When this is done, one may still be outraged at a particular horror of war, yet may morally accept it in order to avert or control a worse evil. In traditional just war language, the *jus in bello* principles of discrimination (avoidance of direct, intended harm to noncombatants) and proportionality of means (use of means not more destructive than necessary to

Moral war, i.e. the
Moral resort to evil to
prevent greater evil
POWER AND THE INTERNATIONAL ORDER

achieve a justified end) provide parallel and mutually supporting approaches to setting such acceptance in a moral frame.
Walzer employs both principles in his discussion of "War's
Means, and the Importance of Fighting Well" (chap. 8). Every
moralist, indeed, must address the problem of how to place the
destructiveness of war—and outrage at this destructiveness—in
a frame that also acknowledges the values that war may protect
and the worse evils it may avert. While constructing or illustrating a full theory of morality competent to undergird judgments
balancing lesser and worse evils or the destructiveness of war
against the good it accomplishes is not the purpose of the media
when they show images of casualties of an exploding bomb or
shell in a street or a marketplace or an apartment house, it *is* the
role and responsibility of those who would have moral judgments matter in international affairs. Lack of attention to the
full dimensions of this responsibility leads to confusion about
the implications of morality regarding the use of military force
and the shaping of proper policy in the post–cold war age. Thus
the tendency of a shifting focus of outrage to displace other
elements in ethical judgment points to the need for a rebirth of
sustained ethical reflection and debate on the nature and role of
military force as an instrument of national policy and international order in the contemporary age.

Realism versus Just War Reasoning

For many policy theorists the only relevant theoretical framework has long been that of realism, with its reliance on national
interest as the ultimate lodestar for piloting the ship of state. For
realists moral concerns are understood as expressions of idealism
that have no place in the nation's policy or actions unless they
have been transmuted into the metal of national interest. From
this perspective the quest for human rights, for example, may or

may not be a proper element in the making of policy and in national decision making; it depends on whether in the case in question seeking respect for human rights serves the national interest. The same can be said for efforts to provide humanitarian relief, to support international law, or to end a civil war. Realists generally have dismissed the idea of world order as hopelessly utopian and support for the United Nations as undermining pursuit of the national interest. In principle, though, realism might imply support for the idea and institutions of world order, so long as such support furthered our national interest. On this view, ideals like world order and human rights are tools to be made use of when advantageous to be and avoided when harmful.

The concept of the national interest is by definition a guide that is dependent on outcomes. If a particular policy or action results in an outcome that is detrimental to the national interest, then it should not have been chosen. To be at its best, then, realism requires a stable historical context which allows for predictability. In conditions of instability, either internal to a nation or in relations among nations, it may not be possible to define accurately what the national interest requires, and accordingly a stable policy for dealing with the instability is not likely to come into being. Realism was well equipped to deal with the stable bipolar reality of the cold war era and with the stability of the nuclear deterrence relationship between the United States and the Soviet Union. The era of change ushered in by the end of the cold war has produced historical instability as the formerly Communist world has broken apart from ethnic, religious, and nationalistic stresses, leading in numerous cases to armed conflicts that have proven the more intractable because of a noted lack of predictability in the effects of policies and actions framed with an eye to the bipolar regime. Indeed, what realism required in the former context—for example, the West's refraining from military intervention at the time of the Hungarian revolution of 1956—may lead to bad policy under post–cold war conditions—for example, the West's reluctance to intervene militarily in the conflicts over the breakup of former Yugoslavia, though doing so might have avoided the worst effects of "ethnic cleansing" and violation of the rights of non-combatants. Whatever its merits may have been in the cold war era, realism is a much less dependable guide to national and international policy in the world as it now is.

Neither utopianism, moral outrage, nor realism provides a useful guide to politics, power, and the international order in the post–cold war era. Both a broader theoretical context for moral judgments and a deeper historical context for policy formulation and decisions are needed. In this book I will argue for a theory of statecraft rooted in just war tradition as responding to both needs and providing principled guidance for both moral judgment and policy. Michael Walzer, underscoring the importance of this tradition in the preface to *Just and Unjust Wars,* linked it directly to common moral understandings and described his task in that book as consciously "to recapture the just war for political and moral theory."[13] Paul Ramsey, whether writing on Vietnam or on nuclear weapons and deterrence, drew on a specifically Christian theory of just war which he argued is implied by the Christian duty to love one's neighbor.[14] Stanley Hoffmann, in *Duties Beyond Borders,* associating the term "just war" with its specifically medieval form, went on to reinvent a contemporary theory of just war point by point, without calling it that.[15]

Indeed, much can be said for the already existing presence and influence, recognized and unrecognized, of just war tradition in contemporary national and international institutions.

International law is historically rooted in this tradition and represents one of the streams of doctrine and practice through which the tradition is influential during the modern era. Rules of engagement for United States and other national forces reflect just war tradition through being in accord with international law, and they may also embody this tradition through its presence in military customs and past practice in war.[16] The influence of just war thinking on United States policy and practice can be seen in the 1983 "Weinberger doctrine," "Six Conditions for Committing United States Military Forces," and in the public debate before and after the Gulf War.[17] James F. Childress has argued that the just war criteria as a whole reflect simply the way people in Western culture think about war and the use of force for political reasons.[18]

Up to now, however, as noted earlier, just war reasoning has largely been focused, like other forms of reasoning about morality, politics, and force, on the problems of the cold war, especially nuclear weapons and deterrence. It is now time to draw out the meaning of this tradition for morality and statecraft in the post–cold war era.

Thinking in Just War Terms
Understanding Just War Tradition

Because of the breadth of just war tradition, there are various ways of thinking in just war terms. In *The Challenge of Peace* the American Catholic bishops employed the concept of just war as a moral theory with roots both in natural law and in Christian theology, but developed and given definitive form by Catholic moral teaching.[19] Protestant theologian Paul Ramsey, who more than any other single theorist deserves credit for bringing a coherent theory of just war to bear in American moral debate through his writings in the 1960s, derived that theory ultimately from reflection on the implications of love of neighbor as developed in classical Christian thought.[20] When in debate with the secular policy community, however, Ramsey spoke of the just war criteria as inherent in the idea of good politics itself, and thus not particularly Christian but arising from the common moral wisdom of humankind.[21] In a similar vein, Michael Walzer developed his understanding of just war as a set of ideas ("the theory of aggression" and "the war convention") generated out of common human experience of the reality of war and reflection on that experience.[22]

My approach, both in my previous work and here, is to focus on the tradition of just war as a body of moral wisdom deeply and broadly rooted in Western ideals, institutions, and experiences. Developed over history as a result of contributions from both secular and religious sources, reflecting the practice of statecraft and war as well as moral and political theory, this tradition has found different expression in various cultural contexts. Its importance as a guide for ethical judgment in matters of statecraft follows from its character as a synthesis of idealist and realist elements from many contexts. To be sure, this tradition has been significantly shaped by religious and philosophical elements, and until the modern period all the major benchmark just war theorists were theologians or canon lawyers. Yet, along with the contributions of Christian thought and practice and of philosophical reasoning, there are others, also of major importance: influences from secular law both domestic and international, from the traditions of military life and the experience of war, and from the practice and customs of statecraft. Philosophy has helped to shape just war tradition, not only as a distinct stream of thought, but as a mode of reasoning attached to religious, legal, military, and political discourse. Dialogue and mutual influence among the various streams has also been

Table 1
Sources and Development of the Just War Tradition

Late classical era: deep roots, early expressions
The Bible (Old and New Testaments)
Roman law and practice
Christian theology: writers such as Clement of Alexandria,
Ambrose, Augustine

Medieval era: coalescence of a cultural consensus
Canon law: Gratian's *Decretum*, writings of the Decretists and
Decretalists
Scholastic theology
The code and customs of chivalry
Customary rights and practices of sovereigns
The inherited idea of *Jus Gentium* (Law of peoples or nations)

16th to 18th centuries: consolidation, transformation, differentiation
Transformation to natural-law base: Victoria, Suarez,
Grotius, others
Theory of international law: Grotius, Pufendorf, Vattel, others
Military codes of discipline replacing chivalric code
Limited war theory and practice: "Sovereigns' wars"

19th century: further definition within distinct streams
Customary international law
First Hague Conference
Origin of Geneva Conventions
Military manuals on the law of war
Popular, philosophical, and religious efforts to restrain or end war

20th century: elaboration and growing interaction
Positive international law:
Jus ad bellum: League of Nations covenant, Pact of Paris,
UN Charter
Jus in bello: Arms limitation treaties and conventions, growth of
humanitarian international law
Military manuals on law of war, rules of engagement
Religious and philosophical recovery of just war concepts
Public debate over war, its meaning and effects

important in shaping the tradition as a whole. At times specifically Christian versions of just war reasoning, such as those of
contemporary thinkers like Ramsey and the American Catholic
bishops, have developed in interaction with one or more of the
other streams of the developing tradition, either influencing or
being influenced or both; at other times such Christian thought
has developed mainly in dialogue with its own internal concerns. The same is true of all the other individual streams, each
considered on its own.

The history of development of just war tradition is accordingly complex (see table 1). But recognizing this complexity is a
way to keep in mind that international law, military guides to
conduct in war, and political conceptions of the place of the use
of force and when it is authorized all historically and thematically help to make up the broad just war tradition alongside
more specifically moral and religious elements. Just war reasoning about the use of force is not properly understood as a collection of abstract moral ideals, alien to political judgments or
military thinking and imposed from outside. By its very nature,
the just war approach to the ethics of the use of force is already
in dialogue with the spheres of statecraft and military affairs.
That there are differences of content and emphasis and tensions
among the various approaches encompassed in just war tradition is also the case, however, and this necessitates an ongoing
and sustained dialogue as the means of developing moral meaning out of the tradition for contemporary issues. Indeed, this
has been true for every period, and the tradition as a whole
reflects the experience of such interaction and dialogue over
history up to our own time.

The purposes of just war reasoning, on this broad conception, have been defined by three levels of practical moral concern: the needs of statecraft, of the responsibilities of command,

Table 2
Purposes of the Just War Tradition

A guide to statecraft
>Theory of the use of force by the political community
>Understanding of the moral qualities of political leadership
>Protection of fundamental rights and values
>Relation of ends to means in political life.

A guide to commanders
>Relation of military command to authority/purposes of political
>community
>Understanding of the moral qualities of military leadership
>Protection of fundamental rights and values in situations of
>armed conflict
>Moral limits on means and methods in conflict situations

A guide to the consciences of individuals
>Claims on moral consciousness of individuals at all levels of
>political and military life
>Definition of responsibility in relation to the use of force by the
>political community
>Definition of the individual's rights and responsibilities in the use
>of force

and of the individual moral agent (see table 2). In the first of
these respects it provides, as Paul Ramsey has argued, a theory
of statecraft that takes account of the connection between force
and politics, establishing criteria for determining when the use
of force for social goods is justified and when it is not, and
setting limits beyond which the justified use of force ought not
to go. In the second respect, just war tradition provides guidance to military commanders, placing their role and responsibilities in a larger context of value to be served by the forces at
their command and locating their right to apply such force in
relation to the ends rightly sought and the destruction of values
to be avoided. Finally, at the level of the individual moral agent,
just war tradition offers moral guidance for conscientiously

weighing the question of participation in the use of force and the degree of such participation.

Thematic Content of Just War Tradition

Looked at as a whole, just war tradition has two major thematic branches, classically denoted by the terms *jus ad bellum* and *jus in bello.* These have to do, respectively, with when it is just to resort to military force and what it is justified to do in the use of such force (see table 3). Contemporary writers sometimes attach their own terminology to these two general themes; thus Walzer, as I have already mentioned, refers to the first by the term "theory of aggression" and to the second by "the war convention," while William V. O'Brien, approaching just war reasoning from a perspective close to international law, employs the terms "war-decision law" and "war-conduct law" for these two thematic branches of the tradition.[23] Other writers, such as the American Catholic bishops, retain the traditional terminology. Whatever terms are used, close attention needs to be paid to the content subsumed in each of them and the emphasis given each element by a particular theorist, as these often differ in detail from one theorist to another and sometimes depart appreciably from the classic form of the just war idea described below.

Historically the *jus ad bellum* has developed around a set of seven principles on how to justify resort to war: the requirement that, to be justified, a war must have a *just cause,* be waged by *proper authority* and with a *right intention,* be undertaken only if there is *reasonable hope of success* and if the total good outweighs the total evil expected (overall *proportionality*), be a *last resort,* and be waged for *the end of peace.* Each of these criteria has a particular meaning as shaped and transmitted by the tradition.

At the same time, there are differences and tensions among the various component streams of the larger tradition and

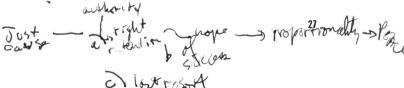

7 ad
Bellom

Table 3
The Just War Tradition as a Source of Criteria for
Ethical Judgment

The *jus ad bellum*: Criteria defining the right to resort to force

1. JUST CAUSE: The protection and preservation of value
   Classic statement: Defense of the innocent against armed attack
   Retaking persons, property, or other values wrongly taken
   Punishment of evil

2. RIGHT AUTHORITY: The person or body authorizing the use of
   force must be the duly authorized representative of a sovereign
   political entity. The authorization to use force implies the abiity to
   control and cease that use: that is, a well-constituted and efficient
   chain of command.
   Classic statement: Reservation of the right to employ force to
   persons or communities with no political superior.

3. RIGHT INTENTION: The intent must be in accord with the
   just cause and not territorial aggrandizement, intimidation,
   or coercion.
   Classic statement: Evils to be avoided in war, including hatred
   of the enemy, "implacable animosity," "lust for vengeance," desire
   to dominate.

6. PROPORTIONALITY OF ENDS: The overall good achieved by the use
   of force must be greater than the harm done. The levels and means
   of using force must be appropriate to the just ends sought.

5. hope of Success

4. LAST RESORT: Determination at the time of the decision to
   employ force that no other means will achieve the justified ends
   sought. Interacts with other *jus ad bellum* criteria to detemrine
   level, type, and duration of force employed.

7. End of peace

between each of them and the thrust of the tradition taken as a
whole. In considering the justification and limits of national or
international use of force in the contemporary context, it is
especially suggestive to consider the differences between these
principles in their broadest form as classically defined and as
they are expressed in contemporary international law, one of the
main component streams of just war tradition (see table 4).

The requirement of *just cause* classically meant one or more

REASONABLE HOPE OF SUCCESS: Prudential calculation of the likelihood that the means used will bring the justified ends sought. Interacts with other *jus ad bellum* criteria to determine level, type, and duration of force employed.

THE AIM OF PEACE: Establishment of international stability, security, and peaceful interaction. May include nation building, disarmament, other measures to promote peace.

The *jus in bello:* Criteria defining the employment of force

PROPORTIONALITY OF MEANS: Means causing gratuitous or otherwise unnecessary harm are to be avoided. Prohibition of torture, means *mala in se.*
Classic statement: Attempts to limit weapons, days of fighting, persons who should fight.

NONCOMBATANT PROTECTION/IMMUNITY: Definition of noncombatancy, avoidance of direct, intentional harm to noncombatants, efforts to protect them.
Classic statement: Lists of classes of persons (clergy, merchants, peasants on the land, other people in activities not related to the prosecution of war) to be spared the harm of war.

of three possibilities: that the use of force in question was for defense against wrongful attack, retaking something wrongly taken, or punishment of evil. Contemporary positive international law seems to narrow this, establishing defense as the only justifying cause for use of force: either defense by one nation or group of nations against an attack by another or internationally sanctioned defense against a breach of international peace. Yet a closer look suggests that the other two classic ideas have been

Table 4
The Just War Criteria in Positive International Law

Jus ad bellum:

JUST CAUSE: National or regional self-defense against armed attack
Retaliation for armed attack
International response to threats to international peace

RIGHT AUTHORITY: *Compétence de guerre* possessed by states; some right to authorize force given to UN Security Council; some recognition of insurgency rights

RIGHT INTENTION: Not explicitly addressed; implicit in above items.

PROPORTIONALITY OF ENDS: In 20th century, a tendency to treat the first use of force as the greatest evil, always disproportionate.

LAST RESORT: Emphasis on international arbitration and/or adjudication; tendency to allow only responsive, or "second," use of force after armed attack.

REASONABLE HOPE OF SUCCESS: Not explicitly treated.

THE AIM OF PEACE: Greatly stressed. Limits on just causes for going to war, emphasis on *jus in bello* restraints, preference for stability over other values. Currently in process of some reevaluation.

Jus in bello:

PROPORTIONALITY OF MEANS: "Hague law," arms limits, bans on means *mala in se.*

NONCOMBATANT PROTECTION/IMMUNITY: Greatly stressed. "Geneva law," various other provisions regarding noncombatants, POWS, "protected persons."
Not treated: injury to noncombatants received due to proximity to legitimate targets, long-term damages due to persisting effects of otherwise legitimate means of war.

(margin handwriting: "old | punishment / retaking / defense → "defense" | new")

absorbed into a broadened concept of defense in contemporary
international usage. A retaliatory second strike, for example,
would classically have been called "punishment of evil"; today it
is categorized as "defense." The use of force to retake Kuwait
from Iraq would have classically been called "retaking something wrongly taken"; in the language of contemporary international law, however, it was "defense" against an "armed attack"
that remained in progress so long as Iraq occupied Kuwait. (The
Falklands War provides a second recent example of this latter
reasoning.) So the underlying ideas remain, though the vocabu-
lary has changed to reflect twentieth-century sentiment that first
use of force in a developing conflict is morally suspect, while
second use is not.

The requirement of *proper authority* (or, as alternatively
stated, "sovereign" or "right" or "competent" authority) limits
the right to authorize force to sovereign political entities—that
is, those with no superior. Classically this requirement developed as a way to restrict the resort to force by denying it to local
strongmen and to individuals bearing arms. Legitimate sovereigns, by contrast, because authorized to use force, could employ it against such local strongmen and marauders wherever
found.[24] Indeed, for medieval just war theorists, the concept of
authority to use force implied the responsibility to use it as
necessary in the service of order and justice and for the punishment of evil, following the often cited text of Romans 13:4b: "for
[the prince] bears not the sword in vain; he is the minister of
God to punish evildoers."[25] In contrast to the contemporary
emphasis on defense as the only justification for resort to force,
this core concept of right authority has the *prima facie* effect of
favoring certain interventionary uses of force in the interest
of internationally recognized standards of justice. One might
argue from it to the right to use force if necessary for such

(handwriting at bottom: First use suspect / 2nd use moral)

purposes as combating international terrorism, responding to other forms of international lawlessness such as the traffic in illicit drugs, or systematic and sustained violations of universally recognized human rights. In positive international law, however, the limitation tends to flow the other way: aimed at restricting the right of states to resort to war with other states, it also restricts the states' right of intervention across the borders of other states, whatever the justifying purpose. States have nonetheless continued to reserve that right to themselves and to practice it; so customary international law is somewhat at variance with the black-letter law. Debate over national authority for intervention in the present context, accordingly, is somewhat confused.[26]

The requirement of proper authority also raises questions about intervention under international auspices. International organizations up to and including the United Nations lack sovereignty in the traditional sense. Without sovereignty, is there any right to authorize force? Classic just war doctrine would say no, reserving that right to sovereign states. Yet, in contemporary debate international authorization for interventionary use of military force is often claimed, though on the basis of consensus (as in the Security Council resolutions relating to the Gulf War and to the United Nations protective force in Somalia) rather than sovereignty. Later in the book I look more closely at the important contemporary issue of intervention and explore some of the alternative arguments that have been made about it on the basis of just war reasoning.

Right intention in just war tradition has both negative and positive meanings. Negatively, it means the avoidance of bad intentions or motivations, as defined classically in this passage from Augustine:

> The passion for inflicting harm, the cruel thirst for vengeance, an unpacific and relentless spirit, the fever of revolt, the lust of power, and such like things, all these are rightly condemned in war.[27]

Positively, it means the intention of serving the goods of proper political life. Augustine's formulation is also the classic one:

> True religion looks upon as peaceful those wars that are waged not for motives of aggrandizement or cruelty, but with the object of securing peace, of punishing evil-doers, and of uplifting the good.

Or again, "We do not seek peace in order to be at war, but we go to war that we may have peace."[28]

As the just war idea first began to be applied to the practice of war in the Middle Ages, the former passage from Augustine was used as a rationale for church sanctions aimed at keeping individual soldiers from fighting with wrong intentions. Well into the Middle Ages, soldiers were required to do penance after combat, in case, during the heat of battle, they had fought with the wrong intention.[29] By the time of Thomas Aquinas in the thirteenth century, though, as Thomas's inclusion of the above passages in his discussion of right intention shows, the concept was linked directly to the purposes of the sovereign authority undertaking the war and was tied especially closely to the purposes of serving justice and establishing peace. Standard contemporary usage follows the example of Thomas in linking the just war criterion of right intention closely to the idea of *the end of peace,* where it refers not to the individual soldier but to the purpose of the state in employing military force. In this context it requires that this purpose be not to serve some aggressive end but to establish or reestablish such goals as international order and respect for human rights. International law has no explicitly

Roman

specified notion of right intention, though arguably one can be read out of other principles expressed there.

Reasonable hope of success, overall proportionality, and *last resort* are, for just war tradition in its classic form, all prudential tests to be applied as additional checks when the above deontological requirements have been met. All are derived historically from Roman practice, and they refer to political prudence at any time and in any culture. International law does not address them specifically, and religious just war theorists have paid little attention to them historically. Yet they have come to figure more prominently in some contemporary just war reasoning, particularly in what Paul Ramsey called the effort to redefine the *jus ad bellum* as a *jus contra bellum* in cold war–era ethical debate: the use of just war categories to deny the possibility of a just war.[30] In this reasoning the destructive capabilities of contemporary weapons are made the core of an argument that any use of force today must necessarily be disproportionate and hence unjust. It follows that there can be no reasonable hope of success, and that contemporary war can never reasonably be a last resort for serving justice, order, and peace, because it will by its nature create injustice, disorder, and more war. The *jus contra bellum justum,* then, though sometimes called "just war pacifism," is really just pacifism. It begins with a presumption against war, and it employs certain dogmatic assumptions about modern weapons to attempt to undercut the possibility of any contemporary just use of force, on the grounds of the just war principle of proportionality.

There are two important problems with this reasoning. First, there is nothing inherently disproportionately destructive in contemporary weaponry. Indeed, sophisticated contemporary guidance mechanisms today allow military targets to be destroyed with far less collateral damage than was the case in earlier conflicts. Second, the concept of proportionality in just war tradition means the overall balancing of the good (and evil) a use of force will bring about against the evil of not resorting to force. It begins with the recognition that a loss of value has already occurred (the just cause) prior to the consideration whether force is justified to restore that value. Rather than implicitly ruling out contemporary recourse to force, then, the moral requirements of reasonable hope of success, overall proportionality, and last resort continue to be useful tests of the wise use of military power in given contexts.

What, then, of the claim made in *The Challenge of Peace* that just war doctrine begins with a "presumption against war"?[31] It is certainly true that such a presumption seems to appear in much recent Catholic thought on war, including a variety of papal statements.[32] Nonetheless, such a presumption is not to be found in just war tradition in its classic form, or even in the specifically churchly theorists Augustine and Aquinas to whom Catholic just war theorists generally refer for authority. The idea of such a "presumption" seems to owe more to the influence of Catholic pacifists on the development of *The Challenge of Peace* and to a general uneasiness with the destructiveness of modern war and the venality of modern states than to the heritage of just war tradition.[33] I would say it more emphatically: the concept of just war does not begin with a "presumption against war" focused on the harm which war may do, but with a presumption against *injustice* focused on the need for responsible use of force in response to wrongdoing. Force, according to the core meaning of just war tradition, is an instrumentality that may be good or evil, depending on the use to which it is put. The whole structure of the *jus ad bellum* of just war tradition has to do with specifying the terms under which those in political power are authorized to resort to force for good—that is, to rectify specific

35

injustices. It is a serious distortion of the meaning of just war tradition to magnify the importance of the prudential concerns included in the *jus ad bellum* so that they diminish the importance of the fundamental requirements of just cause, proper authority, and right intention.

The *jus in bello* is defined by two concerns: discrimination, or avoiding direct, intentional harm to noncombatants, and proportionality of means—that is, avoiding needless destruction to achieve justified ends. Both concerns are given concrete contemporary form in the law of armed conflicts; most important, discrimination is embodied in the Geneva Conventions and Protocols, and both discrimination and proportionality are served in the various weapons limits established by international agreement and customary practice.

Historically and thematically, the *jus in bello* concerns have taken second place to the *ad bellum* criteria, since only after the decision is made that a particular use of force is just can one turn to the question of how to fight justly. Influential contemporary ethical reasoning, beginning with Ramsey's focus on discrimination as the uniquely Christian element in the just war idea, has tended to erase this prioritization and even to invert it (as in "just war pacifism"), so that the decision regarding whether to resort to force is made to depend on whether the anticipated use can pass exacting tests of discrimination and proportion. Such reasoning, though, is quite at odds with the structure and history of just war tradition as a whole.

While the roots of the just war *jus in bello* lie in the Middle Ages, the major development of this attempt to limit the conduct of war has taken place in the modern period. Medieval efforts to establish protection of noncombatants developed only slowly, and the first weapons limits failed to change the empiri-

cal face of combat. More is owed to the code of chivalry from
this period than to the efforts of the canonists and theologians.[34]
New emphasis was given to the *jus in bello* early in the modern
period, particularly in the thought of Grotius, where this emphasis complemented a redefinition of the *jus ad bellum* so that,
in practical terms, it was assumed to exist whenever the sovereign of a nation formally declared war and published the just
causes for his action.[35] Both Grotius and his predecessor Vitoria
stressed noncombatant immunity, as had the medieval code of
chivalry; by contrast, the customary *jus in bello* of the limited
wars of the eighteenth century put the priority on lowering the
overall damage of a war, providing for noncombatant protection as implied by proportionality, not as an absolute right implied by the principle of discrimination.[36] In international law
the establishment of noncombatant immunity as a right and
noncombatant protection as a responsibility of belligerents has
come only with the development of the Geneva Conventions
and Protocols beginning in 1863 and with the growth of international humanitarian law in the period since World War II.[37]
These international rules are supposed to be observed by all
nations, though in practice there is not universal agreement,
and in civil conflicts they have often been entirely ignored.

The kinds of armed conflict which have become commonplace today pose serious challenges to the effort to restrain the
conduct of war; such conflicts include "holy" wars, civil wars,
and other internecine conflicts in which it is often claimed that
there are no real noncombatants. To my mind, such claims are
examples of special pleading; but at the same time, moral reflection has to take seriously where to draw the line between those
who may be directly, intentionally targeted and those who may
not. Indeed, the question of how to ensure the protection of

1863
Geneva

immunity ~ proportionality
(discrimination)

noncombatants is one of the most important moral issues posed by contemporary armed conflict. In later chapters I treat this issue in some depth.

Considerations of discrimination and proportionality rightly belong in responsible planning for potential uses of force, for it is a moral obligation to anticipate how to serve just ends by just means. This means that, alongside concerted efforts to ensure observance of noncombatant rights and protection, there is a moral dimension to weapons development, strategy, and tactics. Conventional arms control efforts have aimed at limiting weapons of unnecessary and/or indiscriminate destructive capability. Yet, in both world wars and in contemporary warfare conventional weaponry has proven its ability to wreak both indiscriminate and disproportionate damage. While one implication of the *jus in bello* concerns found in just war tradition is to ensure that weapons at hand are used discriminatingly and proportionately—that is, to ensure that the tactics and strategy of warfare respect these moral limits—I would argue that there is also a *prima facie* obligation to develop weaponry that is inherently more discriminate and relatively less destructive, such as by incorporating "smart" weapons into military readiness for various kinds of contingencies, as well as by improving accuracy and lowering yields of other types of arms. Finally, the *jus in bello* together with the *jus ad bellum* implies efforts to restrict the availability of arms of all kinds to parties who may misuse them.

Conclusion

This chapter began by showing the need for a renewed moral debate over the use of military force in the contemporary age. I noted that the last major debate over morality and war, which took place in the early 1980s and had to do chiefly with nuclear weapons and deterrence strategy, did not anticipate either the changes in international relations that have come about with the end of the cold war or the changes in the nature of war that have become typical today. My focus in this chapter has been on identifying these changes and their impact, showing what is needed in moral analysis and debate to address them adequately, and arguing for the use of just war reasoning to assess and deal with the particular moral problems posed by contemporary warfare.

I would stress that I do not think of this endeavor as one of "applying" just war principles or rules as if they were fully understood and fixed for all time to the changing vagaries of warfare. Rather, carrying on a moral argument by engaging just war tradition is to contribute to the ongoing development of that tradition by entering into a critical dialogue with the wisdom it contains. This wisdom, which has come to be classified in terms of the several criteria identified and discussed above, is itself the product of historical experience, as the implications of justice in the use of force are drawn out in the context of good statecraft. So, looked at one way, this is a book about the need to address morally the problems posed by contemporary war; looked at from the opposite perspective, it is a book about the development of moral understanding and, specifically, the contemporary meaning of just war tradition. Taken as a whole, just war tradition has to do with defining the place of the resort to force in statecraft and with specifying the limits of justified uses of force. A body of historical wisdom, reflection, and precedent attaches to each of the criteria that make up the classic *jus ad bellum* and *jus in bello,* defining their meaning with a great deal of clarity and precision. Yet just war tradition, like the field of law in the Anglo-Saxon legal tradition, is not fully defined at any time by these criteria understood as principles or by a static understanding of their meaning as developed in past wisdom, reflection, and precedent. Rather, the meaning of the tradition or any part of it at any given time and with reference to any given context or problem must be developed in dialogue with the principles it expresses, the precedents it embodies, and the moral wisdom it reflects. Thus, besides providing a broad and deep foundation for moral reflection on statecraft, this tradition also provides a proper forum for exploring the implications of that reflection for policy choices and actions taken in the international sphere. In turn, the tradition itself is thereby expanded and renewed. The discussion which follows has both these purposes in mind.

2

Thinking about Resort to War in Just War Terms

In the previous chapter I discussed the right to resort to armed force in just war tradition (the *jus ad bellum*) as this has come to be defined through seven moral concepts: just cause, competent authority, right intention, reasonable hope of success, overall proportionality of good over harm, last resort, and the goal of peace. Both historically and in terms of the inner logic of the just war idea, though, these seven moral criteria are not all of equal importance: the first three have priority over the others. The primacy of these three ideas in foundational just war thought is illustrated by Thomas Aquinas's statement of the *jus ad bellum*, a statement reflecting the consensus of both Scholastic theology and the canon law of his time, in language that included only these concepts. "In order for a war to be just," Thomas wrote, "three things are necessary." He goes on to list sovereign authority, just cause, and right intention, linking each irement to the thought of his predecessor Augustine.[1] Sim-, in this chapter I will explore these three most fundamental elements of the just war conception of when resort to armed force is justified, attempting to draw out their meaning for the possible use of military force in the present day.

Giving special attention to the importance of just cause, proper authority, and right intention does not mean that the remaining four traditional requirements for moral resort to force are unimportant, only that their position is secondary within the logic of just war tradition. That resort to force must reasonably be expected to succeed, that it must reasonably be calculated to produce more good than the evil it necessarily causes, and that, given the uncertainty of such expectations, it should be a last resort when no other means will produce the desired result are all prudential tests that pertain to good decision making in the practice of statecraft at any time and in any place; Augustine in fact brought them into Western just war theory from Roman practice. These prudential tests are of a qualitatively different character from the deontological criteria that a decision to use force must have a just cause, must be determined by a person or a body of persons having competent authority within a sovereign political unit, and that the purpose must be governed by a right intention. For Augustine, to whom the concept of right intention in just war tradition can be traced, the goal of peace was a positive indicator of such intention, which he also defined negatively by listing a number of wrong intentions to be avoided.[2] To separate the goal of peace from the requirement of right intention adds nothing to the just war *jus ad bellum* that is not already present; it simply makes more explicit a concern that is already there.

Anyone seeking to take seriously the moral requirements of just cause, competent authority, and right intention must also come to terms with the four remaining concerns that have come to be defined today as distinct criteria for judgment within the just war *jus ad bellum*. Yet the priority of the first three criteria must also be respected. It is one thing to argue that a particular use of force (for example, insertion of limited military force to protect humanitarian relief efforts in an ongoing armed conflict) meets the requirements of just cause, competent authority, and right intention but cannot reasonably be expected to succeed and may cause more harm than good; this is how the *jus ad bellum* criteria should be properly brought to bear on a given decision. It is quite another thing to argue that lack of reasonable hope of success or proportion of good over harm—let alone that all military force, under current conditions, will inevitably be disproportionate—removes all moral justification for use of force; this is a misuse of the *jus ad bellum* criteria.

Because of the priority of the first three criteria in just war thinking about resort to armed force, the focus of this chapter is on them. Yet good statecraft, after ensuring that these three concerns have been satisfied, will still have to test whether use of force otherwise justified can meet the prudential tests and fashion its final course of action accordingly. Extreme cases may exist in which the only moral course is to take action that is imprudent; examples of such action include the resistance to the invading German forces by the Poles, the Dutch, and the Belgians at the start of World War II. Such examples illustrate the ultimate priority of the deontological tests (in these cases, the test of just cause in particular) over the prudential ones. But most cases are not so extreme, and in less clear circumstances the prudential tests serve as a check on foolhardiness among those entrusted with the burdens of statecraft, even as the deontological tests serve as a check on their propensity to egotism. Both sorts of concerns have a valid place in decisions as to

43

whether resort to force is justified; yet satisfaction of the requirements of just cause, competent authority, and right intention (including the aim of reestablishing peace) has a greater moral priority than does satisfying the prudential criteria of the just war *jus ad bellum*.

In the following discussion I explore the moral content of the ideas of just cause, proper authority, and right intention in three steps. The first is to examine the core *jus ad bellum* ideas in terms of the meaning assigned to them during the period when just war tradition coalesced as a cultural consensus in Western culture, the Middle Ages; here I will focus on the core ideas as discussed by Thomas Aquinas in the passage cited above. The second step is to follow these ideas as they developed in the modern period, with focus on the implications of changes in the concept of statecraft and of the face of war as reflected in moral thought on war. The third step is to assess these ideas in the contemporary context. Here I will focus on two issues: first, the difference between typical contemporary uses of military force and the image of modern war as an inherently and necessarily destructive holocaust found in important recent moral thought on war; and second, the changing relationship between states and the international order as exemplified by the United Nations.

A Classic Statement of the Three Core Criteria: Thomas Aquinas's Question "On War"

While the roots of just war tradition can be traced back to the thought of the fourth-century Christian theologian Augustine of Hippo and even further, into the culture of classical Rome and the wars of Israel as depicted in the Old Testament, the earliest coherent, systematic statements of the idea of just war were a product of the Middle Ages. The formative period covered approximately three centuries, from the publication of Gratian's magisterial collection of canon law, the *Decretum,* in 1148, to the work of such writers as Honoré Bonet and Christine de Pisan, writing during the Hundred Years' War. Various sources, including customs of statecraft and study of Roman legal theory and practice, fed into the developing idea of just war; but the most central contributions were made by canon law and theology, which mostly focused on the question of justified resort to force (later to be called *jus ad bellum*) and the code and customs of chivalry, which mainly affected conduct during armed conflict (the *loi d'armes* or *jus in bello*).[3] Because the focus of this chapter is on the former question, our concern in the early development of just war thought is with the churchly theorists and the *jus ad bellum* as they defined it.

Thomas Aquinas's position provides an easily accessible window into the normative conception of the justification of armed force during this critical period in the development of just war tradition.[4] Composed during the latter half of the thirteenth century, Thomas's observations on justified resort to war followed and reflected the creative work of the canonist Gratian and his two generations of successors, the Decretists and the Decretalists. These canonical writers had drawn heavily on Augustine on just war, and Thomas did so as well. In building on the canonists' work and their use of Augustine, Thomas helped to embody, rationalize, and extend the developing consensus on moral use of armed force. While the influence of the canonists overshadowed Thomas's thought on war during his own time, by the dawn of the modern period, theorists like Vitoria and Suarez looked no further than Thomas for the authoritative statement of justified resort to armed force.[5] Thus Thomas's position is doubly useful, since it is both accessible and at the center of the development of medieval Christian moral thought on the just war idea. In the following discussion of his statement

authority vs. just cause

of the core *jus ad bellum* ideas, I will also make reference where helpful to the canonical consensus which he presupposed but did not himself elaborate.

For a war to be just, Thomas writes, "three things are necessary. First, the authority of the sovereign by whose command the war is to be waged." While twentieth-century just war thought typically lists just cause first among the criteria for justified resort to force,[6] for medieval theorists the question of authority to employ force more often came first, as it did with Thomas. The order of the listing might signify nothing, but for medieval just war thinkers it reflected the fact that the problem of who actually might authorize resort to force was a major question for the shape of social order. Indeed, there were two distinct questions. First, at what level in the feudal hierarchy did a person have the right to employ armed force on his own authority? The problem here was the claims of members of the lower nobility, individual knights and men-at-arms, and even on occasion townspeople and peasants to have the right to use arms on their own responsibility as they determined. In practice, this led to a high level of social violence and fragmented—often unjust—rule by local warlords or armed gangs. These claims were opposed by the higher nobility and by the Church, leading to efforts by both (such as the Peace of God movement beginning in the south of France in the late tenth century) to impose social order by restricting the right to authorize armed force to the highest level of secular rule in a defined region. The second question was whether authority to employ such force extended to lords of the Church (the Pope, bishops in their dioceses) or only to secular rulers. The theoretical answer to both questions and the resolution of the underlying issue of social structure was importantly the result of the work of the canonists of the late twelfth and early thirteenth centuries. Thomas's language reflects their solution: the authority necessary to justify use of armed force is *sovereign* authority—that possessed by the rulers of recognized sovereign political entities.[7]

While this medieval debate has the particular flavor of its context, the same two types of fundamental problems have endured to the present day: Do religious leaders have the right to initiate "holy" war against perceived enemies of their faith? Do local ethnic minorities or other groups of people with their own identities and grievances against the established order have a right to take up arms to establish their own autonomy? The medieval response, that the right to resort to armed force should be limited to sovereign temporal powers, has also turned out to be the most enduring response to these continuing problems, embodied in customary and positive international law and the structure of the international order. For this reason, and not just because of its importance in the medieval context, this idea of sovereign authority as constituting right authority for the use of armed force should be looked at carefully. → *under*

Summarizing the position that had already become standard by his time, Thomas justified the restriction of authority to use the sword to sovereigns for three reasons: first, private individuals do not need to resolve disputes by appeal to the sword, because they may appeal to their superiors and ultimately to the sovereign; second, sovereigns have the responsibility to maintain internal order and justice in their domains; and third, sovereigns are responsible for defending the common weal against external enemies, and both these responsibilities imply the right to employ armed force. Thus, he argues, citing Augustine (from *Contra Faustum*, xxii.75), "The natural order conducive to peace . . . demands that the power to declare and counsel war should be in the hands of those who hold supreme authority." This line of argument remained essentially unchanged from the

Middle Ages, through the modern period and the development of the state system up to the present.

It is important to note in Thomas's discussion the relationship between authority to have recourse to the sword and the responsibilities of the sovereign to maintain order and justice. This linkage was typical of medieval political thought. It did not so much empower the ruler to do what he pleased with the armed force at his disposal as lay on him the burden of having recourse to such force as a necessary tool of sovereignty. This understanding of the right to use the sword carries forward to the conception of just cause: the sword may be used only against those "who deserve it on account of some fault," Thomas writes, amplifying his meaning by citing a passage from Augustine (from *Quaestionum in Heptateuchum*, Q. x, on Joshua) that was also familiar from the canonical writings: a just war is one that seeks to punish evil or restore something that has been unjustly taken. These two justifying causes add to the responsibility of defense already stated to define the idea of just cause in terms of three responsibilities of political leadership: to maintain order by defending against internal wrongdoing and external attack, to restore justice by punishing those responsible, and to retake any persons, properties, or powers wrongly seized by evildoers. There is no substantive difference between this language and Michael Walzer's contemporary term for the *jus ad bellum*, the "theory of aggression."[8]

One highly respected twentieth-century commentator on the just war idea in Thomas and in Scholastic theology as a whole argues that the justification for use of armed force there follows from the concept of "vindicative justice"—that is, the restoration of justice by vindicating those who have been the victims of injustice in some form.[9] On this conception, the ruler's authority to use the sword follows from his role as "minister

"Vindicative justice"
(Restoration of justice
always a response to injustice —
JUST RESORT TO ARMED FORCE
"aggression")

of God" (Romans 13:4) to execute God's justice in his temporal sphere of rule and responsibility. This concept further emphasizes the role of armed force as a tool of good statecraft which may be used against injustice when necessary. In the previous chapter I took issue with the arguments of "just war pacifism" and the slightly softer but related concept of a "presumption against war" in just war theory. In the position laid out by Thomas, which represents faithfully the reasoning employed by canonical thought as well, these ideas simply are not present. *right* Rather, there is a conception of armed force as an instrumentality of good or evil, and it is defined as good when used in accord with the responsibilities of sovereign rule to set right the wrongs imposed by others—especially those wrongs imposed by wrongful use of armed force.

The third idea which Thomas identifies as necessary for just resort to the sword is a right intention, which he defines as intending "the advancement of good, or the avoidance of evil." Persons not holding sovereign power (and the associated responsibilities) by definition cannot have such an intention. But sovereigns too may misuse the power of the sword; thus Thomas again makes use of the language of Augustinian tradition in defining wrong and right intentions. The former include "motives of aggrandizement, or cruelty"; or, more fully, "[t]he passion for inflicting harm, the cruel thirst for vengeance, an unpacific and relentless spirit, the fever or revolt, the lust of power, and such like things." By contrast, a right intention has the object of "securing peace, of punishing evil-doers, and of uplifting the good." Thus Thomas, following the line of reasoning established by Augustine and the canonists, linked the idea of right intention to the goals of medieval political theory: a just and therefore peaceful political order. The goal of peace is not to be achieved, on this conception, without justice; it does not

> war has no positive goodness
(in service of Just Peace)

49

stand alone, but in a necessary relationship with the responsibilities of rulership which justify the sovereign's right to have recourse to the sword.

Thus Thomas comments further: "Those who wage war justly aim at peace, and so they are not opposed to peace, except to the evil peace"—that is, the tyrannical order that is imposed by the unjust. The aim of peace, he continues, also implies care in the way force is employed even against those who deserve it; this is as close as Thomas came to the stipulation of a *jus in bello*. For him, right conduct in war would follow from the virtuousness of its purpose and of those who fought in accordance with that purpose. Limitations on the actual use of justified force are implied here, but are not developed in the form of rules, as in canon law, the chivalric code, and later just war tradition. Thomas's treatment makes clear the logic, though: the first question to be decided is whether resort to armed force is justified, and that is done by taking account of the three requirements of sovereign authority, just cause, and right intention. Then one moves to the second question, which is how the justified force may be justly exercised. Again, this is a logic diametrically the opposite of that of "just war pacifism" and its argument that defines the *jus ad bellum*, the right of recourse to armed force, by the *jus in bello*, the expectation as to whether or not the force in question may be expected to be used entirely justly. Thomas's position is more clearly approximated in international law, though the language of the law is different from that of Thomas's moral discourse: the right of recourse to armed force belongs to states under certain specified conditions, and violations of humanitarian law and the laws of armed conflict do not take away that right, though they may subject violators (up to the leadership of the state in question, if warranted) to punishment.

In *Duties Beyond Borders* Stanley Hoffmann identifies just

war reasoning as a phenomenon of the Middle Ages, but then undertakes to establish rules for contemporary statecraft and use of armed force that look remarkably like those developed by medieval just war theorists.[10] At various points in my discussion of the position laid out by Thomas I have linked that position to contemporary conceptions, to underscore the continuity of the moral conceptions in some cases or to criticize certain mistaken moral reasoning in others. In both sorts of cases my purpose has been to make plain that the issues dealt with by medieval just war theorists are very much like those confronted by statesmen in the present day, and to suggest that the responses worked out by the medieval theorists deserve to be taken seriously in the present context as well. Indeed, my broader point is one I have made many times in my work on just war tradition: properly understood, it carries conceptions of statecraft and the role of armed force in good government that take various specific forms over time but remain fundamentally stable. This tradition is, as a whole, a repository of the way in which Western culture has come to think of the values which political life exists to support, protect, and foster; the role of military force in the service of those values; and the limits on the use of such force. From this perspective, the question of the just use of military force today is one that may rightly be approached by looking at earlier historical reflections on the same question, so that the answers both reinforce the core values carried by the tradition and reveal wrong turns in past and present arguments about the place of the use of force in statecraft.

The Just War Question in the Modern Era: The Emergence of the Modern State and the Phenomenon of "Modern War"

The coalescence of just war tradition took place in a historical context in which the concept of sovereignty was more often *the Modern*

associated with the person of the ruler of a political entity than with the entity itself, and in which the form of warfare was limited both by available resources and by the dominant ideologies of the Church and the chivalric class. The development of just war tradition in the modern period has been marked by fundamental changes in both politics and the character of war: in the former by the rise of the modern state and the system of international order linked to it and in the latter by the emergence of totalistic forms of warfare drawing on the full resources of states and motivated by ideologies in which the cause of the nation at war is understood in ultimate, all-or-nothing terms. The changed understanding of the political system, which can be glimpsed in the thought of Grotius and the Peace of Westphalia that ended the Thirty Years' War in 1648, is more conventionally dated to the time of the Congress of Vienna in 1814–15. Empirically, the shift in the idea of sovereignty from the individual who wields it to the state on whose behalf it is wielded has been a gradual one, which, if the emergence of powerful dictators as heads of state in the twentieth century is taken into account, has not yet been fully completed. More important, though, is the emergence of the legal idea of the state as international person, whose status, responsibilities, and powers are independent of the personalities of those who govern it. This is the sovereign state of the modern state system.

It is this legal shift that Grotius anticipated in his *De Jure Belli ac Pacis* (*The Law of War and Peace*), first published in 1625 during the Thirty Years' War. In this work Grotius rethought the inherited just war tradition, transforming it into a theory of the law of nations, the theoretical basis on which modern international law developed. For the purposes of the present discussion, what matters most in this is Grotius's reconception of the *jus ad bellum*.

52

First, on the matter of authority to make war, Grotius held to the requirement that it be sovereign authority; yet in various ways he located the basis of sovereignty in the political entity governed, not in the person or persons who govern. The subject of sovereignty is the state, he declares in one place, and not any particular person;[11] again, he sharply distinguishes the private interests of a ruler from the public interests of the state for which he has responsibility;[12] elsewhere, he argues that both the right of resistance and the powers of sovereignty are subject to the state.[13] Heavily influenced by the example of classical Rome, he in other connections speaks of "sovereign power" as deriving from the "people" of a state.[14] The conception of the law of nations that he developed built on this recasting of the nature of sovereignty, though the state system it anticipated did not emerge until as much as a century later.

An important consequence of this new conception of sovereignty was that the exercise of sovereign power in regard to the use of armed force became more formalistic and less moral in character. While medieval theorists had assumed that a sovereign would make plain the moral rationale (that is, the just cause) for his resort to force, or that such just cause would be self-evident, Grotius made it a requirement of his *jus ad bellum* that war be formally declared by the sovereign authority on behalf of the state.[15] Further, he redefined the idea of just cause itself as rooted in the right of self-defense, thus effectively collapsing the inherited categories of punishment and recovery of property into the third traditional just cause, defense. His aim, as he states explicitly, was to distinguish wars based on self-interest of one sort or another from wars rooted in "motives of justice."[16] This made the initiation of armed hostilities more subject to objective judgments (presumably outside observers could easily tell when there had been aggression and thus that *compétence de guerre —*

defense was justified) and less dependent on the particular judgments of an individual sovereign, which might be influenced by particular interests, dislikes, or ideological biases. Finally, Grotius did not discuss the concept of right intention as a requirement of the *jus ad bellum* except insofar as it was implied by the purpose of defense. But he did explicitly grant that the resort to arms for defensive purpose might be preemptive, if the threat were certain and immediate.[17]

Grotius's aim in this reformulation of the *jus ad bellum* was to hedge about and diminish the possibility of religiously motivated uses of armed force such as had torn Europe apart in the wake of the Reformation. He thus emphasized the rights of the state as a sovereign entity, narrowed the cause of justice to the purpose of self-defense, and recast the whole notion of justification of recourse to arms in terms of law, rather than morality. What he did not foresee was the ease with which this idea would, in the following century, transmute into the idea of *compétence de guerre*, whereby each state claimed the right to determine when its interests were threatened and initiate war accordingly. Nor did he foresee how, beginning with the wars of the age of the French Revolution and of Napoleon, the character of war would itself change to become much more totalistic and destructive, so that efforts would build to restrict even further the right to go to war, or even to deny it entirely.

In Grotius's thought the right to make war was given to states by the law of nature; shortly, other theorists, including Locke in England and the French *philosophes*, would argue for a conception of the rights of man based also in nature. These two theoretical developments came together in the two great revolutions of the end of the eighteenth century, the American and the French. These revolutions had a substantial impact on the idea of the *jus ad bellum*. The first form of this impact was on the

54

idea of the authority necessary to resort to armed force. On the traditional conception, which Grotius had begun to modify, revolution was inherently unjust, since the requisite sovereign authority was lacking. The American and French revolutions challenged this conception in the name of the authority of each individual, based on that individual's natural rights, to enter into a collective defense of those rights even against sovereign power. The second major impact of these two great revolutions on the *jus ad bellum* idea was the development of a kind of messianism whereby those who had established the right to govern themselves came to believe they had a right to expand that cause. While this messianism took both American and French forms, the more immediate impact on the idea of just resort to armed force came from the French Revolution and took the form of the exporting the Revolution. Geoffrey Best comments:

> "Liberty" and its revolutionary accompaniments "equality" and "fraternity" were goods it could seem a duty and pleasure to extend to others. So self-evidently good were these principles that, when they failed at once to catch on in neighbouring countries, surprised French revolutionaries ran rather quickly to explain the failure in simplified terms of conspiracies, oppression, and wickedness."[18]

More important, they undertook to export the Revolution by force of arms, a task taken up by Napoleon (though his rule was revolutionary in a very different sense from that of the Jacobins). More broadly, the conception of war justified by national purpose expanded into a new doctrine which Clausewitz termed "national war": the kind of warfare Napoleon waged, the closest empirical example he knew of his ideal of "absolute war." This was war in which the utmost exertion of the powers of the nation were utilized to carry on war "without slackening for a moment until the enemy was prostrated."[19]

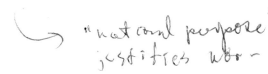
→ "national purpose" justifies war —

However laudable the initial goal of extending the rights of man to all societies, once the idea of war justified by national purpose was established, it was easily co-opted for any form of nationalistic goals, whether the imperialism of the nineteenth century or the demagoguery and totalitarianism of the twentieth. Coupled with other developments—the idea of *compétence de guerre*, the conception that the nation at war had the right to draw on the entire resources of the nation to make war, the conception that only total victory over the enemy is acceptable, and the new developments in the technology of war made possible by the Industrial Revolution—the resulting form of war was deeply unlike earlier more limited forms of war.

By the time of the American Civil War of 1861–65 and the Franco-Prussian War of 1870, various forms of reaction had begun to take shape. One form of such response focused on trying to limit the destructiveness of war; this was the line taken by the American theorist Francis Lieber and the U.S. Army's General Orders No. 100 (1863) and by the contemporaneous first Geneva Convention: these developments sought to strengthen the limits imposed by the *jus ad bellum* of Western tradition.[20] The other line of reaction aimed at the idea of a *jus ad bellum*, the justification of the right to make war, and took the form of a rejection or restriction of this right. Both those who would abolish war entirely and those who would limit states' right to go to war made use of a growing critique of the institution of war itself as inevitably horrible, needlessly destructive of lives and values, and fed not by a search for justice but by the venality of states and their political leaders.

The just war idea as a concept of Christian moral thought has accordingly suffered. In Protestant thought this latter line of development led to a widespread adoption of pacifism, especially by religious elites, and to a criticism of the state system.[21]

In Catholic thought a form of pacifism has emerged as well, but the main line of moral doctrine has resulted in a somewhat modified version of the just war heritage. This line of development began with a document prepared for Vatican Council I in 1870, criticizing large standing national armies as fostering a spirit of militarism and leading to "hideous massacres" that the Church could not regard as just wars.[22] Such criticism of the destructiveness of modern war has continued through pastoral statements of successive popes from Pius XII through John Paul II down to the "presumption against war" language of the United States Catholic bishops.[23]

The reaction to modern war in international law has produced a *jus ad bellum* that explicitly limits the right of states to employ force except in self-defense, but which allows internationally mandated uses of force in response to certain types of threat.[24] Otherwise the status of the *jus ad bellum* of international law is much the same as outlined theoretically by Grotius in 1625. Thus the concerns of just war tradition remain present there, though truncated, in legal form.

The rise of the modern state and of totalistic war form the immediate backdrop for reflection on the question of justification in contemporary resort to armed force. In what follows I will argue that these developments have colored twentieth-century conceptions too much, and that the picture of war and statecraft painted by the reaction against totalistic forms of war undertaken for *raison d'état* badly distorts the understanding of contemporary warfare and the possibility of justified uses of armed force in the service of justice, international order, and peace.

Justification of Uses of Armed Force in Contemporary Context

While classic just war theory envisioned the political community, under the authority of its sovereign head, as the central actor in the employment of armed force to combat injustice, twentieth-century legal and moral thought in the just war tradition have sought to limit the right of individual states to resort to force, while reserving a somewhat larger latitude to international organizations—in particular, the United Nations. The limitation placed on individual states represents a response to modern developments in the conception of the state and the character of warfare that together have had the effect of making war seem more an instrument of injustice than of justice, more a source of destruction of lives and values than a means of protecting them. In the following discussion I will first explore the implications of this change and certain problems associated with it in the turn away from the state and toward international authorization for the use of armed force; then I will argue for a new focus on the role of the state in the use of force in the service of justice, viewing this through the lens of the fundamental just war idea of *jus ad bellum*.

The United Nations Organization and the Use of Armed Force

In positive international law the attempt to restrict the right of states to initiate the use of armed force on their own authority began in the aftermath of World War I, when the League of Nations Covenant set up arbitration procedures aimed at staving off the possibility of war among member nations. Subsequently the Pact of Paris of 1928 bound its signatories not to initiate war against one another, though it left open the option of using armed force in defense against attack. Continuing along the same path, in the wake of World War II the United Nations Charter prohibited member states from "the threat or use of force against the territorial integrity or political independence of any state" (Article 2), while granting the power of self-defense against "armed attack" to all nations, acting individually or col-

lectively (Article 51). At the same time, the Charter gave th
Security Council the power to authorize force in cases of threa
to "international peace and security" (Chapter VII). Thus, in
positive international law the right to engage in offensive uses of
force, in the sense of military actions across borders, was located
in the United Nations itself—in particular, within the Security
Council.

I have already indicated how in moral thought the modern
conception of the state and the destructiveness of modern war
had initiated a reaction by the latter third of the nineteenth
century, establishing patterns of criticism of the state and of war
that have endured to the present. This development has been fed
in the twentieth century by the experience of the two world
wars, by the American experience in Vietnam, and by the development of nuclear weapons. For many opponents of modern
war, a much-quoted statement by Pope John XXIII in the en-
cyclical *Pacem in Terris* might stand as at least a minimal expression of their position: "in this age which boasts of its atomic
power, it no longer makes sense to maintain that war is a fit instrument with which to repair the violation of justice."[25] Other
moral criticism, as I have noted, focused on the venality and
"militarism" of modern states. But the same moral reproach was
not leveled at the United Nations, which for critics of the modern state and the state system could be held up as transcending   *right*
their failures. That the United Nations could, under the conditions of the cold war, authorize military force only in peacekeeping operations, that the forces in question would be always small
and lightly armed, and that resort to them was relatively infre-
quent helped to insulate the international organization from the   *v*
criticisms of modern war directed at the military establishments
of powerful states.

Moral thought shaped by visions of the militarism and

venality of states, not to mention those of internationalists, and focused on the United Nations as the beginning of a new world order in which the state system would vanish neglected to take adequate account of the fact that real power was not located in the international organization but remained with the individual states and the groupings of states that formed around a common purpose. Hence these efforts to find in the United Nations a form of statecraft in which states play a subordinate role were utopian, based on an imagined reality that did not yet exist and downplaying the reality that did exist.

The relentlessly negative portrayal of the state as an institution both disregarded the positive attributes of the state system and ignored differences in the way specific states were constituted and how they behaved. On the other hand, an uncritically positive attitude toward the possibilities of international order overlooked the fact that the structure of order defined through the United Nations was not one that could stand alone; rather, it depended on viable states—particularly the great powers seated in the Security Council—to function. Further, this positive attitude toward the United Nations did not take account of the fact that under the conditions of the cold war this organization was not able to do the best it could in living up to the role envisioned for it in the Charter. The end of the cold war removed this latter problem and set the United Nations free to act in accord with the provisions of the Charter: the right to intervene, by force if necessary, in conflicts where no peace had been established, in order to set right conditions deemed to pose a threat to international peace and security.

Yet paradoxically, being set free to act in this way made plain the more fundamental limitation inherent in the character of the United Nations as an international organization: that it lacks in itself the attributes necessary to make it capable of effectively

UN (or non-sovereign) has NO just war capacity —

2

acting out this role stipulated in the Charter. It lacks cohesion, so that policies and decisions have led to inconsistency in its dealings with the conflicts it has addressed. It lacks sovereignty but depends on agreements among its sovereign member states. It lacks an effective chain of command for military forces it may place in the midst of an ongoing conflict, so they cannot be an effective arm of international statecraft. All these features that the United Nations Organization lacks are in fact necessary characteristics of the state as a political institution, and their absence at once shows the limits of the role of the United Nations and the continuing importance of states in the international system. All the deficiencies noted are first and foremost defects in sovereign authority; but since without such authority there is no entity competent to determine just cause and undertake military action on its behalf, this lack means that the United Nations as an institution cannot have a *jus ad bellum* in the fundamental just war sense. Legally, the lack of these characteristics undermines the positive-law definition of just cause whereby certain rights are reserved to the Security Council while being denied to individual states or other organizations or groupings of states. Empirically, the record of United Nations–authorized military intervention in Somalia and in Bosnia has brought these problems to light.

At the same time, the press of events has produced a nascent customary international law that preserves the form of the existing positive law while reflecting the continuing rights and responsibilities of states and proceeding from the fact that viable states possess what the United Nations does not: competent authority to formulate policies and reach decisions regarding the just use of force, to exercise command over such force, and to assess their rights and responsibilities relative to ongoing conflicts even when they have not themselves been party to these

UN → Devolves auth. to Coalition

conflicts. Many commentators regard customary international law, based on the collective attitudes and actions of states, as the real international law, not that which is written down in positive form *unless* it is backed up by state attitudes and behavior. So it is especially important, I think, that the recent crises in Kuwait, Somalia, and the former Yugoslavia have brought into being a process whereby the rights of just cause reserved to the United Nations in positive international law have been extended to individual states and coalitions of states to give them rights to use military force across national borders which the positive-law concept of just cause sought to deny them. The three cases I have mentioned exemplify this development in different ways. The legal grounding of the response to the invasion and occupation of Kuwait, where this extension was first evident, was admittedly mixed. While the coalition action was carefully defined so as to fit the conditions of Article 51 of the Charter, whereby groups of states are given the right collectively to respond to an ongoing armed attack (in this case, Iraq's ongoing military occupation of Kuwait), Security Council authority was also sought and obtained for the coalition's action, an authority that was not strictly required under the terms of Article 51.[26] Somalia too provides a mixed lesson, in which the United States and other individual nations contributed forces under the legal authority of the United Nations and in accord with its definition of just cause; yet, in the case of the United States forces, the chain of command was American, and the United Nations possessed only an ineffective command authority over the other national forces present. The problem of an effective chain of command carried over into Bosnia both while the intervention there was entirely a United Nations operation and after it became a mixed UN–NATO cooperative effort. The Dayton Accords achieved a different state of affairs, in which the responsibility shifted le-

a new authority
(security council)
+ NATO

gally to maintaining the peace agreed to by the conflicting parties, and in which the military Implementation Force (IFOR)
and its successor the Stabilization Force (SFOR) were made up
of NATO troops under NATO command. This carries the development I have described to what may be a new state of equilib-
rium, in which regional alliances employ interventionary force
with the formal authorization of the United Nations and in
accord with the just causes reserved to that body in positive
international law, causes going beyond what is allowed such
regional alliances by the same body of positive law.

Now, while I have had a good deal to say about the question
of authority, these reflections bear simultaneously on the question of just cause, since these two elements of the *jus ad bellum*
are closely intertwined. Encapsulated within the development I
have sketched is a significant expansion of the *de facto* conception of just cause for major states and powerful groupings of
states able to shape Security Council decisions. Whatever the *de
jure* limits on the right of a state or a group of states to engage in
the use of force across national boundaries, if Security Council
sanction for such action can be obtained, the result is effectively
the same as if the states directly possessed the right to such
action. This possibility has been in existence since 1945, but it
was limited in the cold war era by the presence of the veto in the
Security Council. In the post–cold war context the logjam of a
party-line veto has given way to a situation in which, in practical
terms, what is required is that the majority of Security Council
members agree to support a particular use of force, while no
one permanent member opposes it enough to veto it. This implies that the extension of the just cause idea I have described
will take place only with coalitions of nations whose core prominently includes a majority of permanent Security Council
members.

a new source of authorization

political, not legal — (shifting by the moment) ← Back to old conception (the power, not rules)

63

It is notable that both NATO and the coalition formed against Iraq in the Gulf War satisfied this condition. While the latter was an ad hoc grouping of nations for a single purpose, NATO's ongoing institutional existence defined by treaty, common interests of the members, and a half-century of history of common cooperation gives it a much more significant potential role. NATO was brought into existence in accord with the understanding defined in the United Nations Charter that regional alliances of states could be formed for a defensive purpose. It was thus defined formally by the same highly restricted positive-law conception of just cause for use of armed force which applied to individual states. The debate over NATO involvement in Bosnia and the gradual growth of that involvement marks a transition away from this conception of NATO's role; it also marks the coalescence of a new definition of just cause for the use of forces under NATO command.

Finally, with the replacement of the United Nations peace-keeping forces by a robust NATO force, and with tactical decisions regarding just cause for use of that force in the hands of those within the NATO chain of command authority, a state of affairs has been reached that embodies the new conception sketched above. The positive legal authority for this force's presence remains that defined by the framework of the United Nations Charter, but the *de facto* authority for the use of force has been delegated to this regional organization, and this regional organization has been given the power to act within the broader framework of just cause which was earlier denied to it—a framework that includes not only defense of self but defense of the rights of others. This is extremely significant in both political and moral terms: politically, in that it embodies a conception of an international political body greater than the individual state, yet not so utopian as earlier conceptions of world order; morally, in that it embodies both the recognition of a concept of just cause for use of military force that goes beyond the narrow right of self-defense and the extension of this concept to a regional grouping of states.

The United States, because of its post–cold war preeminence, is positioned to be significantly affected, as recipient of both benefits and burdens, by this *de facto* redistribution of the right to resort to force for reasons other than national defense against armed attack. At the same time, the nature of the shift implicitly requires that decisions to resort to force for such causes be subject to the test of approval by the other powers that make up the permanent membership of the Security Council and participate in such regional security groupings as NATO or ad hoc coalitions that may be formed in response to particular crises. This suggests that the states involved in such groupings must share more than simply common interests; it implies that they must agree that common values are at stake. Thus there seems to me to be a tilt here toward support for broadly recognized rights and humanitarian needs, a point to which I will return below.

What this developing *de facto* state of affairs implies for major powers acting in their own spheres of interest, either unilaterally or at the head of regional groupings of states, also seems clear. Whether it is the United States employing military force in the Western Hemisphere (as in Grenada, Panama, and Haiti) or Russia in the Caucasus (as in Chechnya and, more limitedly, elsewhere) or France in its former colonies in central Africa, the restrictive limits of the *de jure* definition of just cause seem no longer to apply—if, indeed, they ever in reality had the force they claimed.

All this bears directly on the possibility of uses of force that are genuinely preemptive, which anticipate the beginning of armed aggression but do not wait for that aggression to take place. Such uses might take the form of actions across a national border in response to perceived security threats while in the process of development or, more broadly, actions aimed at ending violations of human rights or other prominent evils that the local authorities either do not address or are unable to deal with. The behavior of states since 1945 has never consistently ratified the intent in Article 2 of the UN Charter to disallow cross-border projections of force except after a first military attack has taken place. Yet there are two new elements in the current scene: first, a recognition that the danger may not be military but may nonetheless threaten national security (for example, the drug trade, terrorism and other hostile acts by the leadership of a foreign country or with their approval and support); second, the possibility of intervention to correct ills that are not themselves directly or immediately threatening to national security but which entail major violations of universal values which the local government has not sought to remedy (indeed, it may itself be the source of the violations) or is unable to remedy. The United States intervention in Haiti exemplifies a national action to set right violations of value which had both these characteristics at the same time.

National Interest and Support for Universal Values as Sources for Just Cause

These last considerations introduce another morally significant element in the developing contemporary *de facto* understanding of just cause for use of armed force: that just cause as currently understood in practice may proceed from concerns of national interest that include, but go beyond, immediate military threats, and in other instances from concern to protect universal values, remedy their violation, and prevent violations from continuing. At the same time, the use of military force that is justified in these ways is not the same as that envisioned in the international-law effort to restrict military action to responses to armed attack. This latter conception envisioned military action as the initiation of war between nations, war that might escalate to become total in its means and draw other nations into it so that it became global; in other words, it reflected the developments in the character of war that began with the age of Napoleon and in the twentieth century led to two world wars fought with totalistic means and purposes. While the redefined just cause I have been describing opens the door to such a form of war as an extreme possibility, in context it has to do with far more restrained and local applications of military force.

Indeed, such uses of armed force are best understood as not to involve the making of war at all but to encourage the establishment of peace: to separate warring parties, to provide or facilitate delivery of food or medical care, to keep peace while a fractured society rebuilds itself, and possibly to support such rebuilding not only morally but materially. Above this level, but still well below the level of all-out war, are uses of military means that might involve interdiction or punishment of organized criminal activities (for example, United States use of air, naval, and military intelligence capabilities against the Latin American drug trade), limited applications of force to discourage and punish aggression (for example, the use of NATO air and UN artillery strikes in Bosnia in the period prior to the signing of the peace accord), or protection of the rights of minorities (for example, enforcement of the protective zones designed to benefit the Shiite and Kurdish populations in Iraq). Also in this intermediate level fall military responses to terrorist activity (for example, Israel's periodic resort to military action in southern Lebanon, the United States air strike against Libya) and preemptive limited military strikes to remove a threat still in the process of developing (for example, Israel's use of air power against an Iraqi nuclear reactor capable of producing weapons-grade fissionable material).

Where, in the above mixture of situations, do interests end and ideals begin? I suggest that in the present environment these are not discrete alternatives but mutually supplemental sources for the idea of justice in just cause for resort to armed force and for a contemporary definition of right intention, as exemplified by the variety of purposes being served in the above cases. Indeed, I would carry this argument further. If the paradigm is that of the black-letter law as stated in the United Nations Charter, that individual states and regional organizations of states may resort to force only in armed self-defense against attack by other armed force, then the argument from national or regional security interests fits well. But if the paradigm is instead that defined by the developing customary law since the end of the cold war, in which the rights reserved in positive law to the United Nations are exercised in a *de facto* manner by regional organizations and individual states, then not only state interests narrowly conceived, but also internationally recognized values must be taken into account.

The effect of this development in international affairs, I suggest, is to create a contemporary conception of the justified use of military force that has much in common with the fundamental just war *jus ad bellum*. Though there are differences between this contemporary conception and that established in just war tradition (thus necessitating a continuing dialogue and moral critique), they are not as great as those between the traditional just war *jus ad bellum* and earlier arguments as to the meaning of international law. On the contemporary conception defined in developing customary law, the criterion of competent authority requires not only sovereignty, but a significant measure

of international agreement, either by formal Security Cour
sanction or at least by the lack of negative sanction (and thus
tacit acceptance) in the case of joint action by groupings of
states. Such approval serves also to ratify the presence of just
cause and right intention. The criterion of just cause is no
longer the very narrow conception of defense defined as second
use of force in response to armed attack but includes uses of
military force, sometimes preemptively, for the purpose of protecting major values broadly held, including formally denoted
"threats to international peace and security." This idea of just
cause could be accurately described in classic just war terms as
including not only defense, but also punishment of evil and the
retaking of something wrongly taken. Finally, the criterion of
right intention is satisfied by uses of military force undertaken
by actors for the purposes described, rather than for purposes of
aggression or national self-interest narrowly conceived.

To return to a theme that is central to this chapter, I regard
the question of justified use of force in the present historical
context to be very different from that posed in the context of
total war. In response to this changed state of affairs, I have
argued that a contemporary *jus ad bellum* is developing in the
practice of the United Nations and of individual states which in
important ways closely matches the concerns addressed in the
original just war *jus ad bellum*. The result has implications not
only for how Americans should think about the policy and
military actions of the United States, but also for how other
peoples around the world should reflect on their own place and
that of their states in the contemporary international order.

From the perspective of persons who continue to regard
states as incurably venal and all uses of force in the modern era
as disproportionately destructive, the position I have defined
will seem an unwarranted and immoral loosening of strictures

Beyond 'total war,'
back to pre-1648 –

against the resort to force. From the perspective of political realism, my argument will, on the other hand, seem to have gone too far, taking too much account of moral concerns, international standards, and values. But between these two perspectives is precisely the territory of just war tradition, an understanding of statecraft in which the use of armed force in the service of justice is both permitted and restrained. Such is the conception of just cause I have sought to define and whose implications I have sought to draw out for the contemporary age.

3

The Context of the Question

The problem of intervention involving military force has emerged as one of the most pressing issues for international statecraft in the aftermath of the cold war. Two related factors have contributed to this. First, the end of the structured superpower rivalry of the cold war removed the restraining and controlling effect that this rivalry had had on local disputes, with the consequence that such disputes have often developed into intense and highly destructive armed struggles characterized by great suffering, displacement of people, societal breakdown, and death in the affected populations. Second, the end of the cold war rivalry has created a space for third-party states and the international community to intervene in these local conflicts to mitigate their destructiveness and to seek to influence their course and outcome, an involvement that might earlier have led to a wider war.

There were, to be sure, local armed conflicts during the cold war era. For those which took place within the sphere of interest of one of the superpowers, the other and its allies were inhibited from intervention even for the purpose of humanitarian relief. Many conflicts outside these immediate spheres of interest involved the superpowers and/or their allies directly or indirectly, with means ranging from clandestine support to provision of weapons and training to proxy warfare. Other simmering conflicts were suppressed or managed by the superpowers or their allies so as to avoid the possibility of escalation. Such activities in some cases masked long-term and deeply felt hostilities and in other cases created or fueled new rivalries or uncovered old ones. With the end of superpower involvement, these antagonisms have sometimes erupted into armed conflict, whether for the purpose of establishing one group as dominant (or even eliminating a rival group), to create a new state or redraw existing boundaries, or simply to revenge past wrongs. Local forces, left free to fight out their differences, have engaged in such conflicts, presenting the international community with repeated cases of armed conflict–created instability and humanitarian need on a massive scale.

The United Nations also, in the context of the cold war, was inhibited in how it dealt with conflicts by the realities of the superpower rivalry. Leaving much of the matter of relief of victims to nongovernmental organizations (NGOs) and private voluntary organizations (PVOs), the United Nations focused on keeping conflicts in check through peacekeeping operations involving United Nations diplomacy and the interposition of forces almost always from nonaligned member states between conflicting parties, following provisions in Chapter VI of the Charter. United Nations peacekeeping during this period developed a characteristic form: it depended on the parties to a conflict achieving a cease-fire and actually inviting United Nations peacekeepers into the region of conflict to monitor the cease-fire. Such a force was interventionary, but dependent on the conflicting parties' cease-fire and their invitation; it was non-belligerent, with no purpose of military involvement in the conflict in question; it was not aimed at imposing a solution to the conflict or rebuilding the society torn by war; it was not for the purpose of humanitarian relief, though it ideally maintained a context in which such relief, as well as rebuilding and reconciliation, might occur. The light arms with which peacekeepers were equipped were comparable to those of police forces, not combat units, and were intended only for protection against unauthorized actions in violation of the cease-fire. The conflicting parties themselves, on this model, bore the responsibility for maintaining the cease-fire and preventing their forces from breaking it, and the peacekeeping forces not only were not mandated to enforce the peace against the military forces of these parties, but they were not designed to do so.

Already with the approach of the end of the cold war these prevailing patterns began to undergo some changes. In Sudan, Ethiopia, Somalia, and other areas of conflict, private relief organizations and agencies began to intervene to provide humanitarian assistance to the victims of conflicts even when there was no cease-fire, they had not been invited by the conflicting parties, and their personnel were not under the protection of the forces in conflict. National support of such efforts also became more open, with military transport for relief supplies being provided in some cases. Attempting to assist the coalition government in Cambodia after the era of the Khmer Rouge, United Nations peacekeepers extended the role of such forces by convoying the relief efforts of NGOs and at times taking on a quasi-belligerent role relative to the parties to the not-yet-settled dispute. With the end of the cold war these trends have continued and become more settled, while new dimensions have also developed.

Nonetheless, the abruptness of the end of a world system deeply shaped by the bipolar superpower rivalry and the eruption and multiplication of local wars totally unlike the nuclear conflict anticipated in much policy, military planning, and moral discourse have meant that inevitably the transition to the new era has been marked by an absence of settled political and institutional arrangements or a moral consensus on what to do. Even as local conflicts have multiplied, so have interventions, pieced together and justified by ad hoc decisions and arguments, often backed by a moral rationale of a similar ad hoc nature.

In this chapter I will examine when intervention in local conflicts by military means is morally justified and what limits such intervention should observe, drawing on just war thinking about the proper nature of statecraft and conditions for justified use of military force in the service of statecraft. I begin in the following section by discussing three examples of explicit just war reasoning directed to the question of intervention: that of Protestant theologian Paul Ramsey in his essay, "The Ethics of Intervention";[1] that of political philosopher Michael Walzer's chapter on "Interventions" in his 1977 book *Just and Unjust Wars*;[2] and that of the United States Catholic bishops in their 1993 statement on peace and war.[3] Ramsey's and Walzer's discussions mark early and late stages, respectively, in the last previous major moral debate over intervention in the United States, that over American involvement in the war in Vietnam. Ramsey's was originally prepared as a paper given in 1965, the year in which full commitment of United States combat troops began, while Walzer's comes from the years immediately following American troop withdrawal. Each reflects this debate, yet both are intentionally moral

analyses and arguments about the problem of intervention
general. The position of the United States Catholic bishops s
cifically addresses the current context, but is heavily influenced
by conceptions framed in the cold war context. All three explicitly connect to just war tradition, though the ways they use that
tradition differ considerably. Together they embody some of the
most serious just war–based thinking about the problem of
intervention in the last thirty years. Following the discussion of
these three moral perspectives on intervention, the third section
of this chapter examines the question of intervention involving
military force in the context of international law, which is itself
historically one of the major streams by which just war tradition
has developed. In the final section I provide my own assessment
of the moral issues associated with military intervention.

Three Moral Arguments on Intervention

"[I]t is the wrong-doing of the opposing party which com-
pels the wise man to wage just wars," wrote the Christian theologian Augustine of Hippo early in the fifth century in *The City of
God*.[4] Later just war tradition, citing another work of Augustine's,[5] explained what this would mean, leading to the fundamental concept of just cause for the use of force as defined by
the need for defense or for vindicative justice.[6] What is most
fundamental in this conception of just cause is that it justifies
the use of force not out of self-interest but for the sake of others:
those who are in need of defense or who have suffered wrongs
needing to be righted. The nature of this obligation was, for
many during the formative period of just war thought, encapsulated in a much-quoted statement by the fourth-century Christian theologian Ambrose of Milan, the mentor of Augustine:
"He who does not keep harm off a friend, if he can, is as much
in fault as he who causes it."[7] The idea of the *jus ad bellum*

defend the neighbor

developed out of this conception of an obligation to defend the neighbor, by force if necessary. The distance between the moral reasoning of Ambrose and Augustine and that of the three examples of contemporary just war thinking about intervention is great in historical terms, but small in terms of the positions taken. The moral justification for intervention in all three of these cases is grounded in a concern for justice focused on setting right wrongs done to others who are not able to prevent such injustice on their own.

Paul Ramsey's Reasoning on Intervention

For Ramsey, in line with the fundamental paradigm of just war thought about the moral use of force in statecraft, military intervention in the cause of justice is "among the rights and duties of states unless and until supplanted by superior government."[8] Were there such a higher order, then the obligation of maintaining justice and the right to employ military means to do so would rest there. But there is no such superior order in the international arena;[9] thus the responsibility rests with states, and in particular with the United States: "The primary reality of the present age and the foreseeable future is that the United States has had responsibility thrust upon it for more of the order and realized justice in the world than it has the power to effectuate" (23). The result is a tension between what can be done and what ought to be done:

> [F]or us to choose political or military intervention is to use power tragically incommensurate with what politically should be done, while not to intervene means tragically to fail to undertake the responsibilities that are there, and are not likely to be accomplished by other political actors. (23)

For Ramsey, the former is simply an expression of the nature of the empirical limits of politics, while the latter expresses the moral obligation that may lead to intervention: not having the power necessary to accomplish the ideal does not imply standing aside from all action but may imply, rather, the obligation to act even with limited abilities to produce limited good. Thus the *right* of intervention follows not from the power, but from the *responsibility*, to intervene; states possess the right only insofar as they experience this responsibility as an obligation to act in the service of justice in the international arena.

With the overall context thus set for moral reasoning about intervention, Ramsey narrows his focus to define the allowable grounds for intervention, distinguishing two sorts: "ultimate," or "just war," grounds and "penultimate," or "secondary," ones.[10] Four considerations define the former: the requirements of justice, order (both "terminal goals in . . . proper politics"), the national and international common good, and domestic and international law. First, posits Ramsey, "the statesman must make a decision about the politically embodied justice he is apt to sustain or increase by his choice to intervene or not to intervene." Second, he must make "an assessment of order as one of the ends power must serve." Third, he must measure whether to intervene or not by the degree to which it serves national and international common good, which "are not always the same." The statesman should seek to make choices that fall in "the area of incidence, or overlap, between them." This limits the practical scope of the obligation: the requirement to serve justice and order does not imply overextension at the expense of the common good (and thus the justice and order) of one's own nation. What needs morally to be done in the world always requires resources far greater than those available. The statesman, observes Ramsey, "is not called to office to aim at all the humanitarian good that can be aimed at in the world. Instead he must determine what he *ought to do* from out of the total humanitarian *ought to be.*" Good statecraft involves careful choices among the possibilities for moral action. A justified intervention, then, is not one that serves this "ought to be" alone, any more than it would be one that served national interest alone. A common area must be found. Finally, Ramsey calls on the statesman to consider the requirements of the domestic legal system as well as international law and international institutions in determining whether to intervene in a specific case. This consideration, as Ramsey further develops his argument, turns out to be less an expression of the "ultimate" or moral grounds for intervention than an opening to his discussion of the "penultimate" grounds.

In the immediate context, though, it is clear that Ramsey wants all four of these considerations to be satisfied; but he does not require that all four be satisfied completely or equally well. Rather, there is a priority among them, with justice not only the first concern in order of priority, but also a concern embedded in the other three. He makes this point explicitly in developing what he means by the statesman's responsibility to law:

> Not all justice is legal justice. Not all order is legal order. The legalities comprise, of course, mankind's attempt to impose some coherence upon the order of power. But such coherence flows also from the justice that may be preserved, beyond or beneath the legalities, in the relative power positions of the nations. (30)

This statement, taken to its extreme, implies that a principled action in the service of justice may trump the requirements of law. Indeed, Ramsey follows the above passage with a discussion that shows some skepticism about international law in particular, criticizing that form of Christian opinion in his own time that looked to international law as the normative reference point for determining justice and order in relations among nations. The proper understanding, Ramsey argues, is in

'International' is not automatically supreme

fact the reverse of this: good statecraft must judge internation
law in terms of the normative goals of justice, order, and the
common good. International law is also deficient by comparison with domestic law: its legalities are "far more imperfect"
and "the social due process for changing the legal system . . .
even more wanting" (31). Yet, as Ramsey further explores the
relation of justice and law in the international arena, he does not
push to the most radical conclusion from this argument, which
is that national action, convinced of its justice, need take no
account of international law. Rather, on this point, as on the
relation between the requirements of justice and available resources, he argues that statecraft should seek to find an area of
common ground (31–33).

Johnson

More light is shed on what he has in mind in the justice–law
relationship in his discussion of the "penultimate," or "secondary," justifications for intervention (33–38). The two he identifies, counter-intervention and intervention by invitation, might
better be termed conditions or cases in which intervention may
be justified.[11] The "ultimate," or "just war," concerns, Ramsey
makes clear, must be satisfied first: "The penultimate justifications finally depend upon the validity of particular decisions
made in terms of just war intervention."[12] But the two secondary
justifications are precisely cases in which intervention is allowed
by international law, and recognizing this clarifies the structure
of Ramsey's argument about the relation between considerations of justice and of law in decisions about intervention. His
position is that the secondary justifications should never be regarded as ultimate in themselves, so no decision can be made on
their basis alone (34). Yet, while account must always be taken of
the ultimate (just war) grounds, it is also the case that "this does
not mean that these grounds are ordinarily sufficient without
having recourse to the secondary justifications" (33–34). Rather,

(Right of intervention) Justice above international law –

79

these latter justifications carry "additional validity" of their own; they set "firebreaks" or "qualitative boundaries" on what may be done (34).

The upshot is a conception of justified intervention as normally requiring both moral ("ultimate," or "just war") justifications and legal ("penultimate," or "secondary") ones. The legal justifications alone are not sufficient, because, lacking prior moral warrant, particular appeals to the right of counter-intervention or intervention by invitation may not aim at justice or order but instead may simply cloak the cynical self-interest of the intervening state.[13] "[J]ustice and order and the relevant common goods are always needed in the justification," writes Ramsey.[14]

But just as it is necessary for the moral justifications to be added to the legal ones, so also the norm for good statecraft is to take account of the latter and not seek to serve only the former. The moral justifications are necessary, Ramsey argues, though "ordinarily" not sufficient in themselves without the additional warrant of those cases allowed in international law. This leaves open as an extraordinary option, in Ramsey's construction of the argument, interventions that meet the moral tests but not the legal ones, but Ramsey does not pursue this possibility, which would open the way to a conception of statecraft in which the right of intervention becomes a form of crusade. Rather, his focus is on what he calls "politically responsible" action (35), action that falls in the area of overlap between the two kinds of justification. This is the area in which the actual choices are to be found, with which good statecraft should be concerned.

Ramsey's understanding of the justifiability of intervention recalls the concept of right intention as defined by Augustine and adopted by his medieval heirs: not an intention shaped by the possibility of gain, superior power, or any other factor based on self-interest, but rather the intent to prevent injustice and to restore justice; this is *right* intention. This way of approaching intervention—or, for that matter, any other state decision, whether involving use of military force or not—is clearly in substantial tension with the approach of political realism, for which national interest should guide decision making. Ramsey's position clearly rules out an exclusive reliance on the latter, but it also places concern for the national good in the context of the moral grounds for which intervention may be justified. In his terms, the national interest properly understood is not distinct from the demands of justice and order or of the international common good. Statecraft must seek to be guided by all three, while taking account of the empirical resources available and respecting the boundaries of action laid out by international agreement in international law. This way of understanding the question of intervention puts the question of its moral justification first, but it also respects the limits of the contemporary international order. We turn now to an understanding of intervention which begins with positive international law as an expression of this order, then explores the justification of intervention in terms of exceptions to a fundamental paradigm.

Michael Walzer on the Justification of Intervention

Arguably no principle is more sacrosanct in the modern concept of international order based on the state system than the inviolability of the borders of a sovereign state. Clearly visible in the assumptions that underlay European balance-of-power politics during much of the nineteenth century, in the twentieth this principle has become embedded in positive international law, where it underpins the idea of *jus ad bellum* narrowed to the concept of national defense. For Michael Walzer this idea is a fundamental element in the "legalist paradigm" of international order, which he defines by means of six propositions:

1. There exists an international society of independent states.
2. This international society has a law that establishes the rights of its members—above all, the rights of territorial integrity and political sovereignty.
3. Any use of force or imminent threat of force by one state against the political sovereignty or territorial integrity of another constitutes aggression and is a criminal act.
4. Aggression justifies two kinds of violent response: a war of self-defense by the victim and a war of law enforcement by the victim and any other member of international society.
5. Nothing but aggression can justify war.
6. Once the aggressor state has been repelled, it can also be punished.[15]

Among the *prima facie* obligations that the principle of territorial integrity imposes on states is nonintervention across the borders of other states. Thus Walzer, in the opening sentence of his chapter on "Interventions," links the general requirement of nonintervention to the legalist paradigm, going on to argue that intervention by military force is almost always forbidden by it, yet may be justified in certain exceptional cases by precisely the same fundamental values that give rise to this paradigm. As Walzer puts it, "those conceptions of life and liberty which underlie the paradigm and make it plausible . . . seem also to require that we sometimes disregard the principle" of nonintervention (86). Specifically, he argues that there are three sorts of cases in which the prohibition of cross-border uses of military force does not "seem to serve the purposes for which it was intended": (1) intervention in civil wars involving states in which there are two or more political communities, when one community resorts to force for the purpose of secession or "national liberation"; (2) counter-intervention in a conflict to offset a prior intervention by another power; and (3) intervention to counter extreme violations of human rights by fighters in the course of an armed conflict or by a government against its people (90). Cross-border uses of military force which are undertaken for one or more of the above reasons constitute exceptions to the *prima facie* rule against such intervention. Yet the justification for intervention in each of these cases also carries with it limits on the actions that may be taken.

Following the methodology employed throughout *Just and Unjust Wars*, Walzer employs historical examples to explore these three exceptional cases in which intervention may be justified: for the first case, the Hungarian revolution of 1848–49; for the second, American intervention in the war in Vietnam; and for the third, the United States' intervention in Cuba in 1898 and that of India in Bangladesh in 1971.

Walzer's discussion of the first case follows closely the nearly contemporary argument of John Stuart Mill. Mill, though generally opposed to intervention, argued that in the case of the Hungarian attempt to secede from the Austro-Hungarian Empire and establish an independent state, two issues mattered: first, that the Hungarians actually constituted a distinct political community able to win its independence and govern itself, and second, that it was prevented from doing so by Russian intervention on behalf of the Empire, which led to the crushing of the rebellion in 1849. Writing about this event ten years later, Mill argued that the British should have counter-intervened so as to neutralize the effect of the Russian action, leaving the matter to be settled by the original parties to the conflict (92–93). Walzer notes that Mill's argument tends "to justify assistance to a secessionist movement at the same time as it justifies counter-intervention, indeed, to assimilate the one to the other" (93). Walzer wants to keep these issues theoretically separate; yet, as I argue below, he does much the same thing as Mill in his own treatment of the Hungarian secession movement and the war in Vietnam. The two issues—whether intervention is justified in support of a secessionist movement and whether it is justified as a response to an earlier intervention in a conflict by another outside party—can in fact be separated theoretically, but the separation is somewhat artificial. Since the Russian intervention was at the request of the Austrian emperor, there is also a third issue involved here, intervention by invitation, which is linked to the other two. Presumably the Russians weighed the justification of the Hungarian independence movement on their own terms before responding positively to the request to intervene, and presumably the British would have done so as well before counter-intervening. The key is the judgment as to the cause; the justification of intervention, whether by invitation or in the form of counter-intervention, has a secondary role. This is in fact the argument we have observed in Ramsey's analysis above, and it turns out in practice to be Walzer's argument as well, though his analytical categories separate support for secession from counter-intervention, and he does not have a separate category for intervention by invitation.

Walzer agrees with Mill on the virtuousness of the Hungarian cause.

> The problem with a secessionist movement is that one cannot be sure that it in fact represents a distinct community until it has rallied its own people and made some headway in the "arduous struggle" [Mill's phrase] for freedom. The mere appeal to the principle of self-determination isn't enough; evidence must be provided that a community actually exists whose members are committed to independence and ready and able to deter-

mine the conditions of their own existence. Hence the need for
political or military struggle sustained over time. (93–94)

On Walzer's reading, the same argument would apply whether
or not the case was one of counter-intervention; if the attempt at
independence met the conditions defined above, then an initial
intervention on its behalf would also be justified: "imagine a
small nation successfully mobilized to resist a colonial power
but slowly being ground down in the unequal struggle. Mill
would not insist, I think, that neighboring states should stand
by and watch its inevitable defeat" (94).

Something still appears to be missing in this analysis, though;
the secession of the southern states in the American Civil War
would seem to fit all the criteria for a distinct political community "ready and able to determine the conditions of their own
existence," as specified in the paragraph above; yet Mill, an oppo-
nent of slavery, did not favor British intervention on behalf of
the Confederacy; nor, I think, would Walzer wish to argue that
other nations should have intervened to enable this effort at self-
determination to succeed. Similarly, Walzer's reference to the
example of a struggle for independence against a colonial power
depends on a prior judgment against colonial rule. The question
of what Ramsey calls "politically embodied justice" in the cause
to be supported seems to require a more substantive answer than
Mill's argument and Walzer's use of it provide.

The case of American intervention in Vietnam, as discussed
by Walzer, presses this question further. Walzer rejects the "official American version" of the justification of this intervention
out of hand. There was no legitimate local government, "a political presence independent of ourselves," in South Vietnam; thus
it was not conceivable that it could "win the civil war if no
external force was brought to bear" on either side (97–98). Thus

the case of the South Vietnamese, for Walzer, failed the test that the Hungarian revolution of 1848–49 passed with flying colors. Since the government of South Vietnam was illegitimate, it is implicit (though not stated by Walzer) that the American intervention could not have followed an invitation or been an action in accord with the terms of treaty obligations of the United States to the South. Nor was this a case of counter-intervention in response to a prior intervention from North Vietnam, Walzer argues. He admits that there was, in the South, "a systematic campaign of subversion, terrorism, and guerilla war, largely directed and supplied from the North" (99). But it was not a prior intervention to which the United States responded. "It would be better to say that the U.S. was literally propping up a government . . . without a local political base, while the North Vietnamese were assisting an insurgent movement with deep roots in the countryside" (99). It is possible, he admits, that the division of Vietnam into two societies might have proceeded the way the division of North and South Korea did, and that the war in Vietnam could have had the character of the Korean War; but, he says, this was not the case (100).

There was, of course, a contrary description of the events and the justifications for intervention, the "official American argument," which Walzer dismisses as implausible and "accepted by virtually no one" (97). But in fact it had been widely accepted by the American public early in the war, and it still had considerable acceptance at the time Walzer was writing. The gradual erosion of support for American military involvement in the war in Vietnam probably had less to do with favoring an argument for Vietnamese self-determination and more to do with the growing cost in American money and lives of this involvement and with revulsion at the type of war this was, as played out on American television. As Walzer himself admits, it may well be impossible "to tell the story of Vietnam in a way that will command general agreement" (97). But his way of telling the story has a different purpose: to describe the situation in such a way as to show when intervention is not justified. He is engaged not in writing a history of the war in Vietnam, but in pursuing an argument on the moral justification of military intervention. But the telling of history and the moral argument cannot be separated in Walzer's method. Just as the case of the Hungarian revolution of 1848–49 allowed him to describe how such intervention may be justified, so that of Vietnam served the opposite, and complementary, purpose.

Walzer's methodology, while often powerful, is also often problematic, since it requires him to do two things at once: to make the moral argument and to interpret what happened historically. The problem in his use of the Hungarian revolution and the war in Vietnam is that his assessment is not self-evident in either case. Both contemporaries and historians have divided over how to understand these cases. Indeed, in both, the decision as to whether to support the political entity in question by intervention hinged importantly on whether it was understood to represent a legitimate political community. Civil wars are typically justified by appeals to self-determination and the legitimate desire for independence from oppression by the other party; such appeals were made in both these historical cases. Determining whether to credit such appeals has to do with more than the criteria assembled by Mill and adopted by Walzer above. When an outside party takes a side, whether for reasons of moral judgment or national interest or some other, this amounts to an acceptance of the claims of that side and the rejection of those of the other. This does not affect all arguments about the justifiability of intervention; but if the argument is made that intervention in support of legitimate secession movements or wars of "national liberation" is just, then the decision hinges on whether the secession is in fact legitimate, or whether a process of "national liberation" of a distinct political community is in fact taking place.

This aspect of Walzer's analysis of intervention corresponds to the necessity of determining "politically embodied justice" in Ramsey's, which also requires a moral judgment that the cause in question is worthy of support. For the case of the war in Vietnam, Ramsey, looking at American intervention in prospect, somewhat cautiously judged that it would be morally justified; whereas Walzer, looking at the intervention in retrospect, argued that it clearly had not been justified. For Ramsey, though, the judgment he made was, methodologically, only a contingent application of his theoretical analysis of the morality of intervention as a tool of statecraft; the particular judgment itself was not central to determining the parameters for a moral intervention, but secondary to it. For Walzer there is also a theoretical core that is independent of particular judgments, though this is obscured by his use of historical cases to develop the theory. In fact, it would be possible to take the other side in the two historical cases he chose, the Hungarian revolution of 1848–49 and the war in Vietnam, and still develop the questions that matter for Walzer in assessing the justification of intervention. Abstracting these questions means losing the sharp flavor of Walzer's moral argument, but it places the applicability of that argument on a more general level.

Another problem in his discussion of these two cases is that they lead him to muddy his categories. When he introduces the exceptional situations in which intervention may be justified, the first two are secession and counter-intervention. When he explores the cases at length, these categories have shifted to secession and civil war (91, 96). But both cases are in fact examples of civil war, and both are cases in which intervention and counter-intervention are at stake. As noted earlier, Walzer faults Mill's discussion of the Hungarian case for assimilating the issues of secession and counter-intervention to each other. But Walzer also conflates his categories. In fact, underlying his discussion are issues that are more fundamental than the categories he defines: the justice of the cause, the likelihood that the just side in the conflict will win, the prior involvement of other third parties.

There are also other issues which Walzer defines by means of his discussion of the two historical cases, but which are of general importance. First, he argues that prudential calculations of costs, benefits, and likelihood of success should be a part of the determination of the justice of intervention (95). This is reasoning very much in the tradition of the just war *jus ad bellum*. Second, he argues that the scope of counter-interventions should always be determined by considerations of "symmetry." As he applies this idea, it requires that counter-intervention be aimed not at winning the war, but rather only at reestablishing and maintaining the balance in place before the first intervention (100). I find this a problematical notion, at odds with his earlier argument about assisting a worthy independence movement to throw off colonial oppression. While consideration of proportionality in the sense of not causing more harm than good is certainly necessary in calculating the justice of intervention, the idea of balance, or "symmetry," has no clear relation to the other moral justifications established.

Walzer's final category of cases that may justify intervention is situations in which there are grave violations of human rights. The intervention that is justified in such cases is "humanitarian intervention" (101ff.). Here, he says, "we don't want the local balance to prevail." This is not a case in which the argument for self-determination can be applied, since the oppression may be so great that what is at stake is much more fundamental: "the bare survival or the minimal liberty" of significant numbers in a given political entity.

> Against the enslavement or massacre of political opponents, national minorities, and religious sects, there may well be no help unless help comes from outside. And when a government turns savagely upon its own people, we must doubt the very existence of a political community to which the idea of self-determination might apply. (101)

This states the moral justification for intervention very clearly; it is "vindicative justice" in a nutshell. It is interesting that Walzer does not apply this reasoning to the behavior of the North Vietnamese or the Viet Cong in the case of Vietnam. Walzer's discussion of the two historical cases of Hungary in 1848–49 and the American involvement in Vietnam does not add to this definition of the moral justification of intervening in the interests of humanitarian ends, but serves mainly to exemplify Walzer's doubt that, empirically, there are any cases of pure humanitarian purpose in intervention. Indeed, he observes that he has not found any, only ones in which there are mixed motives, with humanitarian ones alongside others. Other tests, then, need to be applied to empirical interventions to determine whether a claimed humanitarian purpose is in fact being served: who the targets of the intervention are, how destructive it is of the society in question, how quickly the intervening force withdraws after ending the humanitarian violations (103–106). Presumably, the prudential tests identified earlier should also apply. One consideration that Walzer does not believe should matter is whether the intervention is unilateral. "The legalist paradigm indeed rules out such efforts, but that only suggests that the paradigm, unrevised, cannot account for the moral realities of military intervention" (108).

The United States Catholic Bishops on Intervention

1983

In their influential 1983 pastoral letter, *The Challenge of Peace,*[16] which focused on the problems of war and peace in the nuclear age, the Catholic bishops of the United States did not address the subject of military intervention. Their focal concern was the possibility of international war, which they regarded as terrible enough if conventional, but which, if it involved the superpowers or their allied blocs, they expected would be a nuclear holocaust (32–33). While they referred their judgments to the moral theory of just war in Catholic tradition, they argued that this theory begins with a presumption against war (22, 26–34).[17] While they denounced aggressive use of military force and accepted the right of defense, they sought to define non-military means of defense, including reliance on nonviolence (22–26). In a major section on the promotion of peace, they identified as critical the need for arms control and disarmament, efforts to minimize the risk of "any war," civil defense, nonviolent means of conflict resolution, and the strengthening of world order (63–76). There was no major section on the possible use of armed force for the promotion of justice.

In November 1993, as a "reflection" on the tenth anniversary of the 1983 pastoral letter, the National Conference of Catholic Bishops issued a new statement on war and peace, *The Harvest of Justice Is Sown in Peace.*[18] Beginning with a "Call to Peacemaking in a New World" (1), the statement includes three major sections, headed by references to "peace," "peacemaking," and "peacemakers" respectively (2, 8, 19). The just war tradition is invoked, and its criteria listed, but nonviolence is explicitly

1993

1993: But justifies intervention
bishops

nowledged as a parallel tradition in Catholic thought (4–5).

hese elements of the 1993 statement are reminiscent of concerns voiced in the 1983 pastoral. But in significant respects the tone and content of this new statement are quite different. In the second section (comprising nearly half the document), laying out "An Agenda for Peacemaking" (8–18), the discussion begins by calling attention to a "challenge" by Pope John Paul II to the international community singling out the cause of justice as linked to peace; it then defines an activist list of what needs to be achieved in the service of these values: securing human rights, assuring sustainable and equitable development, restraining nationalism and eliminating religious violence, building cooperative security, and shaping responsible leadership by the United States, as the preeminent world power. The large subsection on cooperative security devotes considerable space to a topic that nowhere appears in the 1983 pastoral: humanitarian intervention. It is the bishops' description of this item and the responsibilities it entails that concern us here.

"Humanitarian intervention," as defined by the bishops, is "the forceful, direct intervention by one or more states or international organizations in the internal affairs of other states for essentially humanitarian purposes," including alleviating "internal chaos, repression and widespread loss of life." The aim of such intervention is "to protect human life and basic human rights" in such contexts. Such intervention, the statement continues, has been termed "obligatory" by Pope John Paul II "where the survival of populations and entire ethnic groups is seriously compromised." Under such circumstances, the Pope sees it as "a duty for nations and the international community" (15).

This is extraordinarily broad, strong language, especially by contrast with the denunciations of the use of military force for purposes of national interest that have become commonplace in twentieth-century Catholic thought and the "presumption against war" defined in the American bishops' 1983 pastoral letter. The 1993 statement continues with a further quote from John Paul II: when diplomatic and other procedures short of force have failed, and

> nevertheless, populations are succumbing to the attacks of an unjust aggressor, states no longer have a "right to indifference." It seems clear that their duty is to disarm the aggressor if all other means have proved ineffective. The principles of sovereignty of states and of noninterference in their internal affairs . . . cannot constitute a screen behind which torture and murder may be carried out. (15)

This is language comparable to Walzer's explicit justification of humanitarian intervention discussed above. Activist in tone and substance, it repeatedly identifies intervention in such instances as an obligation not only for the international community but also for individual states. In the addresses from which the quoted passages are taken, the Pope clearly had in mind the context of contemporary local armed conflicts in which the suffering of noncombatant populations had multiplied and in which, in some cases, noncombatant populations had been targeted as a means of making war. The American bishops themselves listed the particular conflicts where such need existed and where, accordingly, intervention seemed justified: "Haiti, Bosnia, Liberia, Iraq, Somalia, Sudan and now Burundi" (15)—a list of such conflicts that has continued to grow.

From the papal statements the American bishops identify "several concerns" which they adopt as the core of their own position: first, "human life, human rights and the welfare of the human community" have a moral priority; second, sovereignty and nonintervention are not absolutes; third, nonmilitary forms of intervention take priority over military ones; fourth, military intervention may nonetheless be justified "to ensure that starving children can be fed or that whole populations will not be slaughtered," aims that "represent St. Augustine's classic case: Love may require force to protect the innocent"; and finally, that the right to intervene must be judged in relation to the effort to strengthen international law and the international community (16).

The bishops comment of the right of military intervention, already grounded in Augustine's fundamental justification of the moral right to employ force, that it should follow the dictates of just war tradition, especially "establishing conditions . . . for a just and stable peace" and not itself becoming involvement in war. Of the concluding concern that intervention should be related to the goal of a strengthened international order, they call for more explicit language on intervention in international law and the development of effective mechanisms through which intervention can operate, and they express a preference for "multilateral interventions under the auspices of the United Nations" as opposed to unilateral actions.

If all the above considerations are taken into account, the bishops conclude,

> humanitarian intervention need not open the door to new forms of imperialism or endless wars of altruism, but could be an exceptional means to ensure that governments fulfill the purposes of sovereignty and meet the needs of their people. (16)

Along with the implicit and explicit references to just war tradition made earlier, this concluding statement makes clear that the bishops do not understand the position advocated as simply "altruism" but in accord with the interests and purposes of political order rightly understood. Their language echoes Ramsey's and reflects that of earlier just war thinkers like Augustine and Thomas Aquinas: sovereignty—that is, political authority—is justified only insofar as it serves the common good of the people governed. Assumed here is what Ramsey states explicitly: that the national common good is linked to the international, and that the good of one people is not distinct from that of another. In any case, the United States Catholic bishops and Ramsey agree on a conception of statecraft as defined by just war tradition, in which idealism and realism are not distinct, but according to which the proper interests of statecraft follow from the fundamental values which government exists to serve.

The 1993 general statement of the National Conference of Catholic Bishops was preceded and has been followed by various statements from individual representatives of the Conference. A striking example is the letter of Archbishop John Roach, head of the bishops' International Policy Committee, to Secretary of State Christopher in May 1993, calling for military intervention in Bosnia.[19] Roach argued that "the United States, with the United Nations and other international bodies," confronts a "moral imperative . . . to protect the lives and basic rights of the people of Bosnia." Intervention would also, continued Roach, serve national interests of various sorts: it would prevent the war from widening, avert a worsening refugee crisis, strengthen international order, and discourage other conflicts based on militant nationalism or ethnic feeling. The intervention should be in accord with just war principles, to make possible the diplomatic achievement of an "enforceable and enforced political settlement" and "political reconstruction," with "a commitment to democracy and basic human and minority rights."

The position staked out by Archbishop Roach here clearly anticipates the position taken a few months later by the United States bishops as a body. It differs in explicitly linking military intervention to the later processes of a peace settlement, political rebuilding, and the goal of a democratic society respectful of rights; but these latter goals also appear in various places and various forms in the formal statement of the National Conference of Catholic Bishops. Fundamentally, the Roach letter urging intervention in Bosnia represents a concentration and particular application of the general position on justified intervention taken in the latter statement. Together, these two 1993 statements illustrate how contemporary Catholic thought has come to understand military intervention as sometimes an obligation that follows from the terms of the just war tradition, a position that contrasts sharply with earlier skepticism that military force could ever be employed justly in the contemporary world.

The Idea of an Obligation to Intervene in International Law

The "legalist paradigm" of absolute territorial sovereignty and nonintervention across borders, even with exceptions such as those argued above, does not reflect fully the historical and contemporary form of the international order. That there is some kind of obligation to provide protection and humanitarian assistance to victims of armed conflicts and natural disasters has long been recognized in international law as well as in moral discourse. While its deepest roots reach into antiquity, in positive international law it is only a bit more than a century old, beginning with the first Geneva Convention of 1863.[20] The oldest international organization concerned specifically with such issues is of the same vintage: the Red Cross, which also originated in Geneva in 1863. Since that time, both positive and customary international law providing for protection and humanitarian relief to victims of conflicts has greatly expanded, and such protection and relief have increasingly been recognized as a general moral duty to be discharged through international, national, and nongovernmental efforts. Since World War II, the growth of human rights law has significantly broadened the field of those who may be deserving of protection and relief, as well as the concept of an obligation to provide them, by interventionary means if necessary. In contemporary international law, then, the locus of this obligation is humanitarian law, that portion of international law that includes human rights law and the law of armed conflicts.

Up through World War II, the chief focus of humanitarian law and moral concern was the protection of noncombatants in international wars and assistance to refugees created by such wars. On the traditional model, the law of war prohibited the direct, intentional harming of noncombatants. Nonetheless, whether direct and intentional or not, armed conflicts do result in casualties to noncombatants and losses of property, livelihood, and other disturbances to civil life. The people affected may be in the area in which the conflict is taking place, or they may flee the conflict and become refugees. The problems and the possibilities of dealing with them differ in the two cases.

For persons in need of protection and assistance within the area in which an armed conflict is taking place, efforts to respond to these needs are defined in the law as first of all the responsibility of the parties involved in the conflict. Each has responsibilities not only to those people favoring its own cause, but to all persons within the area over which it has control. Some specific responsibilities are spelled out in international law, but more broadly the field of responsibility is defined by a broad international consensus on the responsibilities of governments, whether *de jure* or *de facto*. The monitoring activities of the International Committee of the Red Cross and the Red Crescent and, informally, those of nongovernmental organizations such as Amnesty International, assist in enforcing the discharge of these responsibilities of the conflicting parties by bringing violations to light and exerting moral pressure. In cases in which one or both these parties fail to live up to their responsibilities, these organizations may be able to bring them to do so. They may also function as channels of relief and may open new channels for additional relief from other organizations. But the work of such organizations depends on the willingness of the conflicting parties to allow them to function, whether as monitors or as providers or facilitators of relief.

This model, most fully detailed in positive international law by the Geneva Conventions of 1949,[21] was developed for international conflicts. Conflicts internal to states, including civil wars, rebellions, revolutions, and use of violence by states against segments of their own population are by definition not international; thus, though moral concerns might be directed toward the victims of such conflicts, the mechanisms of monitoring and enforcement developed for international conflicts did not extend to these. Indeed, it could be argued that the rules laid down by the Conventions did not apply in non-international conflicts.

The Geneva Conference of 1974–77 attempted to change this state of affairs by means of its Protocol II extending the law of war to include civil wars involving dissident armed forces under responsible command, where both these forces and those of the recognized government were to be bound by the law.[22] This Protocol, however, has not been ratified by major nations, including the United States; so its provisions have not attained the status of *lex lata,* positive international law. Nonetheless, they have a real value as a statement of *lex ferenda,* that which would be desirable as positive law, and despite their lack of formal ratification, they reflect a growing international concern to bring the behavior of parties to conflicts inside states under scrutiny, subject this behavior to the same sort of restraints as are applied to international armed conflicts, and provide protection and assistance to the victims of such conflicts.

This effort has proceeded alongside the development of international concern to define and protect human rights. From Article 55 of the United Nations Charter to the Helsinki Conventions, numerous specific definitions of human rights have been advanced, and while these differ in various particulars, the underlying theme of them all is by now well established: that human rights exist and constitute a claim to protection and humanitarian relief from suffering.

Myres McDougal and Florentino Feliciano, in one of the standard contemporary works on international relations, argue that the attempts to regulate violence and to extend the protection of human rights are closely related elements in the quest to establish a "minimum world public order" and note that both have been important objectives of international organizations.[23] Nonetheless, there are important countercurrents to both.

First, the effort to extend the humanitarian law of armed conflicts to all forms of such conflicts, not just those between states, runs against customary and positive legal tradition in two particularly important ways: it implicitly diminishes the idea that national borders are inviolable by making internal conflicts subject to international laws, and it undercuts the right of sovereign governments to deal however they will with dissident groups and their populations as a whole. Both threaten to replace absolute sovereign authority with an international regime of law. The prospect of intervention across the borders of a state by one or more other states to enforce international law and/or to protect victims of violations of such law represents a violation of the traditional idea of sovereignty, and it might be argued to constitute a just cause for war. Humanitarian relief efforts in a state without that state's permission by nongovernmental organizations, including private voluntary organizations, avoid this last problem associated with national or international intervention across a state's borders, but at the same time, persons undertaking such assistance in a hostile environment cannot be protected by forces from other nations without the same problems arising.

Second, the attempt to establish international protection of human rights has been hampered by the existence of two essentially different conceptions of the source of such rights. One conception, deriving from Western liberal political theory, understands those rights to be vested in individuals by nature. On this conception, no government can revoke or impair such rights. The other conception, associated with Marxist–Leninist political theory but also adopted by some non-Communist authoritarian states, understands human rights to be vested in communities rather than individuals; so governments have the right to abrogate or deny specific human rights to individuals when the rights of the community justify doing so. The two theoretical conceptions lead to opposite conclusions both as to what constitutes an unacceptable violation of human rights and as to whether interventionary action to support and protect human rights is ever justified. On the first conception, the criterion for deciding whether a violation exists is what is done to the individual; given such violation, a *prima facie* justification exists for interventionary action to correct that violation, and whether and how to take such action becomes a matter for prudential calculation. On the second conception, the criterion for deciding whether a violation exists is whether the state constitutionally protects human rights, and interventionary action in a state which does so on behalf of individuals whose rights have been suspended, abrogated, or revoked by the state is never justified. This conception, then, reinforces the traditional idea of the inviolability of national borders to interventionary action by other states or by international organizations.

With the collapse of communism as a political ideology and the breakup of the cold war "second world," the Western conception of human rights as grounded in nature and vested in the individual has gained ascendancy as the working doctrine of international order. The conception of human rights as pertaining to communities, by contrast, has increasingly become associated with the claims of ethnic, religious, and national groups seeking their own autonomy or their own states, and thus with the conflicts engendered by such claims. So the debate between the two conceptions of human rights lives on, though the partisans of each side have shifted: now it is the proponents of universalism and international order against the proponents of particularist community identity and ethnic, religious, or national autonomy in a framework of independent (and inviolate) states.

One significant outcome of the development of a universally applicable international humanitarian law has been some erosion of the traditional rule against intervention across state borders against the will of the target state. The new rule, though not firmly established, seems to permit such intervention for humanitarian purposes recognized in international law, even if the intervention involves the use of force within the borders of the target state and even against the government of that state. But the principles on which this development is based are still not accepted universally; moreover, the development has succeeded as a reflection of contemporary historical conditions, so support for intervention to protect and succor victims of conflicts and to enforce the law of armed conflicts could disappear in a different historical context.

The Justification of Intervention: Conflicting Obligations

The above discussions examine arguments that an obligation exists, both in morality and in international law and practice, to protect the victims of conflicts and to provide them with humanitarian assistance, and that this obligation extends in certain kinds of cases to intervention, by force if necessary, to ensure these ends. In other words, the obligation to the victims of conflict defines a right to protect and assist them on the part of the international community and even of individual states. In some cases this obligation is understood as extending as far as imposing order by force on societies torn by conflict, so as to end the conflict and remove the causes of harm to those victimized by it.

Now, if there is such an obligation, why not go ahead and act on it? Why should the United Nations acting collectively through the Security Council, or even individual states capable of acting on their own, not aggressively pursue the protection and humanitarian relief of victims of conflict, intervene militarily to serve these ends, seek an end to conflicts up to the point of military action to impose peace, and impose a new order on conflict-ridden societies, to make them peaceful members of the new world order? The problem is that the matter is far from being so easy. Nor is it simply a problem of lack of resources or of will, though there is a straightforward moral rule of thumb that no one is obligated to do something that is out of his or her power to do. A more serious problem is the clash of obligations. Besides the obligation just described, other obligations which limit the ability to respond to conflicts as indicated also exist in morality and law and are recognized in the behavior of nations. These other obligations may for convenience be divided into three kinds: obligations to the international order, obligations to the political communities which may contribute to the ending of conflicts and the succor of victims, and obligations to the victims of conflicts and other members of their societies as well.

Obligations to the International Order
Maintaining the territorial ideal of sovereignty

One such obligation has already been introduced: that of not violating established and recognized national borders. I will not treat this at length here, since I have already said a good deal about it. Like much else in international behavior, this is an ancient rule of thumb, reflected in the common doctrine that defense against attack or raiding across borders is a justifiable reason for taking up arms. The modern version of the doctrine of inviolability of borders, as it exists in positive and customary international law, may be dated to the Treaty of Westphalia in 1648, which ended the last of the European religious wars, the Thirty Years' War. This treaty is generally regarded as establishing the beginning of the modern state system. After this point, religious differences and, by extension, ideological differences were no longer to be counted as causes for war.

The doctrine of inviolability of borders thus, when it originated, spoke to two different concerns. First, it was a means of rejecting, in the name of secular sovereignty, ideological claims rooted in religious belief and the possibility of war waged to enforce such belief. Second, it established the rights of sovereignty in terms of territory, an unambiguous criterion transparent to all concerned, rather than other criteria more open to judgment, such as the sovereign's character or behavior. The territorial definition of sovereignty overrode not only religious preference, but also other possible criteria, such as ethnicity and language, as unambiguous and transparent as territory. Defining sovereignty in terms of territory assumed the possibility of not only multi-religious, but also multilingual and multiethnic states. This, as we shall see in a moment, has come under some attack in the present context.

The doctrine of inviolability of borders secured the idea of sovereignty but has never prevented conflicts over who was legitimate sovereign of a particular territory. Indeed, the doctrine has never been more settled than in the twentieth century, when it has come to constitute the centerpiece of efforts to create an international order and to end war by denying the right to initiate use of force by one state against another across the latter's borders. This doctrine is central in the Covenant of the League of Nations, the Pact of Paris, and the Charter of the United Nations.[24] At the same time, the twentieth century has posed some of the most serious challenges to the concept of sovereignty rooted in the inviolability of state borders. These are of two sorts.

First, the idea has reappeared that states should be defined by common cultural features of their population, like a common ethnicity, language, religion, history, or tribal affiliation. Beginning with the concept of self-determination as advanced by Woodrow Wilson at the end of World War I and incorporated into the Versailles Treaty, this idea has achieved a secure place in liberal political thought, but it has had somewhat mixed results in practice. Its uneven application in the Versailles Treaty fed animosities that helped to lead to World War II; its adoption by former colonial states has fed civil wars over and over again as multiethnic states created by the colonial powers have lapsed into warfare among their constituent peoples; and in the form of the Soviet concept of "wars of national liberation," it became a source of cold war conflict.

Ironically, then, some of the very sources of conflict that the Peace of Westphalia sought to put to rest—notably, ideologically

borders — vs — ethnic-cult
(to prevent self-det THE QUES
religion/ideology)

THE QUESTI

charged rationales for conflict based on religious differenc/
ethnic heritage—have again appeared with new vigor
form of arguments for self-determination, leading to conflicts
aimed at creating "ethnically pure" states, revised national borders, and new states created out of old ones. At the same time,
parties seeking to form their own national states do not want to
challenge the *idea* of states with inviolable borders, since once
they have achieved their goal of their own state, they want to be
protected by this international norm.

The second challenge to the Westphalian idea of sovereignty
as tied to the inviolability of state borders is the ideology of
world order, especially as expressed in the claim of universality
for international law and for ideas such as inviolable human
rights for all individuals. In the previous section I discussed the
tension between the concepts of state sovereignty and world
order and marked the growth of the latter as against the former
in certain kinds of cases. At the same time, however, this remains far from representing an established international consensus, and the norm of sovereign rights based on territorial
inviolability remains dominant in theory and in most of international practice.

The end result is that the concept of sovereignty as tied to the
idea of inviolate territorial borders remains a central element
in the contemporary international system, so that intervention
across borders for humanitarian reasons must be clearly defined
and carried out so as not to violate this norm. The intervention
may not be for imperial purposes—that is, to take over the target
society for the benefit of the intervenors. Rather, it must be to
reestablish the status quo or to lay the groundwork for the
inhabitants of a state to reestablish a common control over their
own future, while protecting them and providing humanitarian

assistance. The intervenors, ideally, will provide these services and get out, leaving the society on its own feet, its sovereignty and its territorial borders intact.

For this reason, the various possible levels of intervention may be ranged along a scale from humanitarian assistance to the victims of conflict to old-style United Nations peacekeeping to new-style United Nations peacemaking to social reconstruction, with actions to advance respect for human rights ranged along this scale. Not all options for intervention are equally allowable in all possible cases. The continuing centrality of the concept of sovereignty tied to inviolable state borders is thus one reason why intervention well along on this scale could be undertaken in Somalia and in Bosnia, where both great need was present and order had broken down or become uncertain, while even flagrant cases of oppression of minorities by secure national governments (for example, Iraq's treatment of the Kurdish and Shiite minorities, Iran's treatment of the Baha'i, China's occupation of Tibet and effort to stamp out its traditional culture, the Russian military's behavior in the civil war against Chechnya) do not lead to international intervention.

Protecting the concept of international consensus

International order is far more robust as a concept in the minds of some theorists than it has ever been in reality. Indeed, it rests on a consensus always in danger of fracturing over particular events and issues. This feature of the international order is well illustrated by the history of the United Nations during the cold war, when the East–West rivalry paralyzed the Security Council, and the idea of international order shifted from the *de jure* United Nations to the *de facto* bipolar regime of the two superpowers. More generally, it is also visible in the perennial debate over just what is to be understood as international law, the positive black-letter content of treaties and agreements or the customary international law visible in the actual behavior of states in the international arena.

In a fundamental sense, both international and domestic law require the consent of those governed for them to have force. Domestic law, however, can also rely on the enforcement powers of the government. At the extreme represented by police states, the consent of the governed is itself coerced, and the hegemonic power of the government both lays down the law and enforces compliance. International law, by contrast, cannot appeal to a world government with sufficient authority and power to enforce compliance. Instead, it depends on a mix of different levels of consensus and reciprocal interactions among states for its force in regulating international affairs. In this mix the agreement of the major powers counts the most heavily—hence the cold war regime, and also the success of the Security Council in adopting a common policy toward Iraq in the Gulf War. Where there is disagreement among the major powers, especially when one of these powers itself is the target of enforcement measures the others wish to impose, the situation is very different, whatever the black-letter content of positive international law.

This leads to a sometimes painful, but nonetheless real, feature of the current international order. Where a major state's own interests are at stake, even a considerable consensus among the other powers is not likely to provide sufficient weight to change that state's behavior or to enlist it in an effort to change that of another state. The record of international efforts to modify China's behavior with regard to human rights exemplifies this. So too does the difficulty the United Nations has experienced in dealing with North Korea over inspection of nuclear facilities. Perhaps the most flagrant contemporary example is provided by the roadblocks the government of Iraq has used to impede or prevent altogether the work of United Nations weapons inspectors in the aftermath of the Gulf War. In such cases as these, the difference between consensus and action, on the one hand, and deadlock and inaction, on the other, may be only a single vote in the Security Council. Military action by a United Nations–sponsored coalition against Iraq in the Gulf War was possible, not simply because of the broad support for such action, but because the Soviet Union chose to support the coalition and not to back its former client state, Iraq. International intervention in a spot like Somalia, which no longer possesses the strategic significance it had during the cold war, is a very different matter from interventionary actions in places where the national interests of major powers are still at stake.

Achieving and protecting an international consensus, especially of the major powers, is thus of great importance for intervention in support of humanitarian values. Some interventions, no matter how urgent the perceived need, simply may not be possible because of the absence of such consensus, or may be delayed by the difficulty of achieving agreement, or may be limited significantly because of the limits of the consensus reached. The cases of Rwanda at the time of the 1994 massacre and of the wars over the breakup of former Yugoslavia illustrate all these problems at various stages. At the same time, not all the powers involved in deciding on a possible intervention need to have the same level of agreement; simple lack of opposition to a measure strongly supported by others is often functionally enough. Nor does a commitment based on such agreement require the same degree of involvement in carrying out actions in accord with the agreement; no Soviet or Chinese troops were in the Gulf War coalition, for example, and until recently, the forces of permanent members of the Security Council were not involved in formal United Nations peacekeeping. The Korean War and the Gulf War employed major-power military forces, but only those from the West. The participation of U.S. forces in Somalia also followed this model. It remains to be seen whether the case of the former Yugoslavia will establish a new model, in which the involvement of troops from the former Soviet bloc along with units from NATO countries signals a changed relation between international consensus and humanitarian military intervention.

The core of the matter is that international intervention for humanitarian reasons depends on the existence of an international consensus that supports such intervention, especially an agreement among the major powers. Even in cases of great humanitarian need, such a consensus may be lacking. In such cases alliances of nations convinced of the need for humanitarian intervention may still form and choose to act on their own, but at the risk of creating international tensions that may aggravate the perceived problem or produce others. For a single nation to act on its own, unless within its traditional sphere of interest, is yet more difficult and more of a challenge to the idea of international order. Indeed, if humanitarian need is judged by international standards of order, then there is an implicit contradiction in a nation's acting alone to respond to that need, disregarding the lack of an international consensus supporting such action.

Obligations to the Political Communities of States that would Intervene

The rationale for humanitarian intervention described above derives from violations of rights or deprivations of fundamental values affecting significant numbers of the people in the social context in question. It is, at bottom, the same rationale that justifies the existence of political communities as such: to protect the rights of their members and to serve them by providing for their fundamental needs. Since no intervention is without cost of some kind, whether of resources, lives, or both, and without some risk to the intervening state as a political community among others, the decision as to whether or not to intervene involves a calculation aimed at reconciling the obligation to those in humanitarian need with the obligation to the members of one's own political community. It is the kind of calculation which evokes great disagreement.

The arguments developed above for humanitarian assistance focus on the needs of victims, so the responsibility to provide relief is greater toward those whose need is greater. Often proponents of such relief seem to assume the capability of wealthy and/or politically powerful nations to provide it, so that domestic needs, if not so pressing, take second place to other needs that are more acute. At this extreme, then, the arguments for humanitarian relief up to and including military intervention resolve the conflict of obligations in favor of those with greatest need, even at domestic cost.

Traditional political philosophy, by contrast, focuses on the obligations and responsibilities within the political community itself, seeking to explain and justify the existence of states in terms of the benefits they accord their citizens. It is a natural question whether all people have an inherent right to enjoy such benefits. Even when this is agreed, as it is by the liberal political theory undergirding the Western democracies, the obligation to secure such benefits is understood as divided among individual political entities. Each of these has its first obligation to its own population, and no one of them is obligated to provide for all. If there is an obligation to protect the rights and secure the basic needs of individuals in other political communities, that obligation is only collective, shared by all existing polities. So political theory clearly puts the first priority on serving the rights and needs of one's own political community.

Traditional Christian moral reasoning splits along the same lines of difference. Both Catholic and Protestant thought assume that Jesus's command to love one's neighbor establishes a primary ethical obligation. Understanding this as an obligation to act for one's neighbor's benefit, however, presents a dilemma: human capacity to love in such a way is finite, and in practice it is impossible to act so as to benefit all neighbors meaningfully and without exhaustion of that capacity.

In the positions discussed above, the Protestant theologian Paul Ramsey resolves this dilemma by tilting toward the obligation to intervene on behalf of justice even when one's resources are not up to the task and when doing so calls for self-sacrifice. Traditional Catholic moral theology defines the degree of obligation to respond to need in terms of the order of proximity established by natural law, so that a state's first responsibility is to its citizens. But this applies only to cases of equal need; when one's own citizens receive their basic needs and more, the lack of basic needs on the part of others, or the violation of their basic rights, imposes an obligation to them to provide relief out of one's own bounty. This underlying reasoning is visible through contemporary Catholic arguments for intervention: the United States and other Western nations are wealthy, stable, and democratic; they can well afford to intervene in external conflicts on behalf of their victims, and so they should do so. (There is, however, an implicit proportional limit: an Archbishop Roach may argue strongly for intervention in Bosnia, but no such official figure has voiced an argument for intervention on behalf of victims of human rights abuses in China. Ramsey too was prepared to apply his reasoning to justify military intervention in Vietnam, but not to initiate general war with the Soviet Union over similar issues.)

My point in this discussion is that there are real obligations both ways: to the victims of armed conflict, political oppression, and other abuses and also to the citizens of each prospective or actual intervening state. In the real world, practical compromises between extreme positions are the stuff of political decision and action, and that is what is called for here. *Contra* the most extreme advocates of humanitarian relief regardless of the domestic cost, the level of sacrifice required must be taken into account in forming a good policy for action. And *contra* the most extreme arguments that charity begins (and ends) at home, a serious case can be made for assisting persons in great need in other parts of the world, when the cost to us is not too great. The problem, of course, remains that with which this section began: how to find the best balance. That, unfortunately, can only be found case by case.

Obligations to the Members of Societies Targeted for Intervention

In terms of the just war tradition, the argument for humanitarian intervention focuses on the *jus ad bellum*, the decision whether to intervene militarily. The criterion of just cause is addressed by the focus on the needs of victims for protection from abuses of their human rights and/or provision of the necessities for living, including food and shelter. The criterion of right authority is addressed by having such intervention take place under United Nations auspices or by an alliance of nations or an individual state in accord with international law, and ideally in the presence of substantial international consensus. The requirement of right intention is satisfied by the purpose of providing humanitarian assistance and, in some cases, assisting in reestablishing domestic order, after which the interventionary forces are withdrawn. The remaining prudential requirements—last resort, reasonable hope of success, overall proportionality of good over evil in the action, and the aim of establishing peace—are also embedded in the argument establishing the right of humanitarian intervention.

There remains, however, the problem of what just war tradition calls the *jus in bello,* the matter of right in the actual use of military force in the situation addressed. In international law and the practice of states, this is dealt with under the auspices of the authorizing body or by the military command structure of the forces involved by the issuing of rules of engagement. More broadly, the conduct of such forces is governed by their own domestic and military law and by the established international law of armed conflicts. This latter, of course, is part of international humanitarian law, that element of international law often cited to justify humanitarian intervention in the first place. Thus there is an element of reinforcing circularity in the implications of this part of international law: it justifies the use of military intervention for humanitarian purposes, and it seeks to limit the conduct of the interventionary forces so that they will not themselves be the source of further damage to humanitarian values.

Within the context of the actual use of interventionary military force, the mere presence of such force may in some circumstances become the source of further harm to humanitarian values and further victimization of the persons to whom interventionary action was meant to provide relief. This situation may arise when conflicting parties within the society begin to regard the interventionary forces as themselves combatant rivals for power instead of neutrals in the conflict. Then one or more conflicting parties may direct attacks at the interventionary forces and/or at the persons under these forces' protection, raising the overall level of the conflict and producing new victims. Such situations are quite common in interventionary uses of military force of all kinds, from United Nations peacekeeping efforts to explicit efforts at providing humanitarian relief.

In terms of the rightness or wrongness of such intervention, the place to address the possibility of armed reaction and the potential for widening the conflict, rather than reducing it, is first of all in the decision as to whether to employ interventionary forces at all; in just war terms, this is a matter of overall proportionality, proportionality in the *jus ad bellum* sense. But there is also the possibility that the actions of the interventionary forces may themselves violate humanitarian values and increase victimization. This is what specific rules of engagement and the broader international law of armed conflicts seek to prevent; in just war terms, this is what the *jus in bello* seeks to avert.

Military action is seldom pure in its effect. Ideally, armed conflicts would involve only combatants and would seek resolution with a minimum of vital harm to the participants. While battle between ships at sea or armies in isolated areas on land (for example, that in the North African deserts in World War II) satisfy the first aim, only gamelike combat such as that of medieval tournaments or the coup counting of American plains Indians exemplifies the second. Interventionary use of military force in support of humanitarian relief in the midst of noncombatant populations satisfies neither ideal aim.

By the terms of the *jus in bello,* combatant forces are to observe two principles: avoidance of direct, intentional harm to noncombatants (the principle of discrimination, or noncombatant immunity) and avoidance of uses of force gratuitously harmful or beyond the level necessary for accomplishing a legitimate aim (the principle of proportionality in its *in bello* sense). The international law of armed conflict embodies these principles in various positive-law forms. In the case of military intervention for humanitarian purposes, these principles also define the obligation to both the victimized who are the direct targets of humanitarian relief and to other noncombatants in the surrounding population. They are to be protected from harm, and measures taken by the interventionary forces should not be such as to cause direct, intentional harm to them or to create gratuitous or disproportionate destruction to their living environment, including the long-term chances for restoration of peace and stability.

Measures taken to avoid conflict between this obligation to avoid such harm as just described and the obligation to provide humanitarian relief include strict rules of engagement and limits on the weapons that interventionary forces have at their disposal. The former tend to prevent the interventionary forces from being drawn into a conflict as combatants, and the latter restrict the harm these forces can do through using their weapons. Unfortunately, both also limit the degree of protection such forces can supply to those persons receiving humanitarian aid, as well as restrict their overall effectiveness in dealing with combatants.

In a traditional peacekeeping situation, in which the outside forces are present with the consent of the conflicting parties, giving the peacekeepers only light arms minimizes the possibility of their being drawn into the conflict as combatants. In contexts of ongoing conflict, however, the interventionary forces have the role not of ensuring a tenuous peace that has already been established, but of imposing various forms of peace in the areas they occupy, creating buffer zones and safe havens, and convoying relief supplies. In such a context the interventionary forces, while having the justifying purpose of ensuring the provision of humanitarian relief, are functionally closer to being formal combatants than in a traditional peacekeeping situation, and accordingly there is good reason to arm them more heavily. In Somalia before the arrival of U.S. troops, the UNOSOM forces were lightly armed on the traditional model, and they could not stand up to the combat forces of the conflicting parties. The United States interventionary force, by contrast, was armed for full combat, with tanks and helicopter gunships. In Bosnia the forces of UNPROFOR on the ground were mostly armed on the traditional peacekeeping model, with full combat capability reserved to the supporting air power. The inadequacy of this model is well illustrated by the case of the fall of Srebrenica, when the Dutch peacekeeping force present did not even have enough firepower to defend itself or to keep some of its members from being taken prisoner and used as hostages to prevent NATO air strikes against the Bosnian Serb attacking forces.[25] While there is the possibility that intervention by combat-ready troops in an ongoing conflict may cause the conflict to escalate or that such combat power, if used in a heavily populated environment, may cause undesired collateral damage, these dangers must be balanced against those of interventionary forces so lightly armed that they can neither do their job nor keep themselves from being made pawns of the superior local power.

Neither the conflict between the obligation not to cause more harm and that to relieve suffering, nor that between the obligation to intervene and the obligation to one's own people, necessarily rules out intervention by military force for humanitarian purposes; the existence of both kinds of conflict, however, shows that such intervention must always be undertaken with care and may not always be advisable, whatever the degree of humanitarian need in a particular situation. An adventurous policy of intervention may, as these potential conflicts of obligation suggest, produce more harm than good in specific contexts of humanitarian need.

Conclusion

The analysis and argument of this chapter have ranged widely, both in order to demonstrate the importance of the question of intervention in the present context and to develop the significant issues within the moral debate and in the development of international law and the practice of states. I draw the following conclusions from this examination of the question of military intervention.

First, humanitarian assistance to the victims of conflict may be imposed by intervention even against the will of the conflicting parties, and there is a *prima facie* obligation to do this.

Second, intervention may involve the use of military force if this is necessary to achieve the purposes that justify the intervention. Preferably such force should be authorized by the Security Council of the United Nations, but since Security Council decisions may be vetoed by a single permanent member, intervention by force may be undertaken by groups of states or even individual states when there is substantial international consensus as to the justifying purpose.

Third, both the provision of humanitarian aid and intervention by force may go forward even when they are not neutral in their effects on the conflicting parties. In practice, such assistance may favor one party against the other up to the point of *de facto* belligerence on the part of the intervening forces.

While the just war concept of force in statecraft as warranted by the service of justice clearly implies that there is a moral obligation to intervene in situations in which there is rampant evil and injustice, other considerations, also related to the limits on justified force imposed in just war tradition, provide reason to be cautious. In particular, intervention introduces a conflict of values that must be weighed carefully in determining whether an otherwise justified intervention may be expected to produce more good than harm. Further, military force in itself may be a justified response to a particular crisis, but it should not be seen as sufficient unto itself as a response to the conditions that led to the crisis; a decision to intervene militarily thus implies a willingness to address these conditions by other means over a longer term. A final concern is that the pro-intervention consensus that has emerged in recent moral debate and in international praxis is somewhat fragile and may easily and quickly change or disappear. This fact does not remove the need to serve justice as a goal of statecraft, but it does represent a limit on efforts to actualize this need through interventionary actions.

Noncombatants and the Harm of War

All warfare weighs on noncombatants. The burden of war
may be relatively light, as when the civilian population of a
nation at war is taxed, in money or labor, to support military
activities, or when civilians in a theater of war are required to
give food and shelter to soldiers, and civilian property is seized
for military use (a burden even if a promise is made to reim-
burse its value). The weight is heavier if the human cost of the
sons, fathers, and brothers (and perhaps the daughters, moth-
ers, and sisters) who go to war is added; I am thinking here of
the hardship imposed on the families of those who go to war
(the latter are henceforth combatants and to be counted in a
different calculation of the burden of war) and the social disrup-
tion that accompanies the systematic removal of these persons
from the civilian population, perhaps never to return or to
return changed for the worse. War may alter ways of life or

governments or national boundaries, and in all these cases the noncombatant populations affected have little or no say in their fate, except to take up arms themselves (and thus become combatants) or to become refugees, exchanging a bad state of affairs for one they hope will be better.[1]

Still, these sorts of burdens are of a different order of magnitude from those imposed by warfare in which one or both the parties to a conflict recognize no distinction between noncombatants and combatants. Such warfare tends to place a disproportionately heavy load upon members of the civilian population, for a variety of reasons: military personnel may be better sheltered from armed attack, while civilians are more exposed; military personnel may have access to more and better food and medical resources; military personnel are able to fight back, a capability which may deter attacks against them, while noncombatants are relatively "soft" targets. At the extreme, one or both parties to the conflict may choose deliberately to target the other side's civilian population as a preferred means of fighting.

Intentional, direct targeting of civilians has been the pattern in much warfare since World War II, and it is a particular problem in the form that armed conflicts have taken since the end of the cold war. When the combatant–noncombatant distinction counts for nothing, and when the civilian population is directly and intentionally targeted as a way of waging war, not only does the burden of the war shift decisively to them, but the means of war may also become uncontrolled, as enemy soldiers engage in murder, rape, torture, pillage, and wanton destruction with the aim of creating terror among those who might expect to be the next victims. In the worst cases, when the aim of such warfare is not terrorization and thus domination of the enemy population, but their removal as a competitor, the means of conflict may escalate to mass killings and even genocide.

This should surprise no one, according to a long line of critics for whom such ways of fighting are inherent in warfare as such and for whom the evil in war is war itself. "Dulce bellum inexpertis" ("War is sweet to them that know it not"), wrote the Christian humanist Erasmus early in the sixteenth century;[2] elsewhere he described what he took to be the nature of war *per se*:

> Consider [war's] instruments, I pray you: murderers, profligates devoted to gambling and rape, and the vilest sort of mercenary soldier . . . . Think, next, of all the crimes that are committed with war as a pretext, while good laws "fall silent amid the clash of arms"—all the instances of sack and sacrilege, rape, and other shameful acts, such as one even hesitates to name. . . . Even so the worst evils fall upon those who have no stake in the war.[3]

Though the model before him was that of the wars of the Renaissance, Erasmus conceived his description as generic to all warfare. Had he lived toward the end of the century, he would have had additional examples of the horrific practices of war drawn from the religious warfare of the Low Countries and France; had he lived on into the seventeenth century, he could have drawn from the further example of the early part of the Thirty Years' War, whose devastation was the worst that northern Europe had known up to that time and whose armies, fighting in the name of religion, routinely targeted civilians of the opposite religion for pillage, torture, and death.

Erasmus was a pacifist who described the evils of war as a way of opposing all war, but contemporaries who were not pacifists could speak approvingly of the nature of war in much the same terms, expressing their belief that this was what all warfare should seek to be. Thus in 1579 Thomas Churchyard, an English courtier, described in glowing terms the methods employed by the English commander of forces in Ireland in dealing with Irish rebels:

[handwritten margin note: military need for avoiding noncombatant death]

> e further took this order infringeable, that whensoever he
> ᴉde any . . . inrode into the enemies Countrey, he killed
> manne, woman, and child, and spoiled, wasted, and burned, by
> the grounde all that he might: leavyng nothing of the enemies
> in saffetie, which he could possiblie waste, or consume.[4]

It is not a long step from Erasmus, the post-Reformation wars of religion, or Churchyard to such contemporary conflicts as those in Bosnia and Rwanda–Zaire, with their examples of the brutality of soldiers and their intentional direction of violence and killing toward noncombatants. One might well conclude that little has changed in the past four centuries or share with Erasmus the belief that brutality and atrocity reflect the inherent nature of war.

Yet, in fact, such descriptions as those of Erasmus and Churchyard do not tell the whole story. Not long after Erasmus, and contemporaneous with Churchyard, the first general orders and manuals imposing military discipline began to appear, reflecting a view of warfare in which the unbridled lawlessness of soldiers was represented as detrimental to military purposes.[5] The consolidation of just war tradition and its development into a natural law–based theory of international law also took place over approximately the same period, from the work of the Spanish Dominican Francisco de Vitoria, a contemporary of Erasmus, through that of the Spanish Jesuit Francisco Suarez, a contemporary of Churchyard, to the writings of the Italian-English legal theorist Alberico Gentili and the magisterial thought of the Dutchman Hugo Grotius early in the following century.[6] All these theorists unequivocally rejected the sorts of behavior that Erasmus and Churchyard regarded as proper to war and defined a conception of war in which noncombatants were not to be directly and intentionally harmed and disproportionate destruction was to be avoided. One point on which Grotius insisted (echoing Vitoria before him) was that no war is ever justified by differences in religious belief; this became a central feature of the new system of states and statecraft put in place by the Treaty of Westphalia that ended the Thirty Years' War.[7] In short, even as war was being practiced according to totalistic means that included intentional depravities of noncombatants, a reaction set in that utterly rejected this.

The result, which drew on a tradition of restraint in war developed in just war tradition, was an understanding of war in which military discipline triumphed over lawlessness, a consensual law of war developed at the core of a new conception of international law, and justifications for war were tied to reasons of state, not religious, ideological, or ethnic differences. This systematic understanding of the purposes of war and the limits to be observed by belligerents in the conduct of war contrasts sharply not only with the practice of war as described by Erasmus and Churchyard and exemplified by the conduct of armies during the post-Reformation wars of religion, but with the practice of much contemporary warfare. Thinking of war in terms of this early modern consensus, which is deeply embedded in contemporary just war thought and international law on armed conflicts, shows what has been lost and what needs to be recovered for the sake of all people who may be involved in armed conflict, for the development of governments without innocent blood on their hands, and for the maintenance of international order and the peace that it fosters. By this standard, such present-day conflicts as those in Bosnia and Rwanda–Zaire do not represent an expression of the inherent nature of war, but a violation of the fundamental principles that define war and the restraints to be observed in its conduct.

The focal concern of this chapter is one particular element

characteristic of many contemporary armed conflicts: the intentional targeting of noncombatants as a means of waging war. I will argue that this represents not only a breach of the law of armed conflict as it exists in contemporary international law, but, more fundamentally, action that violates fundamental moral concerns for justice and fairness in the conduct of warfare. These concerns may be expressed in a simple moral argument that often recurs in just war thought on the treatment due to noncombatants: these people do not themselves directly participate in the activities of war, and so they should not have the harm of war directed at them. In short, the denial of a distinction between combatants and noncombatants is wrong, both morally and in international law; and the direct, intentional targeting of noncombatants as a means of waging war is an even more fundamental violation of the justice that moral tradition and law seek to protect. Thus it is a matter of grave urgency when participants in contemporary armed conflicts directly, and often preferentially, target noncombatants.

In the following section I examine the idea of noncombatancy and the protections due to noncombatants as they have developed in Western moral tradition and in positive international law. This, in turn, leads to an examination of two particular contemporary ways of waging war against noncombatants: warfare against refugees in the Rwanda–Zaire conflict and war against cities in the conflict in Bosnia. The conclusion raises the question of how to preserve noncombatant immunity as an ideal and an operational concept in contemporary and future warfare. In a later chapter I look more closely at a related issue: the question of war crimes and the relation of war crimes proceedings to the preservation of the status and protection of noncombatants.

Noncombatants and Their Protection:
Moral Arguments and International Law

A distinction between combatancy and noncombatancy, to-gether with the idea that noncombatants should be treated differently from combatants in war, is widespread in world history and culture. Such a distinction appears, for example, in the practices of Aztec society, in the foundations of Hinduism, in ancient China, in the Japanese code of *bushido,* and in Islamic law.[8] In Western culture, as I have argued above, the ideas of noncombatancy and of noncombatant protection run deep in moral tradition and in the customs and laws of war. In the contemporary world the form that these ideas have taken in positive international humanitarian law (including the law of armed conflicts and human rights law) derives importantly from this Western base in just war tradition and, in functional terms, represents a broad (if not universal) international consensus. For this reason, violations of the spirit and letter of the law in particular armed conflicts should be taken very seriously, for they represent a threat to this consensus and thus open the way toward making all warfare more indiscriminate and more destructive of values, lives, and property.

The development of moral and legal doctrine on warfare in the Western tradition assumes that noncombatants will inevitably be harmed as a result of war, even just war. As a practical matter, the complete avoidance of harm to noncombatants is impossible except under very special circumstances: naval battles on the high seas, land warfare in unpopulated areas such as the North African deserts during World War II, air combat, and now also the use of weaponry against space satellites and intercontinental missiles. Because real wars, with such exceptions as these, take place over territories inhabited by noncombatant populations, the destruction that war causes extends to these populations as well, sometimes causing general destruction and loss of life, while at other times almost randomly affecting some persons and places while leaving others untouched.

Indirect, incidental harm to noncombatants as a result of military actions directed at an enemy's armed forces, however, is not the same, either morally or legally, as harm caused by actions that directly and intentionally target noncombatants. Even unintentional collateral harm to noncombatants, moreover, should not go beyond certain limits. The first distinction follows from the definition of the idea of noncombatant immunity itself, often stated in recent moral discourse as the principle of *discrimination*. The second distinction follows from a different principle, that of *proportionality of means:* acts of war should not cause damage disproportionate to the ends that justify them. Together, these two concerns define the *jus in bello* of just war tradition, that part of the tradition having to do with what may rightly be done in fighting a justified war. The same principles are implicit in the requirements of positive and customary international law on war. Sometimes a third limiting concept is advanced: *no Carthaginian peace*—that is, no devastation that leaves a land uninhabitable after the war is over.[9] While this is a reminder of the limits that justified warfare should observe in an age when chemical defoliants or nuclear radiation, or even indiscriminately sown land mines designed to look like pebbles, can render large regions unfit for habitation, I understand the requirement of "no Carthaginian peace" already to be implied by the principle of discrimination. After a war is over, all are noncombatants, and ongoing harm to them violates the immunity from harm they should then enjoy.

In the previous chapter three contemporary moral arguments advanced on just war terms were used as reference points for thinking about military intervention in the present context: those of Protestant theologian Paul Ramsey, political theorist Michael Walzer, and contemporary Catholic moral teaching. These same three sources are also helpful for laying down a basis for moral thought on noncombatancy and the protection due noncombatants in war.

Recent Catholic moral thought on harm to noncombatants has focused on the problems posed by weapons and tactics of mass destruction, especially the counter-city bombing of World War II and the direction of strategic nuclear weapons at targets in urban areas. Thus the *Pastoral Constitution on the Church in the Modern World,* one of the major documents from the Second Vatican Council, includes the following statement:

> Any act of war aimed indiscriminately at the destruction of entire cities or of extensive areas along with their population is a crime against God and man himself. It merits unequivocal and unhesitating condemnation.[10]

The 1983 pastoral letter of the American Catholic bishops made this statement the focus of a condemnation of "total war," which it regarded as "demanded by the principles of proportionality and discrimination."[11] The bishops continued:

> [T]he lives of innocent persons may never be taken directly, regardless of the purpose alleged for doing so. . . . Just response to aggression must be discriminate; it must be directed against unjust aggressors, not innocent people caught up in a war not of their making.[12]

A few paragraphs later the bishops defined discrimination further:

> The principle prohibits directly intended attacks on non-combatants and non-military targets. . . . It is not always easy to determine who is involved in a "war effort" or to what degree. Plainly, though, not even by the broadest definition can one rationally consider combatants entire classes of human beings

such as school-children, hospital patients, the elderly, the ill, the average industrial worker producing goods not related to military purposes, farmers, and many others. They may never be directly attacked.[13]

Building on this foundation, the 1993 statement of the National Conference of Catholic Bishops defined noncombatant immunity in more general language: "Civilians may not be the object of direct attack, and military personnel must take due care to avoid and minimize indirect harm to civilians."[14] Later the bishops applied this judgment directly to the use of air forces against ground targets:

> For example, the targeting of civilian infrastructure, which affects ordinary citizens long after hostilities have ceased, can amount to making war on noncombatants rather than against opposing armies.[15]

But it is not only air forces that may be used in such a way, and the more general underlying principle is what stands out here: making war on noncombatants is morally wrong.

Added to these specific references to the requirements of discrimination in just war doctrine are the concerns we have discussed in the previous chapter, those concerns for "human rights and the welfare of the human community" that justify military intervention when necessary "to ensure that starving children can be fed or that whole populations will not be slaughtered."[16] While the discussion of the requirements of discrimination is intended to let societies at war know that war should not be directed at noncombatants, this latter way of framing the issue focuses on the moral obligation to react when others directly and intentionally violate the immunity due noncombatants. Both sides of the issue are equally important: one should not make noncombatants direct, intended targets in fighting a war, and violation of this rule justifies the use of military force to stop it and reinstate protection of the noncombatants at risk.

For Ramsey, the idea of noncombatant immunity is at the core of the idea of just war. Since, as he argues, following Augustine, the justification for warfare follows from the need to protect the innocent neighbor from unjust attack by an aggressor, armed force may be used only against the aggressor; there can be no justification for attacking some innocents in order to protect others. Hence the very same considerations that justify resort to armed force also imply that such force cannot rightly be directed at noncombatants. "Thus," Ramsey writes, "was twin-born the justification of war and the limitation which surrounded non-combatants with moral immunity against attack."[17] This limitation, he continues, defines the distinction between legitimate and illegitimate military objectives: the former may never include direct, intentional attack on noncombatants. Their "moral immunity" may never be given up.

At the same time, though, Ramsey takes pains to reject two lines of argument that might seem to follow from this fundamental position: that any harm to noncombatants renders war unjust and that modern warfare necessarily harms noncombatants, since the structures of modern society make it impossible to distinguish them from combatants. Both are arguments associated with the position he variously calls "just-war pacifism" and "modern-war pacifism."

Yet the "distinction between combatant and non-combatant," Ramsey writes, "never supposed that the latter were to be roped off like ladies at a medieval tournament."[18] As to the matter of distinguishing noncombatants from combatants, it is not necessary to know "who and where the noncombatants are" in order to know that indiscriminate warfare—warfare directed at noncombatants—can never be justified. Rather, "[w]e have only to know that there *are* noncombatants—even only the children, the sick, and the aged—in order to know the basic moral difference between limited and total war."[19] Thus Ramsey makes exactly the same point encountered above in the stated position of the United States Catholic bishops.

What is morally allowable in warfare is use of force against legitimate military targets. This may proceed even though there are noncombatants in the immediate area who may be harmed by such attacks, who are not "roped off" in some other place.

> The principle of discrimination is shorthand for "the moral immunity of non-combatants from direct attack." This does not require that civilians never be knowingly killed. It means rather that military action should, in its primary (objective) thrust as well as its subjective purpose, discriminate between directly attacking combatants or military objectives and directly attacking non-combatants or destroying the structures of civil society as a means of victory.[20]

The reasoning that Ramsey employs here is the moral "rule of double effect," which he adopts from the thought of Thomas Aquinas. This rule Ramsey defines as follows: "The death of an innocent man might be brought about, without guilt to the agent, as the unavoidable yet indirect effect of an action whose primary intention and physically independent effect was to secure some good."[21] Applied to the conduct of war, this means that justified acts of war—acts against combatant targets—do not violate the principle of discrimination or noncombatant immunity even if they harm noncombatants, provided that such harm is genuinely collateral—that is, indirect and unintended.

At this point in Ramsey's argument a further principle of limitation comes into play, that of proportionality of means, the second *jus in bello* principle. Even acts of war directed against legitimate targets violate this principle if the harm done to noncombatants is so great as to exceed the good that destruction of the legitimate target would represent. Again, this is a line of argument taken up by the United States Catholic bishops. Thus noncombatants are protected by both the moral principles that define the just war *jus in bello*. The first principle, discrimination, gives them an exceptionless moral immunity from direct, intentional attack; in cases where they are at risk of indirect, unintended collateral harm as a result of a legitimate military action, the second principle, proportionality, works to minimize the magnitude of that harm. Thus it may, in some circumstances, rule out an otherwise justified attack on a legitimate military target. More generally, though, considerations of proportionality imply what Ramsey in one place calls "rational, politically beneficial armament"[22]—that is, weapons and uses of weapons in accord with the fundamental purpose of statecraft and of war as an instrument in the service of statecraft: to serve justice.

In Michael Walzer's similarly restrictive approach to noncombatant immunity, the central principle is human rights. The rules for moral conduct of war, he argues, "are simply a series of recognitions of men and women who have a moral standing independent of and resistant to the exigencies of war. A legitimate act of war is one that does not violate the rights of the people against whom it is directed."[23] Combatants give up their right not to be harmed by themselves threatening harm; noncombatants are people who have not done so and thus still possess that right. Like Ramsey, Walzer rejects the argument that no distinction between noncombatants and combatants can meaningfully be made. Even when the people in question are citizens of a state that has wrongly gone to war, they retain their rights as noncombatants unless they themselves become soldiers. Nor do their sympathies change their status; only their actions can do so. Nor do claims of military necessity justify harm to noncombatants: as "men and women with rights," noncombatants "cannot be used for some military purpose, even if it is a legitimate purpose," and much less if the purpose is illegitimate. The rights of noncombatants place an obligation on soldiers: they "cannot violate the life and liberty of enemy civilians" (137). Again, a "legitimate act of war is one that does not violate the rights of the people against whom it is directed" (135).

For Walzer too, the moral rule of double effect means that the rights of noncombatants are not violated by military actions aimed at legitimate targets but which endanger nearby noncombatants. The presence of noncombatants, though, requires soldiers to take "some degree of care . . . not to harm civilians" (152). For Walzer, as for Ramsey and Catholic moral teaching, the allowance of indirect, unintended harm to noncombatants is not a license not to take account of the presence of noncombatants in proximity to legitimate military targets. But, while Ramsey and the Catholic bishops invoke proportionality as the guiding moral criterion at this point, Walzer also invokes discrimination, as he argues that the rule of double effect should be understood in such cases as requiring a "double intention": first, that the "good" be achieved; second, that the foreseeable evil be reduced as far as possible. "Simply not to intend the death of civilians is too easy" under battle conditions, Walzer continues. "What we look for in such cases [that is, cases in which noncombatants are harmed by operations against military targets] is some sign of a positive commitment to save civilian lives." The "proportionality rule" is not all that is involved here, since soldiers too may not be harmed disproportionately. But "civilians have a right to something more." This "something more" requires, on the operational level, that if saving civilian (noncombatant) lives requires risking those of soldiers (combatants), "the risk must be accepted." But the preference is not absolute; here again proportionality must be considered (155–56).[24]

Walzer's way of analyzing the requirements of the rule of double effect echoes and further emphasizes Ramsey's basic argument that the justification of what a soldier does in war is that he uses armed force to protect the innocent. While Walzer arrives at this point by a different route, with a different basis for his moral argument, both he and Ramsey agree that the justification given the soldier for his use of arms is not absolute; it comes with risks. In becoming a soldier, an individual accepts those risks, for he cannot fulfill his duty otherwise. For both Walzer and Ramsey this duty extends to the protection of noncombatants, on whichever side they may be found and in whatever circumstances they may be placed with regard to military activities. It is difficult to imagine a position more opposed to the one in which noncombatants are the preferred targets in war.

The idea that right conduct in war is defined by the moral principles of discrimination and proportionality is quite recent. In fact, it was Ramsey who introduced these terms into the discussion of morality in warfare. That they have become so generally accepted in subsequent moral debate is a mark of the extent of his influence as a contemporary just war theorist. Classic just war thinkers proceeded differently, though, defining noncombatant immunity by identifying various classes of people, normally engaged in peaceful pursuits in wartime, who should not be harmed but allowed to continue with those pursuits. The early lists of noncombatants also routinely added that their property was also not to be harmed.[25] By the eighteenth century, in the writings of Locke and Vattel, this had matured into a broader idea: that cities and towns of no military value should not be bombarded; that even within cities that are

legitimate targets harm should be avoided to particular build-
ings associated particularly with civilian life, such as churches,
hospitals, and culturally important structures; and that the economic base for civilian life be spared direct destruction, including especially damage that would render an area unable to
support habitation.[26]

Early just war thought sought to limit the destructiveness of
war in two other ways: by declaring certain days associated with
religious obligations illicit for fighting (the Truce of God) and
by outlawing certain especially destructive weapons: siege ma-
chines, bows and arrows, and crossbows. Neither of these endured for long, but the latter has recurred in the law of war. So
has a theme which did not appear until the writings of Locke
and Vattel in the eighteenth century: that certain targets should
be avoided because of their purpose to serve human needs
and/or values.[27]

The method and language of positive international law on
the protection of noncombatants follows these early just war
models, rather than the model of argument from moral principles. To be sure, principles may be read through the law, but the
focus in the law is elsewhere: on identifying the classes of people
who are to be protected from harm in war, on specifying how
various sorts of such people may be treated (both foci being
subjects of the Geneva Conventions and Protocols and known
as "Geneva law"), and on limiting the overall harm from war by
restrictions on certain weapons, targets, and means of fighting
(treated in various Hague Conventions, Rules, and Protocols,
collectively known as "Hague law"). In addition, since World
War II, specific sorts of acts have been identified as crimes
against peace, war crimes, and crimes against humanity, including direct attacks on noncombatants and, in particular, the act
of genocide ("Nuremberg law").[28] These provisions of interna-

tional law are relevant, not only as markers of specific international agreements, but as carriers of a moral tradition of restraint in war, by means of stating that tradition, on which it builds, in a consensual and operational form.

If a summary statement of such a complex body of material is possible, then this language from the 1907 Hague Convention on the Laws and Customs of War on Land does it well: "The right of belligerents to adopt means of injuring the enemy is not unlimited."[29] More particularly, war against noncombatants in which they are singled out for attack represents a *prima facie* violation of the protections contained in the 1949 Geneva Conventions and the 1977 Protocols and is a "crime against humanity" as defined in Nuremberg law; it may also, as in the Cambodian civil war and the war in Rwanda–Zaire, constitute genocide.[30] War directed against cities may violate not only Geneva law but also elements of Hague and Nuremberg law. In the following discussion I make general reference to such types of violation in order to emphasize the convergence between international law and moral argument. As the focus of this book is on the moral issues raised by contemporary warfare, I leave the matter of specific violations of particular aspects of international law to the two war crimes tribunals established for these conflicts.

Making War on Noncombatants: Two Contemporary Cases

In this section I examine two contemporary, but different, forms of warfare against noncombatants: war against refugees, as exemplified by the conflict in Rwanda–Zaire, and war against cities, as exemplified by the use of siege warfare against government-held cities in the Bosnian conflict. These are important not as unusual or exceptional cases of stepping beyond the rules of war, but for just the opposite reason: they reflect types of warfare against noncombatants that have become commonplace in contemporary armed conflict. But they are particularly egregious examples of such types of warfare.

War against Refugees: The Case of the Rwanda–Zaire Conflict
Overview of the development of the conflict

While the deep history of conflict between Hutu and Tutsi in the region of Rwanda, Burundi, and Zaire/Congo reaches back much earlier, the warfare against refugees which developed first on Zairean soil during 1996–97 and then in northwest Rwanda beginning in late 1997 constituted the final phases in an ethnically based armed conflict which began in Rwanda in 1994, when, following the suspicious death of the Rwandan president in a helicopter crash, members of the majority Hutu tribe initiated a widespread slaughter of Rwandans of the Tutsi tribe and of mixed Hutu–Tutsi blood. The methods employed were both bloody and indiscriminate, killing more than half a million people. Foreign military intervention slowed the slaughter and provided protection to some portion of those threatened, but large numbers of Tutsi escaped only by becoming refugees in neighboring countries, particularly Uganda and Tanzania. The following year a Tutsi military force struck back from bases in Uganda and with Ugandan logistical support. This Tutsi force was composed largely of former members of the Rwandan army, which had been dominantly Tutsi. It proved to be both better led and militarily superior to the Hutu military that opposed it, so that soon the tables were turned, with Hutu refugees, along with Hutu regular and irregular soldiers, being driven into enclaves and fleeing as refugees across the border into Zaire. Again foreign military intervention and diplomatic pressure from individual countries and the United Nations were brought to bear; as one element in the effort to end the conflict, a war crimes tribunal was established under United Nations auspices to try captured Hutu who were suspected of participating in the original massacre. This stage of the conflict ended with the setting up of a Tutsi-dominated government in Rwanda and control of the country by the Tutsi-based military.

At this point the critical development of the conflict shifted to neighboring Zaire, where approximately a million Hutu refugees had fled, among them former militiamen who had sheltered themselves among noncombatant refugees during flight. In fact, the Hutu combatants continued to shelter themselves in this way even after they regained enough strength and cohesion as a fighting force to begin launching raids across the border back into Rwanda in 1996. Both the presence of the masses of refugees and the military activity of the Hutu fighters led to sporadic conflict with the Zairean army. In October 1996 the ongoing war was widened when the new Tutsi-dominated Rwandan army entered Zaire in response to the cross-border raids. This became a nucleus of a variety of forces, notably including Zairean Tutsi and members of the simmering Zairean rebellion led by Laurent Kabila. In turn, the nature of this combined force changed character, with the Rwandan incursion army becoming part of a broader military structure at least nominally headed by Kabila, whose aim was to overthrow the Mobutu government of Zaire. Thus the cross-border fighting involving Rwandan Hutu and Tutsi forces evolved into a civil war in Zaire, with additional support for the anti-Mobutu forces coming from other neighboring countries.

The specific direction of the war against refugees developed during this stage in this broad and changing conflict. Since the radical Hutu militiamen worked from bases in the refugee camps and were thus sheltered by the presence of the refugees, the military action of the Rwandan incursion force was necessarily directed initially against camps near the border. Reports from this period are mixed, but as significant numbers of Hutu refugees were forcibly repatriated in Rwanda or allowed to return under the eyes of Tutsi military and civilian officials (albeit also in the presence of United Nations and NGO observers involved in the refugee relief effort), it is possible to judge that at this stage a war directed specifically at the refugees themselves had not yet begun. But, as the conflict continued, it became clear that the Hutu fighters in retreat were in fact moving large numbers of refugees with them, using the refugees both for support and as shields. Actions against the Hutu fighters in turn became less discriminate, and at some point along a spectrum in this period of the conflict, it is proper to say that the targets ceased to be the radical Hutu fighters themselves and became the various masses of Hutu refugees as a whole. That is, the initial action against the radical Hutu militias based in the refugee camps evolved into a war against the Hutu refugees themselves. Indeed, this process escalated; the worst reported atrocities come from after the victory of the rebel forces and the installation of Kabila as head of state in Zaire, formally renamed Congo.

Subsequently the tables turned again, as the Kabila government proved unable to enforce order in the northeastern regions of Congo, near the border with Rwanda. Bands of remaining Hutu militiamen reconstituted themselves there, strengthened by new recruits from predominantly Hutu northwestern Rwanda. Beginning during the final months of 1997, the Hutu fighters engaged in terroristic attacks from their bases in Congo across the border into neighboring Rwanda, specifically targeting Tutsi refugee camps in that area.[31]

At many stages in this developing conflict serious moral issues were at stake. The initial anti-Tutsi violence in Rwanda by radical Hutus was large-scale and indiscriminate, perhaps genocidal. By contrast, the Tutsi counterattack and takeover of the country seem to have been directed properly at the Hutu military forces. Nonetheless, those Hutu who chose to become refugees clearly believed they needed to do so. Here the critical moral question is why they fled, and no clear or universal answer can be given. The radical Hutu militiamen certainly had reason to fear retaliation or, at the least, capture and trial as war criminals. The case of the civilian Hutu who fled is more complex. Whatever their reasons, though, the militias quickly co-opted the civilian refugees for their own purposes: to provide a shield and a base for recruitment, supplies, and attacks against the Tutsi. The Tutsi response (the incursion of the newly constituted Rwandan army into Zaire) was again initially aimed at the militias, not at the refugees as a whole. Yet the Hutu fighters, in retreat, made sure to keep large numbers of noncombatant refugees around them, thus making it difficult for the Zairean and Rwandan armies to launch discriminate attacks against the fighters. As the war in Zaire escalated, the refugees as a whole became the target, not simply the combatants. At this stage the aim seems to have become that of killing Hutus, just as the original conflict in Rwanda began with the aim of killing Tutsi and people of mixed blood. According to reports from the war, this represented a conscious policy choice. A particularly telling account comes from the *Washington Post:*

> U.N. Officials and Congolese officers in Kabila's army say its highest priorities—which have remained prominent—were to remove the Hutus from the border with Rwanda and to crush the radical Hutu movement by killing as many Hutu refugees as possible.
> In interviews, Congolese soldiers fighting for Kabila indicate that the massacres were ordered by the Rwandan army officers who dominated Kabila's officer corps. [Names of such officers follow.] . . . In some places, the population was involved in the killing. In other areas, . . . the local population says it was shocked by the mayhem.[32]

The author of this report continues by describing his own witnessing of a cleanup effort at one of the camps, Kaese, where a systematic massacre of refugees had taken place.

While the radical Hutu militiamen bear moral blame for their actions during most of the conflict (for their initial violence against non-Hutu noncombatants and for their later violation of the rights of Hutu noncombatants by intentionally drawing them into the circle of harm), the deliberate killing of Hutu refugees *en masse* is blameworthy in itself and is not excused by earlier radical Hutu actions. Further, any conscious policy decision to pursue the deaths of the refugee masses as such would itself have been a serious violation of the moral and legal obligations of the opposing military forces and the rights of the noncombatants in morality and international law.

The subsequent reconstitution of Hutu militia bands and their own attacks on Tutsi refugees does not change this. In the first place, insofar as the Hutu militiamen are regarded as belligerent combatants in an ongoing civil war, they have no justification for attacking Tutsi noncombatant refugees. From the Tutsi side, even the expectation that the Hutu militias would once again return to such attacks provided no justification for lack of observance of the principle of discrimination in attacks against Hutu refugee camps.

At this writing, late in 1998, no consensus of judgment has emerged as to whether the killing of Hutu refugees was ad hoc retaliation for the earlier killing of Tutsi or whether it was a conscious policy decision, either by the Rwandan officers in Laurent Kabila's forces or by Kabila himself. There is, however, too much evidence of this war against refugees to deny that it took place. Similarly, the later Hutu attacks against Tutsi refugee camps are well attested.

Is this a case in which the rule of double effect applies, so that no attack could be made against the enemy fighters without secondary, unintended harm to the noncombatants? The method of the attacks in Zaire and their extent to all the Hutu who could be reached argue otherwise, and it seems equally clear that the attacks against Tutsi refugees were directly intended. These were not cases of remote bombardment with weapons that cause considerable collateral damage, such as artillery, or by means of air strikes, but killing by individuals at close range using rifles and knives. Nor did the combatants on either side make an effort to spare noncombatants; the latter were deliberately included as targets. In both respects the war against the Hutu refugees mirrors the initial war of the radical Hutu against Rwandan Tutsi and mixed-blood populations, and the later attacks by reconstituted Hutu militia bands carries the pattern to a further stage. So is the slaughter of noncombatant refugees morally justifiable as an act of retaliation in kind? Sometimes retaliation can be argued to be justified, but only if it is relatively immediate, intended as a deterrent to further such action by the enemy, and the only available means—that is, a case of military necessity. The deliberate killing of Hutu noncombatant refugees by Tutsis and Tutsi noncombatant refugees by Hutus satisfies none of these tests; rather, the former was an act by those who had already won the war and who had no immediate need for deterrence, so were not acting out of military necessity; while the latter seemed to serve no military purpose, only ethnic hatred and revenge. Further, does the fact that, during the Zairean phase of the conflict, the noncombatant refugees were in close proximity to the radical Hutu fighters and in some respects served their purposes excuse the action against them? No, because the refugees had no real choice in the matter. Finally, does the assumption that the noncombatants sympathized with the goals of the fighters justify their inclusion as targets? Again no, because mere sympathy, including in this case shared ethnic identity, does not change one's status from noncombatant to combatant.

In short, none of the moral arguments that allow some harm to be inflicted on noncombatants during war excuse what took place here: the war against refugees during the Rwanda–Zaire conflict of 1996–97 constitutes a clear violation of the moral standards for the immunity from direct, intended harm owed noncombatants and of the existing rules of international law providing for their protection. Just as the conflict began with the direct, intentional killing of Tutsi and mixed-blood Rwandan civilians, so it continued with the direct, intentional killing of Hutu, and then Tutsi, civilian refugees. At its beginning and its end, this was a conflict in which the killing of noncombatants was not collateral, but a deliberately chosen means of prosecuting the war. This is what requires to be noticed, and means should be developed to counter such behavior in future conflicts; otherwise the restraints put in place by moral reflection and international law will erode, and the world as a whole will be worse off.

War against Cities: Siege Warfare in the Bosnian Conflict

Siege warfare, once a dominant form of war, belongs to a conception of war as having the purpose of possessing territory. Beginning with Clausewitz, however, the main thrust of strategic thought has understood the aim of warfare in terms of a different purpose: destroying the enemy's armed forces or rendering them unable to fight. In the twentieth century the face of war has been deeply marked by the development of mechanized forces able to move quickly to bypass fortified places and of air power able to reach over defensive lines to destroy not only military forces but also their supporting infrastructure. Prominent and decisive examples of such warfare include the German *Blitzkrieg* at the beginning of World War II, the strategic bombing campaigns later in the same war, the air strikes against Iraq in the Gulf War, and the coalition forces' sweeping mechanized envelopment of the Iraqi forces to end that conflict. Yet, despite the evolution of such forms of war, some places must, after all, still be possessed to be controlled because of their strategic value; this need has led to memorable and bloody sieges like those of Leningrad and Stalingrad in World War II and Dienbienphu in the First Indo-Chinese War, sieges whose outcome was decisive for the course of the war. Sieges of population centers have also constituted a major element in the wars that have followed the breakup of former Yugoslavia, the conflicts over the secession of Croatia and of Bosnia, and these sieges too have had a decisive character. Especially important from the standpoint of ethical reflection is the development of these latter sieges as a form of warfare against noncombatants.

While siege warfare raises particular and pressing moral problems, it is largely ignored in recent writing on the ethics of war. Among contemporary theorists, Michael Walzer is the only major contributor to ethical analysis of war to have directly treated the subject of sieges.[33] Nor did the sieges of Leningrad and Stalingrad during World War II occasion the kind of ethical reflection that was directed to strategic bombing. Indeed, apart from Walzer's discussion, for ethical reflection specifically on sieges, one must go back to Vitoria at the beginning of the modern period, in whose writings there is a brief discussion employing the rule of double effect to excuse collateral harm to noncombatants from efforts to take a besieged city.[34] This same lesson could also be drawn, by analogy, from recent ethical analyses of the moral issues in strategic bombing, and clearly these analyses, along with more general discussions of noncombatant immunity, are relevant to moral reflection on sieges. Yet, as we shall see, the siege of Sarajevo raises significant issues not encountered, or encountered the same way, in these or other contexts, and these issues need to be addressed directly.

Ethics is not the only arena in which siege warfare has been ignored or given only limited or indirect treatment. In military theory the parameters of the treatment of siege warfare are substantially where they were set by the two magisterial theorists of the Napoleonic period, Jomini and Clausewitz.[35] International law has sought to prevent certain kinds of military actions that might be employed in sieges, notably bombardment of undefended places and damage to cultural property;[36] but, as in moral thought, the focus of concern has not been sieges as such, and the provisions set in place do not directly address the full range of problems raised by siege warfare. In international law, as well as in ethics, it is necessary to approach questions of war conduct during sieges not only in terms of those elements that speak most directly to siege warfare, but also from a broader perspective of efforts to restrain the destructiveness of war.

The nature of the sieges of Bosnian government-held cities was fundamentally marked by the overall purpose and character of the Bosnian War. This was a war over control of territory and over who would populate that territory, issues which each party to the conflict understood, or came to understand, totalistically. That the war would develop into one in which the major battles were over cities followed from three other factors: one of demographics, one of terrain, and one of military capability. As regards the demographic factor, at the beginning of the war, the major urban areas were dominated by populations that supported the Bosnian government, while the strength of the Bosnian Serbs lay mostly in rural areas, particularly in the east and northwest. As regards the factor of terrain, Bosnia is a land of mountains and valleys, with few and limited routes of maneuver for large military forces. Control of territory thus confers a major military advantage as well as accomplishing a political goal. The cities and major towns are important politically, not only as population centers, but as the dominant economic centers for the valleys in which they are located and the surrounding mountain areas, while militarily they are important as junctions of lines of communication and supply. The heights around the urban areas are important, correspondingly, for the superiority they give to whoever controls them, either to attack or to defend the cities and towns below. Finally, as regards military capability, neither party to the conflict had the power to destroy the other's forces, partly due to external intervention, but partly because of the character of the forces of the warring parties. The strength of the Serbs lay in their possession of tanks and artillery taken over from the former Yugoslav army, while that of the Bosnian government forces consisted largely in infantry. The latter were mostly irregular infantry incapable of large concerted action, but capable of guerilla-like actions that could frustrate the movement of the Serb armor and artillery and, especially in the center of the country where their strength was greatest, prevent the Serb forces from descending into the valleys. At the same time, the relative strength in armor of the Serb forces enabled them to seize and hold strategic positions from which emplaced artillery, including the guns of stationary tanks, could bombard government-controlled areas. For both sides, the need to occupy and defend territory strained their resources and dictated their military decisions.

The Bosnian Serb forces, with their superiority in tanks and artillery and their control of the high ground around the eastern cities and Sarajevo, had the ability to wage a form of warfare by strategic bombardment of the government-held cities. After encircling and strangling the eastern "safe havens" of Srebrenica and Zepa, they were eventually able to take them by storm.[37] Sarajevo was a different matter; it bordered on this region and, in addition, was of such strategic importance as the major city of Bosnia and the seat of the Bosnian government that its defense was vital to the government forces. Thus the Serbian forces' effort to take Sarajevo never developed beyond siege warfare carried on by methods including choking off supplies to the city, strategic bombardment of various sorts, and sniping at human targets.

What limits, if any, should be observed in the bombardment of a population center? In the apologetic for strategic bombardment developed originally in the 1920s by Giulio Douhet for aerial bombing, strikes against populated areas are depicted as a means to shorten a war, thus making it less destructive overall, by undermining support of the enemy's military forces among his population in general. This reasoning is directly at odds with the idea that noncombatants should never be attacked directly and intentionally. There is in fact no historical case in which bombardment of cities has worked out as Douhet and his disciples predicted. In any case, while the Bosnian Serb forces' bombardment of Sarajevo and the eastern cities held by the Bosnian government included instances of direct targeting of noncombatants, the primary purpose of this bombardment was not simply to undermine morale, but, in line with the classic aim of siege warfare, to gain control of the city.

What is morally problematic about siege warfare depends in part upon the nature of the siege. Near the beginning of his discussion of sieges, Michael Walzer cites the historian Josephus's account of horrific suffering and death during the Roman siege of Jerusalem in 72 AD, then comments as follows:

[T]hat is what a siege is like. Moreover, *that is what it is meant to be like*. When a city is encircled and deprived of food, it is not the expectation of the attackers that the garrison will hold out until individual soldiers . . . drop dead in the streets. The death of the ordinary inhabitants of the city is expected to force the hand of the civilian or military leadership. The goal is surrender; the means is not the defeat of the enemy army, but the fearful spectacle of the civilian dead.[38]

This is a picture of siege warfare as inherently war against noncombatants. As Walzer observes, "The principle of double effect . . . provides no justification here. These are intentional deaths."[39] Indeed, one could go further and argue that the double effect in such a case is reversed, so that the noncombatants are the primary targets of the siege, while the combatant forces, better able to shelter themselves than the noncombatants, receive their greatest damage indirectly through the effect of the siege on the noncombatants.

Yet there is an alternative approach to siege warfare, which Walzer introduces by reference to the Talmudic law of sieges as summarized by Maimonides in the twelfth century: "When siege is laid to a city for the purpose of capture, it may not be surrounded on all four sides, but only on three, in order to give an opportunity for escape to those who would flee to save their lives."[40]

If this, and not that of the Romans' siege of Jerusalem, were the form taken by siege warfare, the results would be bad enough, but how to apportion the blame for noncombatant deaths would still depend on the circumstances. If the civilians present have freely decided to stay because it is their normal place of abode, they are truly noncombatants, and there is no justification for harming them directly and intentionally as part of the siege. (This is the situation traditionally addressed in moral analysis through the rule of double effect.) Second, if the civilians present participate materially in the defense of the city, they lose their noncombatant status while they are acting in this way (for example, assisting in digging a trench or building a wall as part of the defensive fortification), but not while they are going about their regular business or in their homes or civilian shelters. A third possibility is that they are present because the defending forces have forced them to be there, whether to use them as shields or to benefit from their labor (a case similar to that of the Hutu refugees discussed above); in this case the defending forces bear a measure of the blame for harm to the noncombatants, but the attackers still have an obligation (in morality and in the law of war) to avoid direct and intentional targeting of noncombatants and to minimize overall harm to them. Finally, there is the possibility with which we began, that the noncombatants are in the besieged place because they realistically cannot leave: either the besiegers have surrounded the city on all four sides, not just three, and drive back civilians who try to leave by firing on them, or they have so devastated the surrounding countryside that would-be refugees know that they could not survive if they left. The second of these cases is not as bad as the first; in either case, though, it is the besiegers who bear the responsibility for harm to noncombatants, since they could choose to provide a way for those who wish to leave to do so.[41]

A siege, then, constitutes warfare against noncombatants in either of two circumstances: first, if the besiegers surround the besieged place on all four sides and thus deprive the noncombatants of the choice to leave, so as to keep them inside in order to defeat the defenders through the harm done by the siege to the noncombatants; second, if the besiegers are unable to close the ring around the city but choose methods of carrying out the siege that affect noncombatants directly and intentionally or which are disproportionately destructive, again for the end of causing the defenders to withdraw or surrender, yielding the city to the besiegers, because of the harm to noncombatant lives and property. The Roman siege of Jerusalem as described by Josephus exemplifies the first case; the siege of Sarajevo exemplifies the second; and the Serb forces' sieges of the eastern "safe havens" exemplify elements of both forms of warfare against noncombatants.

In mid-1995, when the Bosnian Serb forces' attack on the eastern cities began, these were already encircled and under siege by the Serb forces. As government-held enclaves in the midst of enemy-held territory, they had become refugee centers packed with noncombatants who had been driven into the cities from smaller towns and rural areas. Their designation as "safe havens" by the United Nations, together with the presence of nominal forces of United Nations peacekeepers, was intended to neutralize the areas in question for the purposes of the conflict. Yet the reality was somewhat more ambiguous; the United Nations forces, small and lightly equipped, were a largely symbolic presence, not actually in control of the areas to which they were assigned, let alone able to defend them. The areas in question continued to harbor Bosnian government forces, who by their presence compromised the supposedly neutral status of these places, and the United Nations forces were not strong enough to police them. Thus, despite the formal "safe haven" status of these areas, their real character was mixed due to the continuing presence of pro-government fighters. Had the latter not been there, the areas in question would have been more vulnerable militarily, but the noncombatant character of these areas would have been unambiguous. The presence of the pro-government forces gave the Serb forces a rationale for attacking the enclaves, though this was an excuse rather than a serious reason; the pro-government forces, handicapped by being cut off from the main government-held areas, posed little if any offensive threat and turned out to have inadequate strength even to defend the cities when attacked. Moreover, given the importance of taking territory as a war aim in this conflict and the history of "ethnic cleansing" by the Bosnian Serb forces, it is unlikely that the "safe haven" status of the eastern enclaves would have protected them even if their character had been unambiguously noncombatant. For this was a war carried on importantly by actions against noncombatants, and the attacks on the eastern enclaves followed a reverse double-effect logic: not to allow only collateral harm to noncombatants while aiming at the fighters (the standard meaning of double-effect reasoning in war), but rather to strike at the fighters through the noncombatants.

Thus the offensives against the enclaves followed patterns established elsewhere in the war. First, there was an increase in artillery fire and sniping, directed not at the defending forces' lines but at the centers of the cities, where the noncombatants were located. After the takeover of the enclaves of Srebrenica and Zepa, males of approximately ten years of age upward were separated and taken prisoner, being treated indiscriminately as combatants, while the women and other children were driven out into other government-held areas already heavily burdened by refugees. Women from these enclaves told stories of rape and mistreatment and of seeing the bodies of dead men hung from trees. Approximately half the noncombatants who had been in Srebrenica were unaccounted for after its fall, by United Nations reckoning.[42]

Several characteristics of war against noncombatants stand out here: direct firing on areas where concentrations of noncombatants were located, the absence of efforts to distinguish combatants from noncombatants in the treatment of the men and boys, the sexual violence against the women, the forced expulsion of all noncombatants, even those who had been residents of the cities in question, and the coalescence of all such actions into a campaign of terror against pro-government noncombatants.

While the cases of the eastern enclaves of Srebrenica and Zepa exemplify war against noncombatants not only in the conduct of the sieges but in the actions of the victors after the fall of the enclaves, the case of Sarajevo exemplifies war against noncombatants during a siege in progress. Let us consider a particular type of action by which noncombatants were both indirectly and directly targeted in this latter siege. From time to time, the Serbian besieging forces succeeded in cutting off the power supply, which in turn shut down the supply of water to portions of the city, or they directly attacked pumping stations or piping to the same effect. This forced the besieged inhabitants of the city to get water from a small number of exposed sites: public taps, even above-ground water mains. When they exposed themselves to do this, the besiegers fired on them.[43]

In thinking about this kind of case in ethical terms, the first thing to note is that cutting off power and water supplies during sieges is as old as the practice of sieges. Such actions are allowed, in traditional moral analysis, by the rule of double effect, if they aim properly at the defenders, even though everyone inside the besieged place is equally harmed by the action. If the defending forces take more than their share of the water or power that remains available, this is their moral burden, not that of the besiegers. But firing on noncombatants in search of water changes the moral situation entirely. In itself it is a plain violation of their noncombatant status; moreover, it argues that the original action against the water supply was at least in part intentionally directed against the noncombatants, aiming to cause them discomfort and to draw them out to where they might become targets of rifle fire or mortars. Cutting the Sarajevo water supply for this purpose raised no question of double-effect reasoning; rather, it constituted a form of direct, intentional attack on noncombatants in the city, with its effects reinforced by the rifle and mortar attacks on those noncombatants who exposed themselves to seek water. Though in trying to get water, the inhabitants chose to make themselves vulnerable to such fire, this did not make them responsible for the harm they risked, for they acted as a result of being coerced. The entire moral responsibility was the besiegers', since they coerced the noncombatants by restricting the water supply, then fired on them when they emerged into open places seeking water. The whole train of actions thus represents a direct, intentional attack on noncombatants, an instance of warfare fought by targeting noncombatants.[44]

Reflections

Both just war tradition and the law of war aim to restrain the destructiveness of war in two ways: by distinguishing noncombatants from combatants and protecting the former from direct, intentional attack and by setting limits on the means that may be used in war even against combatants. War against noncombatants, as exemplified in the cases discussed above, violates both these forms of restraint. That the practices illustrated by these cases are widespread in contemporary conflicts raises an obvious question: what is the future of such efforts at restraint?

In recent debate on war it has often been argued—and not only by actual and putative war criminals—that the idea of noncombatancy is meaningless in contemporary war. Persons who oppose all contemporary warfare on moral grounds have frequently used the same argument, citing two factors in particular: that the complex, interconnected nature of modern society blurs the combatant–noncombatant distinction in numerous ways, so that it has become irrelevant, and that the destructiveness of modern weapons, especially weapons of mass destruction, renders talk of discrimination meaningless. But neither factor makes for a convincing argument when examined closely.

On the first point, the line distinguishing noncombatants from combatants may move about from time to time, and there have always been ambiguous cases or cases similar to those named in the law or in moral listings of noncombatants but not actually found there. Further, the functional roles of civilians in war differ, not only from one historical period to another, but from culture to culture, and even within a culture from army to army, depending on its structure. Moreover, some noncombatants in some armies are uniformed (for example, chaplains and medical workers in the United States armed forces). All these are arguments not that the concept of noncombatancy is meaningless or irrelevant in modern warfare, but that it needs to be understood and applied with care and precision in any war in any age. The point of the distinction, after all, is to require active moral effort to identify noncombatants so as to spare them from direct, intentional harm. In the cases discussed above, the effort is just the opposite: to target enemy noncombatants directly and intentionally *as noncombatants* (in the Bosnian sieges) or to reject the distinction altogether (in the war against refugees in the Rwanda–Zaire conflict).

As to the second argument against the combatant–noncombatant distinction in contemporary war, I have focused on the cases above precisely because they have *not* involved weapons of a kind that may be argued to be inherently indiscriminate; rather, the weapons used in these two forms of contemporary warfare against noncombatants (mostly knives, bayonets, and bullets) become indiscriminate in their effects only when the combatant wielding them has made a choice to use them indiscriminately. That choice and the resulting action are immoral in any and every war in any or every time, past, present, and future. Even knives can become weapons of mass destruction when they are used intentionally and directly to kill masses of people. The point of insisting on a distinction between noncombatants and combatants is exactly to avoid this.

Another justification for war on noncombatants is often offered in contemporary warfare: all the members of the opposing group are equally enemies because of ideology, religious belief, ethnicity, or some other cultural factor, so that the combatant–noncombatant distinction is irrelevant. The war may be directed to all of them alike. From the standpoint of moral tradition and international law on war, this is not so much an argument for a contrary position as a denial of the fundamental perspective of morality and law. In fact, there are two opposite claims about war here, one holding that all war is necessarily total, the other holding that common moral rules apply even in war. Specifically on war for the sake of religion, but by extension also on war in the name of secular ideologies, the earliest direct statement of the latter position comes from Vitoria in the sixteenth century: "Difference of religion is not a cause of just war."[45] This judgment has been a standard for statecraft in Western culture throughout the modern period. While Vitoria's immediate concern was to deny that religious difference can justify going to war, his rule also extends to how one fights a war: the noncombatant–combatant distinction is not erased by common religion or ideology, since people may not justly have war waged against them because of such matters of belief or culture. A more general statement on maintaining the noncombatant–combatant distinction comes from Emmerich de Vattel in the eighteenth century:

> Women, children, the sick and aged, are in the number of enemies. And there are rights with regard to them as belonging

to the nation with which another is at war, and the rights and pretensions between nation and nation affect the body of the society, together with all its members. *But these are enemies who make no resistance, and consequently give us no right to treat their persons ill, or use any violence against them, much less to take away their lives.*[46]

There may be a particular tendency for warring parties to treat enemy noncombatants and combatants alike in civil wars, where differences of culture, ethnicity, or belief are often what separates the warring parties. An episode from the American Civil War provides a useful example of the application of the understanding laid out in just war tradition and the law of war. In 1863 Union General Rosecrans, commanding forces in Tennessee, requested official guidance on how to treat the civilians in the area where his forces were located. General-in-Chief Halleck replied in writing, distinguishing three classes of civilians that Rosecrans's forces might encounter and the correct treatment of each type.[47] The first class that Halleck distinguished consisted of Union sympathizers, who were to be left entirely alone by the troops. The other two classes were persons known or assumed to be Confederate sympathizers. "There is no such thing as neutrality in a rebellion," Halleck wrote. Lacking knowledge to the contrary, sympathy for the Confederate cause was to be assumed; but such sympathy was irrelevant as regards how the people in question were to be treated by the soldiers in Rosecrans's command. What *was* important was their actions, not their attitudes. Halleck's second class, then, consisted of people who, while Confederate sympathizers, "so long as they commit no hostile act and confine themselves to their private avocations," are not to be molested by the military and whose property is not to be taken, except for military necessity. The third class, "[t]hose who are openly and avowedly hostile to the occupying army, but who do not bear arms against such forces," may be treated more severely, having their property seized as punishment for particular acts of resistance, being subject to confinement as prisoners of war, or being expelled "as combatant enemies." In short, this last class could be treated as combatants because of their actions, but not the second class, who only had enemy sympathies. It need hardly be pointed out how different this understanding of the rights of civilians in an occupied place is from that of the Bosnian Serb occupiers of areas populated by Bosnian Muslims or other government sympathizers.

In moral terms, the argument that allows warfare to be intentionally directed against noncombatants in such conflicts as those in Bosnia and in Rwanda–Zaire is simply wrong: what combatants *do* may make them liable to have armed force used against them, not what they *believe* or *who they are* ethnically or religiously; likewise, what noncombatants do *not* do—participate in the making of war—means that they should not have war made against them, whatever their beliefs, ethnicity, religion, or sympathies.

Preserving the noncombatant–combatant distinction is basic to the moral conduct of war, but just war tradition and international law also seek to limit the means of war so that they do not cause destruction out of proportion to the justified goal. What it is wrong to do to combatants certainly cannot be done to noncombatants; the rule regarding the former protects the latter. Consider some examples: combatants rendered helpless are to be made prisoners of war and treated humanely, not killed or tortured; noncombatants, who are by definition helpless, deserve no less. The use of poison gas or chemical or biological agents against combatants is prohibited in the law of war[48] (more generally, poison is prohibited as *mala in se* in the moral tradition); thus such means may not be used against noncombatants either. To use against combatants means calculated to cause unnecessary suffering is forbidden in the law of war;[49] similarly, such means are forbidden in dealing with noncombatants. These are all examples of the principle of proportionality in action, and they apply quite apart from concerns having to do with discrimination. Moreover, proportionality imposes a further positive obligation to seek to accomplish justified military objectives by the least destructive means. Where the distinction between noncombatants and combatants is recognized, this implies making an effort to minimize the harm done to noncombatants impeding the objective; but even when such a distinction is denied, this obligation works against, for example, the utter destruction of a town or the driving out of all inhabitants from an area in order to possess it.

Finally, the use of weapons of mass destruction against an enemy is wrong because it would violate both discrimination and proportionality.

Why should parties to a conflict observe such restrictions on their means of fighting, if their goal is to win? Posing the question this way assumes the answer that winning requires total war. But just war tradition and the law of war reject this conclusion. They are not simply expressions of abstract ideals with no connection to the real demands of political action; rather, the moral tradition and the law reflect historical experience both of war and of statecraft, and in the case of the law of war, the rules laid down also express formal agreements by states based on their own interests and values. Fundamentally, the limits that the moral tradition and the law of war set on the conduct of war aim at making sure that war does not destroy everything that is worth living for in peacetime. "[W]e go to war that we may have peace," and not the opposite, wrote Augustine, continuing with this counsel: "Be peaceful, therefore, in warring, so that you may vanquish those whom you war against, and bring them to the prosperity of peace."[50] The underlying point, which Augustine saw clearly, is that the way a war is waged determines the kind of peace that is achieved. Unjust conduct in war prevents the achievement of a just peace—that is, a genuine peace. Bringing a conflict to a close in such a way that the parties are able to achieve reconciliation and thus cooperate in rebuilding their society or societies depends importantly on how they fought each other during the armed phase of their dispute.

For this reason, the goal of peace and stability in domestic and international affairs, it is vitally important to maintain the restraints on the conduct of war embedded in moral tradition and in international law on war. Doing so affects everyone, as does failure to do so. This places the discussion of justifications for military intervention in an earlier chapter in new light: it is the obligation of the international community, as well as of individual nations within that community, to seek to prevent unrestrained conduct in war, especially the extreme case of warfare against noncombatants. While individual states and the international community as a whole should seek to discharge this obligation by means short of military action, this purpose justifies such action when necessary. Intervening to help the victims of such conduct in war, then, is not simply a humanitarian action oriented to the good of those victims; it also serves the cause of international peace and stability. In such cases, not acting is the worse evil.

5

Placing the Influence of Culture among the Causes of Warfare

One of the most striking characteristics of contemporary local wars is the influence of tribal or ethnic membership, history, religion, ideology, and other cultural factors among their causative factors. The Somalian conflict, still smoldering, has been largely a war for hegemony among clans; the 1996–97 Rwanda–Zairean conflict began and ended as a tribal war, the latest stage in hostilities between Tutsi and Hutu; the wars of the breakup of former Yugoslavia have been fed by a strong perception of fundamental differences in religion, historical experience, and orientation to Eastern or Western culture; the behavior of the Khmer Rouge in the Cambodian civil war drew on a radical Maoist ideology; both the Middle Eastern conflict and that in Sudan include differences of religion, language, ethnicity, and history among their causes; both the conflict in Northern Ireland and that in Sri Lanka have drawn on religious difference and differing perceptions of a common history; the Chechnyan war for independence from Russia was importantly motivated by religious and cultural differences; and so on.

This should not have been so, according to realist political theory, which identifies interests, not values and ideals, as the proper motive forces in politics and its extension, warfare. This should not have been so according to critics of the cold war, who understood local conflicts as expressions of the superpower rivalry and expected them to wither with the end of the cold war. This should not have been so according to the expectations of social-scientific study of the causes of wars, which focus on quantifiable factors as what bring wars into being. And above all, this should not have been so according to the expectations of Enlightenment modes of thought, which look for a world order based on common truths accessible to all people through a reason unfettered by dogma and prejudice.

Neither of the two great theorists who initially shaped the concept of political realism, Hans Morgenthau and Reinhold Niebuhr, was ignorant of the influence of values on the definition of political interests; their intention was to lay down a course for politics that took as central the structures, needs, and interrelationships of political communities, by contrast with a politics that appealed to ideals abstracted from such realities. Realism has changed since these origins, so that its dominant contemporary form, when it argues for a politics based in pursuit of national interests, defines those interests in terms of such factors as economic well-being, relative power in international relations, and national security, while excluding from the picture factors associated with ideals or values. Applied consistently, this perspective leads to a conception of domestic politics curiously truncated for a society in which support for high ideals has played a central role both in moments of national crisis and in the ongoing development of American life. When this perspective is applied to other societies, it leads to a similar discounting of the importance of values, ideals, and other cultural influences on their perception of their own interests and on their behavior domestically and internationally. Specifically criticizing one manifestation of contemporary realism, the pattern in United States foreign policy of underestimating religion as a factor in the political behavior of some countries and regions, Barry Rubin argues that this has at times "led to incorrect analysis and erroneous policy responses that have proven quite costly."[1] Rubin highlights the assumption "that religion would be a declining factor in the life of states and international affairs" as a major factor in this mistaken analysis and policy.[2] From the perspective of this assumption, not only is religion not supposed to be an important element in a contemporary state's domestic and international politics, but the presence of religious influences on a state's or a people's political behavior is dismissed as an expression of atavistic primitivism that needs to be transcended. Though Rubin is speaking specifically about the case of religion, his analysis applies, by extension, to other forms of appeal to cultural particularity, such as those noted above among the causative factors in contemporary conflicts.

Underlying the assumptions of contemporary political realism as applied to the outbreak of armed conflict is an approach to understanding the causes of war that stresses the importance of factors that can be measured and quantified, as opposed to those that cannot. For Quincy Wright, who pioneered this approach,[3] measurable factors included the absolute and relative sizes of populations and economies, the rates of change of each, the geography of political units, access to raw materials and the ability to utilize them productively, access to trade and involvement in trading, and so forth. For Wright, as for successive generations of social scientists who have studied the causes of war in these terms, the advantage to be gained by precise quantification and analysis of such factors would be the ability to predict when war might be expected to occur. Such knowledge would allow wise statecraft to avoid war by making changes in important causative factors or their interrelations, or to prepare for a war that could not be avoided. While Wright and his colleagues sought to take account of the knowledge of war afforded by cross-cultural study involving a broad range of disciplines, including history, theology, and social psychology, they did not regard these disciplines as holding promise for predicting future behavior. To be sure, Wright noted, the study of history aims to develop "generalizations true of a particular time and place of the past," but to employ such generalizations as guides for the future is to misuse them. Predictive guides, by contrast, must "accord not only with the observations on which they were based but also with all future and past observations unknown at the time the generalization was made." Such guides, he believed, could be obtained only through study of quantifiable factors in societies by means of social-scientific method.[4]

There is a fundamental accord between this understanding of what is most important in the study of the causes of wars and the approach of realist political theory to political decision making. Historically, moreover, both realism and the social-scientific method employed by Wright, his colleagues, and his successors in the study of the causes of war are part of the legacy of the Enlightenment, which sought to identify permanent truths by means of freely operating, unprejudiced reason, and then to apply the knowledge thus gained in the conduct of human affairs. Thus the Enlightenment, which began as a quest for knowledge not distorted by religious dogma and prejudice, drove toward a conception of right action as behavior in accord with such knowledge, a morality and a politics within the frame of "practical reason," to borrow the term Kant adopted to his own purpose. Realism's effort to define politics in terms of interests, with its rejection of ideals and values, echoes the Enlightenment's effort to define rational knowledge as distinct from dogma and prejudice.

From this perspective, much contemporary warfare, with its appeal to differences of tribe, ethnicity, religion, history, ideology, and other cultural factors, is difficult to understand and deal with. In terms of an interest-based conception of politics, wars in which the influence of cultural factors looms large are dangerously irrational, unpredictable in their beginnings, and often extreme in their conduct.

Unpredictability in origin and extremity in conduct are indeed characteristics of contemporary warfare as exemplified by the cases depicted above; yet surely such characteristics apply to warfare in general, not just wars such as these. It may be that the approach of realism so truncates understanding of the cultural context in which conflicts begin and wars are fought that it overstates the unpredictability and irrationality of conflicts inflamed by strong cultural differences between the adversaries. If so, then it provides a poor guide for a prudent statecraft that seeks to avert the start, and mitigate the destructiveness, of armed conflicts in which such differences are a significant part of the overall context of the conflict, and perhaps among the causative factors of hostility between the conflicting parties. Rather, dealing with such conflicts requires taking into account the values, histories, ideals, and belief systems of putative or actual adversaries, assessing these and other such cultural factors as among the causative factors that may lead to warfare and may tend to make the practice of war more destructive.

One may argue in different ways for an understanding of

conflicts that takes seriously the influence of cultural or civilizational differences between adversaries. That religion in particular must be included among the factors that may both inflame and mitigate conflicts is the argument of several recent studies, including the collection of essays, *Religion: The Missing Dimension in Statecraft,* in which the Rubin essay cited earlier appears.[5]

An argument for taking into account a broader range of cultural or civilizational factors is made by Samuel P. Huntington in his widely discussed "clash of civilizations" hypothesis, which takes contemporary wars shaped by cultural or civilizational differences as harbingers of the nature of future conflicts.[6] For Huntington, among the causative factors in contemporary warfare named at the beginning of this chapter, only the influence of ideological difference belongs to the past; that of the others, reflecting deep divisions between and among major civilizations, need to be taken into account as possible factors in future conflicts. Huntington's argument is distinctive, not only in the breadth of what he includes, but also in his controversial prediction that conflicts in the future will be characteristically rooted in civilizational differences. "Conflict between civilizations will be the latest phase in the evolution of conflict in the modern world," Huntington argues (22). Such conflict, on his analysis, represents a new historical stage, by contrast with three earlier periods: that following the Peace of Westphalia, when conflicts were characteristically among princes; that following the French Revolution, when conflicts were among nations; and that of the period after World War I, when "the conflict of nations yielded to the conflict of ideologies" (22–23). Now history is entering a new phase, that of the conflict of civilizations. Huntington is pessimistic about the shape of war in this new era: civilizational differences are "the product of centuries" and "will not soon disappear"; "[t]hey are more fundamental than differences among political ideologies and political regimes." While these differences will not necessarily lead to war, "[o]ver the centuries, . . . differences among civilizations have generated the most prolonged and most violent conflicts" (25).

As many critics have noted, Huntington's reading of history and his prediction of the future are less than convincing.[7] Moreover, if contemporary realism errs by limiting the factors that may contribute to wars in one way, then Huntington's vision of the future also does not take full account of reality, though what it stresses and what it minimizes are just the opposite of what contemporary realism stresses and minimizes. While it is important to insist on the need to take cultural or civilizational differences into account in seeking to understand the causes of conflict and the ways conflict may be played out, this must not be understood as an argument that cultural difference leads inevitably to conflict. Indeed, Americans above all should understand from experience how cultural differences within a larger social context can add vibrancy, texture, and creativity to both public and private life. Further, specific cultural characteristics can, as I will argue further in the next section, assist in the building of bridges between diverse cultures and help to ameliorate conflicts that do arise. Still, the contemporary and historical evidence is that cultural differences do figure importantly in some wars, and that these wars cannot be fully understood without exploring what this means. The most thorough and inclusive way of doing so is not to concentrate specifically on such differences, however, but to understand them as part of a larger range of causative (or potentially causative) factors in the creation and development of conflict.

The goal for informed statecraft, then, should be to take account of the whole range of potential causative factors for conflict, both factors reflecting differences in cultural characteristics such as values, ideals, beliefs, and historical experience and those reflecting the realist's "interests." My aim in this chapter is to draw attention to the importance of cultural factors of various kinds in contemporary conflicts and to begin to assess what this implies for preventing and restraining such conflicts.

I would emphasize that there is nothing inevitable in the influence of cultural factors on conflict that leads to more violent and more destructive forms of conflict. While the contemporary examples cited above suggest such a connection, it is also the case that cultural factors themselves often provide sources and incentives for restraint in pursuing conflict.[8] Both sorts of influence may or may not be visible in any particular conflict, but a potential way of seeking to mitigate the worst conflicts rooted in cultural factors is to explore the mitigations implied by these same factors or other elements in the cultures in conflict.

In the remainder of this chapter I take up the relation of cultural factors to conflict in two particular ways, focusing on Western culture and the culture of Islam. First, I look more closely at the problem of universal claims made by these cultures as a causative factor in conflict, exploring how such universal self-understanding may become a factor in avoiding the initiation of warfare. Following that, I bring Western and Islamic culture into a comparative conversation over the question of what is allowed in the waging of war, showing that powerful cultural restraints exist in Islam as in Western culture, and that there are significant overlaps between the two.

Claims to Universality and Conflicts between Cultures

The concept of culture is at once simple and complex. Broadly speaking, a particular culture is a grouping of people sharing certain characteristic features, such as a common language or related languages, ethnic background, religion or other normative belief system, history, geographic location, institutions, customary behavior and associated expectations, perhaps a sense of destiny in the world, and a common sense of belonging or identity.[9] Among these features the role of religious or other normative belief systems has emerged as particularly important for defining major cultures and for understanding the role of cultural differences in relation to conflict. Differences of religion appear among the causative factors of some of the most enduring and destructive contemporary conflicts, while religions and the value systems and institutions they generate are the focus of a variety of recent approaches to understanding the importance of cultural differences in generating conflict and seeking to ameliorate or end it.[10]

Normative belief systems, including those of institutional religion, are closely tied to the establishment of personal and group identity, a factor which has obvious importance for understanding how cultural differences can translate into enmity, hostility, and conflict. Within the broad list of characteristic features that define a culture, the quest for identity encompasses other features, including the way history is understood, the significance of the group's geographic place in the world, and its cultural destiny (its place in the cosmos). These, in turn, reflect a normative belief system which may or may not be religious in the institutional sense, but which, even if secular, functions in the place of religion. Thus appeals to fundamental values that are part of the normative belief system may be definitive in a situation of conflict, differentiating one's own group from the adversary, giving the group cohesion, and providing a sense of mission. For the individual, such appeals unite him or her to the group as a whole, through its past, present, and future, and define his or her own responsibility within that group's corporate life. The quest for identity in cultural terms thus leads through other features characteristic of the culture in question to a system of beliefs through which the self and the group of which one is a member are placed in history, in space, and perhaps in the cosmos. The consequence, in short, is to encounter the culture's distinctive religion, though that religion should not be confused with the religious institutions of any particular time or place; rather, the point is that the placement of the self and the group in time, place, and eternity is functionally what religion is about.

In present context this understanding of religion and its relation to culture provides a focus for investigating one particular feature of culture in relation to conflict: whether claims to universality that originate in religion tend to lead to conflict and are properly used to justify conflict. The two particular cultures on which I focus here have both been strongly shaped by religion, though in different ways; they have often been represented, moreover, (as by Huntington) as being inherently on a collision course. In the case of the culture of the West, the influence of institutional Christianity runs deep, though today it has largely taken the form of secular values, while in the culture of the Islamic world, the influence of religious values remains more explicit. I argue that in both cases the appeal to religious universality has principally to do with shaping a secure identity within the particular culture, a function that, rather than leading to conflict, may facilitate cooperation between cultures.

Each of these two cultures claims universality. The form which this claim takes in the West is rooted ultimately in the theology of history laid out by the Christian writer Augustine's *City of God* early in the fifth century; that of Islam is rooted in the understanding of history laid down by the magisterial Islamic jurists of the ninth and tenth centuries (second and third centuries A.H.).[11] These are different conceptions in many respects, but they include similar, if competing, ideas of the final end of history: for Augustine, that this end will be marked by the ultimate triumph of the city of God over the city of earth; for the Islamic jurists, that the end of history will be achieved when the *dar al-islam,* the house of Islam, completely triumphs over the *dar al-harb,* the house of war (the non-Islamic world). Each process is understood as inexorable, each outcome inevitable. The end of history for both cultural traditions is at once the achievement of human fulfillment in both personal and social terms and the culmination of historical change, understood as leading to strife. While Augustine's original conception focused on the transformation of the world as a result of the action of God's grace in individual souls, medieval political theorists transformed his understanding of history into a theory of politics that included a program for the growth and expansion of Christian culture. The subsequent secularization of this religiously based theory of the state did not take away its inherent sense of mission to achieve hegemony in the world; it merely changed its rationale. The Islamic jurists' conception was political from the start, tied closely to their support of the 'Abbasid dynasty of caliphs and its success in the world; nor, subsequently, has it lost its combined religious-political character or its efficacy as a rationale for extension of empire. Is the cultural difference between the West and the world of Islam, then, not inevitably, as Huntington among others seems to hold, destined to lead to conflicts over hegemony, as each culture seeks to accomplish its universalistic destiny? To answer this question, let us look more closely at each concept and how it has functioned historically within the two cultures.

The core statement of the concept of universality in classic Muslim juristic thought is the jurists' conception of the normative Muslim state.[12] This they defined as a unified religio-political

169

community extending across all Islam, headed by a single leader deriving authority from the mantle of simultaneous political and religious leadership first borne by the Prophet Muhammad. In this conception, the success of this state in the world is linked to the success of the divine plan. The goal of peace for the world will not be reached unless and until this historical community is extended throughout the world. The inner character of this ideal state is revealed by the term used by the jurists to refer to it: *dar al-islam,* the "house," or territory, of submission to God, and hence the territory of peace. All strife, on this conception, originates elsewhere; so the jurists described the non-Islamic world collectively as *dar al-harb,* "house," or territory, of war, a territory not at peace within itself because it is not at peace with the will of God. The jurists expected that, because of the character of the *dar al-harb,* there would be conflict between the Muslim state and non-Muslim political entities, though such conflict was not inevitable in every relation with individual parts of the non-Muslim world.

In both historical context and purpose, this theoretical description of the normative Muslim state and its associated statecraft was linked to the rise and consolidation of the 'Abbasid caliphate and the opposition faced by the early 'Abbasid caliphs from both within and outside the Muslim world. Internally, the chief problem was to establish caliphal authority; this the jurists did theoretically by deriving the authority of the caliph from that of the Prophet, on terms defined by existing Muslim tradition. For their part, the early 'Abbasid caliphs strengthened their authority as political leaders by attending to their role as *imam,* leaders and defenders of the faith, patronizing the juristic schools as one way of doing this. At the same time, the 'Abbasids learned relatively early that successful leadership in warfare against the non-Muslim world implied the presence of the

Prophet's blessing on them, and thus his authority to rule. The jurists envisioned the caliph as at the head of the *dar al-islam* in the striving (*jihad*) on behalf of the faith which, in relations with the *dar al-harb*, could be expected to take the form of war. They had an actual example to hand in the form of the Caliph Harun's decision to assume personal leadership in warfare on the frontier between his domain and that of the Byzantine Empire.[13] By succeeding as a *ghazi*, a warrior for the faith against the *dar al-harb*, Harun cemented his authority as caliph of the *dar al-islam*.

Putting the jurists' theoretical construct alongside the historical experience of the early 'Abbasids, then, suggests that the claim to universality for the *dar al-islam*, as formulated by the jurists, had two sides. On the one hand, it described the Muslim community in its relation to the purpose and end of history in such a way that each individual Muslim could take pride in his or her membership in the *dar al-islam*. On the other hand, it solidified the nature of that community as a political entity, able to engage confidently in relations with other political entities with which the Muslim state was in competition. The jurists' conception of these relations was not a recipe for war, for no such recipe was needed. Their view of the world, reflecting its empirical character, was much like that which Hobbes expressed much later in the context of Western political thought: an ongoing war of all against all. In this context the *dar al-islam* had a mission, as the jurists described it: to extend peace where there was war. At the same time, individual Muslim inhabitants of the *dar al-islam* could anchor their personal identity in the identity of this society organized around submission to God, and thus representing an island of peace in a strife-torn world.

Historically, the universal political unity envisioned by the classical jurists never came into being. Rival caliphates multiplied as Islam spread and was consolidated in regions remote from the core Islamic lands of the Middle East, and the empirical existence of a plurality of Muslim states has been the reality ever since.[14] If the jurists' claim of universality for the *dar al-islam* is taken literally as requiring a single political entity, then, historically, the project has failed. But if we focus instead on the function of the juristic conception as providing unity and identity within cohesive Muslim political communities, the picture is somewhat different, and more positive.

Muslim communities in parts of the Islamic world far away from the capital of Baghdad and the core Islamic lands experienced the same threats from outside and the same pressures posed by internal rivalries as were faced by the early 'Abbasids and addressed by the jurists in their theoretical construction of the Muslim state and its role in history. The functional success of the juristic model of religio-political society as a unified bulwark against the *dar al-harb* and as a focus for individual Muslim identity was in fact what was universalized across the Islamic world as local rulers adopted the title of caliph and thus associated their own rule with the ideas of religious warrant and universality.

While the juristic conception of normative Islamic statecraft never matched historical reality even at the start, it was nevertheless enormously successful as a vehicle for giving religious authority to the rule of a multiplicity of princes, whether they styled themselves caliphs, sultans, amirs, or kings. While the idea of universality contained in the juristic conception of the caliphate could be employed as an ideological rationale for extending a prince's own dominions, it could also provide the rationale for a settled understanding of membership in the Muslim community wherever Islam spread.

To be sure, there is a basis in the classical juristic model of statecraft for the idea that Islam's claim to universality implies continuing conflict with other cultures, particularly the West. The concept of *jihad* and the associated tradition regarding legitimate rule were used in the justifications of wars against colonial powers in the nineteenth and twentieth centuries.[15] Similarly, *jihad* is invoked today as a way of arguing legitimacy by such different claimants as Islamist radicals from Palestine to Sudan to Algeria, warlord-rulers like Saddam Hussein, Shi'i clerical spokesmen for revolutionary Iran, and the Saudi assembly of clergy during the Gulf War. The normative juristic model of statecraft had linked political legitimacy to religious warrant, had connected the religious claim to universality with the idea of universal political rule of the Muslim state, and had transformed the meaning of *jihad* from a religious concept of striving on the path of God into a rationale for warfare on behalf of the ends of this political community. The claim to universality, on this ideal model, is inseparable from the claim to legitimacy, and both are inseparable from the practice of *jihad;* since all are at once religious and political in nature, the language of statecraft is necessarily that of religion.[16] Thinking of the juristic model in this way transforms the idea of universal religious sovereignty into an ideology for the legitimacy of the state and the right to wage war, an ideology that has been employed not only against non-Muslim societies but often against rival Muslim rulers making similar claims, both historically and in the contemporary cases of the Iran–Iraq War and the Gulf War.

Even so, when looked at closely, present-day appeals to the tradition seem to have more to do with legitimizing the government of the state in question than with an actual claim that this government, rather than any other, represents the proper center for an expanding, ultimately universal, *dar al-islam*. That is, these contemporary uses of the traditional language exemplify the sort of usage found earlier in the legitimizing of plural

Islamic states, when regional rulers adopted for themselves the title of caliph and associated themselves with the idea of a universal *dar al-islam* with the aim of giving legitimacy to their rule over their own particular realms. While the core juristic idea had been to identify the domain of the 'Abbasid caliphate centered on Baghdad with the *dar al-islam,* the adaptation of this idea by local rulers led to a somewhat different conception: a universal *dar al-islam,* to be sure, but a plurality of legitimate Muslim states each with its own head. Functionally, this is the meaning of the normative tradition on statecraft to be read from both Muslim history and contemporary examples such as those cited above. In practice, this has allowed states to describe their legitimacy in traditional terms, identifying their own sovereignty as belonging to the universal *dar al-islam,* while at the same time accepting a plurality of empirical states.[17]

By contrast with Islam, to understand the claim to universality in Western culture, it is neither necessary nor proper to think of this idea in specifically religious terms, though historically it is rooted in such terms, and thematically it bears many marks of religious influence. Since the beginning of the modern period, the main line of Western political theory and practice has explicitly rejected appeals to religion to validate the state, to justify war, or to conceive of the shape of relations between and among states. The ideal of universal harmony, defined throughout the Middle Ages by reference to the *tranquillitas ordinis,* the ordered peace, of Augustine's *civitas Dei,* in the modern period has become transformed into a different kind of ordered peace, the idea of a concert of nations able to achieve world order. This conception has taken different forms, as exhibited by the various "perpetual peace" theories of the eighteenth and early nineteenth centuries, the development of the theory and practice of international law from Grotius to the present, the creation of the League of Nations following World War I, and the effort since World War II to structure international relations by means of multilateral treaties, regional alliances and unions, and the United Nations Organization. Except for some forms of the perpetual peace idea, the absence of religious justification in these various efforts to achieve international order and peace has been considered a virtue, and competing religious claims to universality have been rejected as translating into particularist rivalries that disturb the harmony of the whole.

As these various examples suggest, not every expression of a secular understanding of politics in modern Western thought has translated into the same *form* of claim as to universality. International legal theorist Georg Schwarzenberger identifies three understandings of law, each of which translates into a different understanding of universal international law: the law of hegemony or power, that of consensus or community, and that of reciprocal interaction between rival systems.[18] Theories of the state and of the international order based on natural law (for example, Grotius and his successors) or natural rights (for example, Locke and his successors, the French theorists of the rights of man) produce a hegemonic impulse no less than appeals to religion. Internal to Western culture, the societies based on such ideals may be described as communities whose laws and institutions express fundamental consensus as to the validity of those ideals (Schwarzenberger's "community law" or "law of consensus"). Attempts to extend such concepts and social structures to non-Western cultures, however, tend to take on the character of the "law of power." Such was the effect of much European and American colonialism, and the development of the idea of international law, originally the "community law" of Western states, into a universal system for international relations was undertaken, often quite consciously, as an element in the spread of "civilization" to non-Western cultures. Schwarzenberger, in works published as late as the 1960s, still spoke of the universal binding power of the international law of war as based in the dictates of "civilization."[19] Fundamentally the same argument is made by other contemporary theorists, such as Myres McDougal and Florentino Feliciano, who speak instead of the universal dictates of "humanity."[20] Theorists who have understood the purpose of international law as extending such presumed universal dictates have conceived the responsibility of enforcing the requirements of this law universally in relations among nations to rest with those nations which properly understood their basis and embodied them in their laws and institutions—namely, those shaped by Western culture—more specifically, the Western democracies.

The debates over how such a conception of universal order should function have changed remarkably little since the perpetual peace theories of the seventeenth and eighteenth centuries. In general terms, these debates have included two features: a conception of a community of nations each of which embraces a common set of values and ideals and incorporates these in their institutions and national behavior, coupled with provisions for dealing with those nations not embracing such standards or behaving accordingly. Two distinct kinds of international structures have developed, incorporating these features in somewhat different ways and degrees: one intentionally open to all nations that by history or choice embody the ideals defining the community, one intentionally defensive against nations repudiating these ideals and guided by others.[21] In the contemporary world, the United Nations, as defined in the Charter, is primarily the first sort of organization, aiming to embrace all the nations of the world in common agreement with the values

embodied in the Charter. Though it makes provisions for dealing with nations that act in violation of these values, these provisions are limited in various ways, and apart from the Korean
police action, only since the end of the cold war has it become
possible to regard them as the regular basis for positive action.
The European Community too is an international structure of
the first sort, though it employs stringent tests for admitting
new members. NATO has historically been a clear example of an
international structure created to defend against a threat posed
by other nations, but arguments such as Czech President Vaclav
Havel's for the eastward expansion of NATO have stressed its
purpose as a community of value, rather than a military alliance
for defense.

As in the case of Islamic culture, but by a different route,
contemporary Western culture's claim to universality has cen-
trally to do with questions of identity. The central issue is not, as
for many contemporary states seeking to identify themselves in
terms of their Muslim character, the security and authority of
regimes, for the core Western societies are well-founded, stable,
and secure; rather, what is central is how to increase international stability and security through the adoption of those values understood as defining Western culture and making for its
success. In terms of the growth of the community of nations,
what this conception produces at its best is not hegemony, but
paternalism. Yet there remains also the second impulse identified above: to defend against nations representing a threat to the
established community and its underlying values or an obstacle
to the extension of this community on its own terms. This impulse tends to feed the potential for conflict with other cultures.

But there is also a further way of thinking about the achievement of universality in modern Western political theory, one

which tends to modulate its more particularist tendencies and mitigate potential hostility among states. This approach is formalist rather than essentialist: it defines universal value in the international political arena as the product of reciprocal interaction among states, whatever their individual understandings of the universal ideal. The conception of a universal international law that results is what Schwarzenberger terms the "law of reciprocity," which rests not on agreement as to common goals, values, or ideals or on the hegemonic power of one culture or society over others, but on negotiation and trade-offs among the various actors in the arena.

At its best, the theory of political realism reflects this understanding. The fundamental assumption of realism is that states rightly act in accordance with their interests; thus, since states have different interests, and various interests have different priorities, they may negotiate their interests so as to produce relationships in which all parties judge their interests to be maximized. While realism denies a place for values in conceiving a desired final result, only at the extreme does this view of politics refuse to allow a place for the influence of values (including, in principle, those rooted in religion) in shaping the concept of interests and the priorities among interests held by the various actors—that is, individual states. Nor is realism the only approach to politics across cultural fault-lines that allows room for reciprocal forms of interaction, provided that fundamental ideals are not thereby disvalued.

Thus we may return to the central question of this discussion of claims to universality rooted in cultural assumptions: whether the different claims to universality found in the cultures of the West and of Islam represent incentives to conflict and barriers to cooperative cross-cultural interaction, or whether these claims, as they have developed in the two traditions, instead provide a way of fostering such interaction. The answer, I suggest, is the latter, demonstrated by examination of the two traditions through their historical practical development, not simply by reference to each tradition's normative ideal as it was expressed originally. It is useful to refer again to Schwarzenberger's three types of "law" to explore this point. Each of these two normative traditions on statecraft, within its own cultural frame, defines a form of "community law"—that is, expresses a value consensus as to the conception of the political community, its leadership, and its purpose. If that consensus is understood in its ideal form, the claim to universality included in it implies hegemony over all systems based on rival conceptions.

In actuality, though, the consensus in each case has developed through a historically defined tradition that includes not only ideal but practical elements, adaptations of the ideal within its own particular cultural frame. In this process each tradition has employed the ideal of universality as a reference point for the normative legitimacy of particular states and communities of states. If, in theory, there can be only one universal ruler of one universal state, then a claim to universal dominion on behalf of a particular ruler or political community becomes functionally a way of claiming legitimacy for the particular dominion of that ruler and/or that political unit. From the standpoint of the ruler and the polity, the issue is not the extent of their domains (though that is implied), but their authority in the part of the world they inhabit. Understood in this way, the concept of universality means not that there can be only one good state, but that there can be many, provided they meet the standards by which the good state is defined in all respects other than worldwide extent and dominion. In Western tradition this conclusion has been reached by means of successive stages of secularization of the political conception based on Augustine's theory of the

179

two cities and the development of an ideal for international order based on free adoption by individual states of the underlying (culturally shaped) values. In Islamic tradition the conclusion described above has been reached not by secularization (which remains problematic and is often perceived, especially among Muslim traditionalists in the Middle East, as part of the threat posed by Western culture), but by a different route: through the historical experience of the growth of functionally autonomous regional rulers claiming their legitimacy to rule from the ideal of the *dar al-islam*.

Among the legacies of each of these normative cultural traditions is admittedly a tendency toward expansionism, when one particular state tries to extend its own conception of virtue to achieve a larger hegemony. But neither tradition, understood through its historical development and not simply by reference to its initial ideal statement, leads necessarily to such political behavior. Indeed, the actual history of each tradition makes a better case for the opposite consequence: acceptance of plurality and reciprocal forms of interaction among states as the proper meaning of normative statecraft.

Finding Cultural Sources for Restraint in Conflicts across Cultural Divides

In the widespread attention that has been given to past and potential future conflict between the West and the world of Islam, a particularly pressing issue has been the use of warfare against noncombatants—by means including terrorism, hostage taking, and assassination—and the link between such warfare and Islamic fundamentalism of various sorts. Many observers would doubtless agree with Robin Wright that such means are part of the idea of *jihad* as interpreted today.[22] More broadly, as argued in the previous chapter, direct and intentional targeting of noncombatants in the course of a conflict has emerged as one of the most problematic features of contemporary warfare in many parts of the world, where it appears as an element of conflicts animated in part by cultural differences between the adversaries. As those examples suggest, a tendency toward warfare against noncombatants seems a problem endemic to conflicts across cultural boundaries, not simply conflicts across the boundary between the cultures of the West and those of the Islamic world.

How is it possible to mitigate this tendency? One way, hinted at in my earlier discussion of Huntington's thesis, involves looking into the adversaries' cultures themselves, turning the tables on the argument for a causative link between cultural differences and warfare against noncombatants. This is a particularly promising approach for major cultures, all of which have traditions on warfare defining right and wrong conduct. The presence of such a body of restraints is well recognized in the case of Western culture, where the tradition in question is that of the just war *jus in bello*. There is much less general recognition of the corresponding traditions in other cultures. In the case of Islam in particular, the popular notion of *jihad* is that it is religiously inspired war without restraints, that direct and intentional attacks on noncombatants are inherent in its very nature. But such a conception reveals a fundamental misconception both of the idea of *jihad per se* and of the restraints on conduct imposed by normative Islamic tradition on those who fight in it. In the following discussion I pursue the comparison begun above, turning to the question of the right conduct of war in the normative cultural traditions of just war and *jihad*.

As the *jus in bello* of Western just war tradition and its connection to the laws of armed conflict as defined in international law have been discussed in the previous chapter, we can here focus on the *jihad* tradition in Islamic culture. This requires that we turn again to the reasoning of the jurists of the eighth and ninth centuries, which forms the core of this tradition. I will focus on the position defined in one of the most important juristic texts from this period, the *Siyar* (law of nations) of the Hanafi jurist al-Shaybani (d. 804–805), who has been called "the Islamic Hugo Grotius."[23] In interpreting Shaybani, comparing him with other important jurists, and relating his position to the tradition on *jihad* as a whole, I pay close attention to the analysis provided by his translator Majid Khadduri[24] and in particular to the work of John Kelsay on the idea of noncombatancy in Shaybani.[25] I also draw on my own more detailed examination of this topic in another context.[26]

For the jurists, and thus for normative Islamic tradition, the idea of *jihad* as the warfare of the Muslim community is a derivative concept, a form of the obligation incumbent on all Muslims as individuals to "strive in the path of God"; in its basic meaning, the word *jihad* refers to this striving, not to warfare. The Qur'an employs this term and other forms of the same root only in this basic sense of effort expended by the individual in following the path of God;[27] warfare in the Qur'an is designated by another word, *qital* (fighting). One tradition associated with the Prophet Muhammad refers to fighting as *jihad;* but warfare is the "lesser *jihad*" by comparison with the "greater *jihad*," the struggle for submission to God in the individual's soul, a striving carried on by heart (faith), hand (good works), and tongue (right speech).

For the magisterial jurists of the early 'Abbasid period, the concept of *jihad* in the sense of warfare was shaped by their understanding of the *dar al-islam* as in a perpetual state of conflict imposed by the *dar al-harb,* the non-Muslim world. In this context juristic usage gave the term *jihad* a particular meaning: the warfare in which the *dar al-islam* collectively engages against the *dar al-harb*. As the jurists developed this particular meaning, they defined the concept of *jihad* as the warfare of the normative Muslim state in terms of several criteria, including the justification required (the threat posed by the *dar al-harb*), the authority necessary (that of the caliph, the authorized successor of the Prophet), and terms of the proper conduct of this warfare. It is this last element that concerns us here: the juristic rules defining what may properly be done and not done in carrying out *jihad* in the sense of the warfare of the *dar al-islam*, the Muslim community.

The importance of right conduct in such warfare is clear in Shaybani's *Siyar*, where it is the subject of the first chapter. The focus there is on traditions ascribed to the Prophet, the original leader of the Muslim community in warfare. Shaybani begins with a statement that sets out the general parameters for right conduct and includes some specific prohibitions:

> Whenever the Apostle of God sent forth an army or a detachment, he charged its commander personally to fear God, the Most High, and he enjoined the Muslims who were with him to do good [i.e., to conduct themselves properly]. And [the Apostle said]: Fight in the name of God and in the "path of God" [i.e., truth]. Combat [only] those who disbelieve in God. Do not cheat or commit treachery, nor should you mutilate anyone or kill children.[28]

Later Shaybani cites several other traditions ascribed to the Prophet which extend the list of those classes of persons not to be directly and intentionally harmed by the Muslim soldiers:

> He [of the enemy] who has reached puberty should be killed, but he who has not should be spared.
> The Apostle of God prohibited the killing of women.
> The Apostle of God said: "You may kill the adults of the unbelievers, but spare their minors—the youth."
> Whenever the Apostle of God sent forth a detachment he said to it: "Do not cheat or commit treachery, nor should you mutilate or kill children, women, or old men."[29]

A few pages later Shaybani adds several other classes of people in accord with a judgment of his teacher, the jurist Abu Hanifa: "the blind, the crippled, the helpless insane . . . should not be killed."[30]

The significance of these passages should not be underestimated because of their spare language. The restraints stemming from statements ascribed to the Prophet had the force of a direct command to all participants in the *jihad*. Those tracing to Abu Hanifa would have been understood as scarcely less imperative, being the considered opinion of one of the most respected jurists of his day and clearly of the same sort as those associated with the Prophet. The result is a definition of noncombatancy and noncombatant immunity in terms of moral obligations imposed by religious law on soldiers participating in every *jihad*. No appeal to principles is made to justify this; rather, the appeal is to the Prophet, him to whom God revealed his will. But a principle is nevertheless understood, and thus Shaybani can attach Abu Hanifa's listing of additional classes of people to those named directly by the Prophet. So too it follows that Shaybani can develop reasoning aimed at interpreting the meaning of the restraints imposed: also in the context of understanding the teaching of Abu Hanifa, Shaybani raises the question of military activity against a city in which there are members of one or more of the named classes of people, responding with a version of the rule of double effect. The Muslim attackers, he reasons, may proceed in their attack, aiming at the warriors from the *dar al-harb;* they are not at fault if their actions harm others, even (for example) Muslim children held as hostages within the city.[31]

Khadduri, citing Shaybani along with several other jurists, notes that the list of noncombatants was further extended by some of them to include monks and hermits, and by others to include "peasants and merchants who do not take part in the fighting."[32] The result is a list of classes of noncombatants much like the lists generated in the West somewhat later, beginning with the Peace of God in the late tenth century and fully developed by the mid-fourteenth century.[33] In their formulations, both cultural traditions reflected not only religion but practices of war as experienced within those cultures, and both traditions continued to develop after their initial coalescence.[34]

An important difference between the Islamic tradition regarding right conduct of war and the just war *jus in bello* that developed in the West is that the former, while forbidding mutilation and killing of people in the classes named, explicitly allowed enslavement of anyone in these classes who might be of use to the Muslim community. This was an element of the broader cultural practice of war which the jurists, including Shaybani, took for granted. Once part of the tradition, it remained, unaffected by subsequent development until well into the present century. What is to be made of this?

Hugo Grotius, commenting on the practices of warfare in the West in antiquity, observed that conquered populations were commonly enslaved and argued that this represented a step in the direction of moderation: not killing but enslavement of the vanquished. Not to be killed is not the enemy's right, argued Grotius, but the result of the victor's mercy, and enslavement of the defeated allowed the victor to obtain some benefit from this mercy, just as he might seize the vanquished's property.[35]

It is a very great step from such a way of treating the enemy to later Western ideas of noncombatancy and noncombatant immunity, but the position defined by the medieval Islamic jurists lies somewhere between these extremes. Indeed, there is a difference in how the juristic writings at the core of this tradition treat the avoidance of harm to noncombatants and the possibility of their enslavement after battle: the former is a direct command, whereas the latter is a permission. Thus in the twentieth century it has been possible for Muslim states to accept the provisions on noncombatancy and noncombatant immunity in international law while letting go of what Grotius regarded as the *quid pro quo* in ancient warfare, enslavement of those thus spared.

Jihad in normative Islamic tradition is war for the sake of religion. But its religious purpose does not translate into license to fight total war against all enemies not of the Muslim faith. Rather, participants in *jihad* are to be limited to those male Muslims who take the faith seriously, and they are to observe certain restraints imposed by the Prophet Muhammad himself and by jurists interpreting the meaning of the Prophet's permissions and prohibitions. The position is clear: there is no justification for warfare directed intentionally against noncombatants in *jihad*. Indeed, Islamic normative tradition on the conduct of war effectively converges with that of the Western just war tradition in that both cultures are able to accept the legal restraints imposed on the conduct of war in international law. Individuals and movements claiming the authority of *jihad* to wage warfare against noncombatants have no true ground in the tradition they claim as their own: *jihad* is war within limits, limits that trace ultimately to the Prophet of God.

Concluding Reflections

This chapter has attempted to find a middle course between two opposing extremes. The first of these seeks to understand and explain contemporary armed conflict entirely on a realist model, by means of value-free conceptions of the adversaries' interests in particular conflicts, without taking into account cultural differences between the adversaries both in the origins of the hostility between them and in the ways they fight once armed conflict has begun. Realism is less a descriptive model of how politics actually works in all social contexts than a prescription for how politics should work in a pluralistic society if it is to achieve the best results for all the members of that society. Ironically, while realist political theory seeks to understand the interests of society as value-free, it in fact depends on a social consensus as to what values are worth pursuing in the form of interests. Yet such a consensus is precisely what is lacking in conflicts over political ends across significant cultural borders. In such contexts, a realism-based effort at mitigating or resolving the conflicts that may arise may succeed by defining the terms of the conflict at a sufficiently general level to allow the adversaries to come to some agreement; on the other hand, such an effort may make a solution or mitigation more difficult by, in effect, seeking to impose hegemonically an understanding of the interests at stake that takes no account of the value perspectives of the adversaries rooted in significant cultural differences between them. In such cases not only are the adversaries situated on different ground from each other, but third parties seeking to resolve their conflict on realist terms are on different ground from either adversary. As a result, realist analysis provides not a common language for resolving the conflict, but a third language that does not translate either of the adversaries' languages adequately.

The true test of any theoretical understanding of the world, in the final analysis, is how well it corresponds to empirical reality, and the presence of cultural differences between adversaries across a broad range of contemporary conflicts calls for a theoretical perspective that takes these differences seriously and attempts to make sense of their impact among the complex of causative factors in the conflicts in question. The pendulum swings too far away from realism's denial of the importance of cultural factors, though, when cultural differences themselves become so central to a theoretical interpretation of conflict that a "clash of civilizations" is predicted as the form to be taken by "the most important conflicts of the future."[36] This view errs in the opposite direction from realism, but it errs nonetheless, in two major ways. First, it so magnifies the adverse effects of cultural difference that it minimizes common factors among cultures and reciprocal interactions between and among people of different cultures. Second, it places so much weight on cultural differences as leading to conflict or inflaming it once it has begun that it fails to take into account those factors within cultural traditions that tend toward the avoidance of conflict and the mitigation of the destructiveness of conflicts under way.

I have argued, against the realist extreme, that the nature of contemporary conflict is such that it cannot be understood properly without recognizing the presence of cultural elements among the factors that combine to cause specific conflicts and affect the way they are fought. At the same time, I have also taken pains to illustrate how, not only in the cultural traditions of the West, but also in Islamic tradition, there are ideals and values which tend to impede open warfare and set limits on the conduct of those particular conflicts that may occur. My choice to focus on these cultures in the above discussions represents a deliberate effort to counteract those arguments which focus on Islamic culture as a source of inevitable conflict with the West.

The perceived tension between these two cultures highlights the influence of religion, and this opens the way to point out those elements in the normative religious traditions of the two cultures which work to prevent and mitigate conflict. The same approach can be brought to bear for other cultural heritages as well. In some respects, though, the case of religion is a relatively easy one. Normative religious traditions are accessible through their doctrines, their ethics, their institutions, their histories, and many other sources; their effects within cultures have already been much studied and often well mapped. Also, as in the case of the two religions discussed above, there may be particular elements that work directly against the initiation of conflict or toward its restraint. Other elements of cultural difference that appear among the presumptive causes of contemporary conflicts are less well understood and are often inherently harder to understand because of a lack of information in depth. Thus to argue that cultural factors tend to contribute to the initiation of conflicts and/or lead to especially indiscriminate and destructive modes of conflict is to direct attention to only part of the whole picture. Rather, more effort is needed to understand the full range of how cultural factors bear on conflict and, more broadly, to understand the normative conception of statecraft within particular cultural contexts. At the end of "The Clash of Civilizations?" Huntington recognizes the need for such broader, less negatively freighted inquiry, when he calls for "the West to develop a more profound understanding of the basic religious and philosophical understandings underlying other civilizations."[37] This is also the message of the essays in Johnston and Sampson's *Religion: The Missing Dimension in Statecraft* and in my own discussion above and elsewhere.[38] But considerably more is needed. Insofar as warfare against noncombatants arises out of ethnic, linguistic, or other cultural differences not rooted in religion, these factors need to be understood in their functioning within the culture or cultures in question. Similarly, insofar as cultural identities shaped by particular constructions of history, claims to place, or other factors tend to foment or inflame conflict, the mechanisms by which these are produced and their effect on group identity need to be investigated and countered. Indeed, the nature of contemporary conflict poses a challenge to develop new and more inclusive ways of thinking about the causes of conflict and of the form conflicts may take. Understanding how religion may function within a given culture in relation to conflict is an important beginning, but only a beginning.

The Problem

Perhaps the most difficult problem posed by contemporary warfare, all in all, is the difficulty of achieving a stable, secure ending to it. The same cultural or civilizational differences that help to bring about and inflame a wide range of contemporary conflicts aggravate and frustrate the always difficult problem of finding common ground between adversaries and achieving a lasting reconciliation between them. Reconciliation is made even more difficult by the residue of injustice, fear, and hatred created by the direct, intentional warfare on noncombatants that has become a typical feature of contemporary armed conflicts. That contemporary conflicts are civil wars adds a further obstacle, since the solution must take one of three forms, each of which has its own problems. First, one party to the conflict may win and the other lose, in which case the losers may be dispossessed of rights, property, and even lives by the victors, leaving a legacy of injustice that may serve as seed for future conflicts. Second, the parties to the conflict may be brought by stalemate or the pressure of third parties to seek to restore the war-torn society; but it is extremely difficult to reunite a society whose internal social glue has already failed catastrophically and can hardly be depended upon to work better the second time. Third, the society in question can be partitioned so as to separate the adversaries from each other; yet this may simply change the form of the conflict, as partitioning itself leaves residues of injustice.

A particular problem in the ending of contemporary conflict and the promotion of reconciliation in its aftermath—and thus genuine peace between former adversaries—is what to do about atrocious conduct during the course of the conflict. Here we have a dilemma: unless some means is found to deal with those persons guilty of such conduct, its effects linger in the guise of mass graves and bitter memories of personal violation to taint any effort at restoring peace; yet, since persons in positions of responsibility and authority within a party to conflict are themselves likely to have condoned, ordered, or participated in atrocities toward the enemy, it is difficult or impossible to secure their agreement to a cease-fire and their cooperation in maintaining the subsequent peace if they are under threat of being brought to justice.

Three recent examples, from the civil wars in Bosnia, Rwanda–Zaire, and Cambodia, illustrate forms of the problem. The first two have already been discussed in chapter 4 above as examples of warfare against noncombatants. Fully adequate responses to these cases of atrocious conduct have yet to be crafted. The Dayton Accords that ended armed warfare in Bosnia were reached only by bracketing out the likely complicity in war crimes of various individuals whose agreement was needed to the Accords, notably Bosnian Serb leader Radovan Karadzic and his military commander, General Mladic. Subsequently, while a war crimes tribunal[1] has investigated atrocities, issued indictments, and carried on actual trials of low-level individuals, the NATO forces charged with implementing the Accords (IFOR) and subsequently stabilizing the settlement (SFOR) have generally not pursued persons indicted by the tribunal because of a judgment that this might reinitiate the armed conflict, with the NATO forces caught in the middle. Second, in the case of the war in Rwanda–Zaire, the unequivocal victory of the Tutsi faction in Rwanda during 1995–96 means that the war crimes tribunal created to deal with atrocities during this conflict has focused on Hutu perpetrators of the warfare against non-Hutus in 1994, not taking account of subsequent Tutsi warfare against Hutu noncombatants after the war spread to Zaire, since the cooperation of Tutsi figures in positions of authority and responsibility would be necessary for the latter effort.[2] Nor does it have jurisdiction over the further phase of this war beginning in late 1997, in which once again Hutu guerillas have struck Tutsi refugees in northwestern Rwanda.[3] Third, in the case of the protracted civil war in Cambodia, the end of the genocidal killings perpetrated by the Khmer Rouge during the late 1970s came as a result of several developments none of which addressed these crimes: a Vietnamese occupation beginning in 1979, a subsequent coalition government established by Vietnam after its withdrawal in 1989, a ceasefire in 1991 and a period of United Nations peacekeeping, and a United Nations-sponsored election in 1993. Even during the period of direct United Nations presence the genocidal killings carried out by the Khmer Rouge were left to one side, since an effort to bring the responsible persons to justice would have prevented the achievement of a cease-fire and the holding of elections. Yet the peace thus secured turned out not to be durable; it broke down, and the elected government came apart in 1996–97, as a result of factionalism within the Khmer Rouge and attempts at alliance with the partisans of the elected co-presidents, Naruddin Sihanouk and Han Sen. The legacy of the "killing fields" remains unaddressed and continues to poison possibilities for reestablishing a national community in Cambodia.

These three cases exemplify in different ways the difficulty of dealing with wartime atrocities in the course of seeking to end armed conflicts. Each conflict in which one or both parties have engaged in such activities has its own particular characteristics. Yet each in its own way poses the dilemma identified above: confronting and dealing with the atrocities seems necessary for reconciliation and a lasting peace, but the cooperation of persons responsible for atrocious conduct seems necessary for a minimal peace between the conflicting parties.

The broad problem of how to end contemporary armed conflicts has generated a very large literature and a new academic discipline, conflict resolution; yet the dilemma posed by war crimes investigations versus cease-fires appears almost entirely in the form of advocacy of one or the other, while dismissing its implications for the one not chosen. This is true not only between international lawyers on the one hand and diplomats and conflict-resolution specialists on the other, but in moral analysis and argument on the subject as well, where calls to end armed conflict as the overweening priority and condemnations of war crimes and war criminals coexist without meeting in a synthesis.

My aim here is to seek such a synthesis, the peace with justice mandated in just war tradition as the only proper end to war. In the following section I focus on war conduct, war crimes, and issues of responsibility in relation to terminating armed civil conflict. In the third section I turn to history for another perspective on dealing with guilt for war conduct in the context of reintegration of the guilty into social life after the end of conflict.

War Conduct, War Crimes, and Justice in the Ending of Armed Conflicts

War crimes proceedings—investigations, indictments, trials, exoneration of the innocent, and punishment of the guilty—respond to the question of how to deal with atrocities committed during armed conflict by treating the acts committed as criminal violations of law and their perpetrators as felons under the law. At first glance, applying this criminal justice model to wartime atrocities seems a straightforward and obvious step. Yet historically, international law has not functioned in the same way as domestic law, and to carry over into the international sphere procedures developed for domestic criminal justice required first that international law be understood not only as consensually binding, but as institutional in a way it has not been until comparatively recently.

While the idea of what is right and wrong behavior in war is very old and well established in the moral and other traditions underlying international law, it was only with the codification of the laws of war which began in the late nineteenth and twentieth centuries that this idea could be said to have a formal legal reference point other than in various domestic legal systems. Even after this codification began, though, the laws of war defined certain types of actions as prohibited or restricted but did not apply criminal penalties to violations. This was in sharp contrast with domestic legal systems, in which the definition of a certain kind of action as criminal is regularly accompanied by the penalties attaching to it. The coalescence of the idea of crimes of war in international law and the forging of a link between such crimes and punishment of guilty persons took place only after World War II, in the Nuremberg and Tokyo war crimes trials (formally the International Military Tribunal at Nuremberg and the International Military Tribunal for the Far East in Tokyo). The precedent of these two sets of trials looms large, but it is almost singular; the *only* war crimes proceedings set up with international sanction since that time have been the international tribunals for former Yugoslavia (established by United Nations Security Council Resolution 827 of 25 May 1993) and Rwanda (established by Security Council Resolution 955 of 8 November 1994; see further notes 1 and 2). These latter two tribunals, moreover, have set a precedent of their own, as the first tribunals created to deal with atrocities in non-international armed conflicts.[4] Because of this relatively limited and recent history, it is not without reason that critics have argued against resort to war crimes proceedings in contemporary armed conflicts, despite the admitted presence of atrocities in the waging of such conflicts. Three significant problems with such proceedings stand out: first, institutionalization of the idea of war crimes trials is still incomplete (for example, they must be established on an ad hoc basis for each conflict addressed, and there is no effective police mechanism for pursuing and arresting persons under indictment); second, the only precedents before the present trials followed an international war, not a civil conflict; and third, such proceedings remain relatively novel in international affairs, the only instances being the war crimes trials of Nuremberg, Tokyo, and the present cases of former Yugoslavia and Rwanda. While there is widespread international support for the current tribunals, as well as for the establishment of a permanent war crimes court, these and other important issues remain to be resolved in order to deal effectively with atrocious conduct that may occur in future armed conflicts.

Nonetheless, building on the long history of prohibited behavior in the traditions underlying international law, the concept of war crimes is now part of positive international law, and the examples not only of Nuremberg and Tokyo but also of the former Yugoslavia and Rwanda trials argue strongly for the acceptance of this concept as part of customary international law, the actual behavior of states. In order to address the argument for war crimes proceedings as a proper response to atrocities in contemporary armed conflicts, let us look more closely at the idea of war crimes as it has taken shape in international law.[5]

The concept of war crimes in international law is defined on the basis of two principal sources. The first of these, the *law of armed conflict,* incorporates the Geneva and Hague conventions and other relevant international declarations and treaties. Among other provisions, this body of law prohibits direct, intentional harm to noncombatants and protected persons and rules out the use of certain weapons deemed to be disproportionate and/or indiscriminate in their effects. Behind the positive law is a stream of normative thought going back through theorists like Grotius to just war concepts of *jus in bello* to ancient sources, as well as a tradition of statecraft that sought to limit the destruction of value brought about by wars. Ranging forward from the positive law are additional protocols and refinements seeking to amplify the limitations imposed and, since the early 1980s, to interpret what had formerly been termed the law of war as applying to all armed conflicts, those interior to a state as well as international.

At the end of World War II the Charters of the Nuremberg and Tokyo war crimes trials introduced a new concept of *crime against humanity,* which extended the idea of war crimes to include not only behavior explicitly prohibited in the positive law of war but also acts (particularly against one's own citizenry) in violation of universal human rights. This second source of the idea of war crimes in contemporary international law, the concept of crimes against humanity, extends in principle to all forms of conflict, domestic as well as international. It too has deep roots in moral and other traditions.

Since 1945, under the aegis of the United Nations, further development of both the law of armed conflict and human rights law and their cross-fertilization have led to their being joined together in the concept of *international humanitarian law*. The idea of war crimes today thus includes both violations of the law of armed conflict and crimes against humanity. This is reflected in the definition of the jurisdiction of the international tribunals established for the conflicts in the former Yugoslavia and Rwanda, which the Security Council defined to be over "persons responsible for serious violations of international humanitarian law" (former Yugoslavia; Security Council Resolution 827 [1993]) and "genocide and other serious violations of international humanitarian law" (Rwanda; Security Council Resolution 955 [1994]).

The concept of war crimes in international law aims both to prevent atrocities during armed conflict and to provide for punishment of persons guilty of crimes of war when they have already taken place. These aims have different force at each of three stages relative to an armed conflict.

1. *Before an armed conflict breaks out,* the concept of war crimes carries the assumption that the values it seeks to protect will be recognized by potential parties to armed conflict, so that these parties will plan potential military actions accordingly and train the members of their fighting units to act so as to observe the laws of war and to respect human rights. Criminal behavior attaching to this stage, it follows, would be a decision to plan the armed struggle otherwise (in the case of political and/or military leaders) or participation in that decision (in the case of

persons at lower levels, on down to individual members of military units), with the emphasis being on the responsibility of persons exercising higher levels of leadership.

2. *During an armed conflict* the concept of war crimes assumes that the leadership (both political and military) of the parties to the conflict will exert control over their armed forces so as to ensure compliance with internationally recognized standards for belligerence, whether the conflict in question is international or domestic. Criminal behavior at this stage lies in acts of omission and commission in violation of these standards, whether by persons in leadership positions or by individuals taking part in the fighting. War crimes tribunals set up during the course of a conflict (as in the case of the tribunal for the conflict in former Yugoslavia) serve both as a means of proceeding against persons who have been involved in planning or carrying out such criminal behavior and also as an effort to prevent the continuation of this kind of behavior by the threat of prosecution and punishment of those persons responsible for it (in the words of the Security Council Resolution establishing the tribunal for the former Yugoslavia, "to contribute to ensuring that such violations [of international humanitarian law] are halted and effectively redressed").

3. *After the conclusion of an armed conflict* the concept of war crimes assumes a continuing effort, at both the domestic and the international levels, to identify persons suspected of war crimes and bring them to justice. War crimes trials set up at this stage, as in the cases of the Nuremberg and Tokyo trials and the tribunal for the Rwandan conflict (whose charge is limited to violations that occurred in 1994), aim at identifying, trying, and punishing persons guilty of violations of international humanitarian law that took place during the course of the conflict in question. An international tribunal is not the only means to this

end, since individual countries have the right to arrest, prosecute, and punish persons for violations of human rights up to and including genocide; Israel's trials of Nazi war criminals provide a prominent example of this. Yet, addressing crimes of war by means of an international tribunal serves the important end of underscoring the conception of such crimes as violations of rules put in place by the international community as a whole, violations that strike at the very framework of international order.

Application of the war crimes model to contemporary armed conflicts such as we have been discussing raises certain questions. First, there is the question as to whether the precedent established by the Nuremberg and Tokyo trials is appropriate for dealing with atrocities in such conflicts, which are typically not international wars but civil conflicts in which the adversaries are divided by major cultural differences. While this is a serious issue, the question is now moot; its answer has already been provided by the creation of international tribunals for the conflicts in former Yugoslavia and Rwanda. Themselves forming a precedent, these tribunals make plain that violations of international humanitarian law are crimes of war not only in international conflicts but in conflicts between elements of the same society, and that the values embedded in such law are to be honored by parties to armed conflict whatever their particular cultural frame.

The answer to a second question remains very much open: what are the implications of war crimes proceedings for the process of bringing peace to the parties in conflict? There may in fact be no simple answer, since this process is a complex one, running from the achievement of a cease-fire through reconciliation of former enemies and the rebuilding of civil society. At

WAR CRIMES AND RECONCILIATION

the beginning of this process, where the concrete problem is how to bring the leaders of the opposing parties to a cease-fire agreement and how to maintain the cease-fire once established, a serious question is whether, as much policy argument would have it, a robust effort to investigate war crimes, identify persons responsible, and bring them before a court of justice is likely to interfere with achieving a cessation to the fighting. The reason, as already observed, is that some of the very persons whose agreement is necessary for a cease-fire may have been involved in the activities that war crimes proceedings would investigate. For such persons, avoiding the initiation of formal war crimes proceedings is a priority, and their position of authority makes it possible for them to seek to bargain away such proceedings in return for a cease-fire agreement. Correspondingly, they may reason that their interest is better served by continuing the fighting, if war crimes proceedings are set in motion. The result is that war crimes proceedings and negotiated settlements to conflicts are set against each other as mutually exclusive alternatives.

The problem is complicated by the fact that in the international arena support for each of these approaches to dealing with conflict and involvement in their implementation come from two significantly different constituencies: for war crimes proceedings, international lawyers and criminal justice specialists and institutions involved in monitoring and enforcing compliance with international humanitarian law; for negotiated settlements focused on ending the fighting, members of the diplomatic community, conflict resolution professionals, and institutions engaged in providing emergency relief and other services. Moral opinion splits between the two.

In general, the latter constituency accepts the idea that the concept of war crimes and attempts to bring war criminals to justice inherently interfere with the process of ending armed conflict. On this view, the fault-and-punishment assumptions associated with the war crimes concept must be replaced by a no-fault model in which the parties to a conflict accept what has gone on in the fighting as past and seek from that point to forge a cooperative future. A modified version of this position would accept lustration of war crimes (that is, making public the nature of such crimes and perhaps identifying those persons responsible—an approach taken in different ways in Chile after the Pinochet regime, in Argentina after the "dirty war," and in the work of the South African Truth and Reconciliation Commission after the end of apartheid).

The rationale for a no-fault position reflects several concerns beyond that of how to end ongoing armed conflict as quickly as possible. One concern reflects the lack of congruence between the context of the war crimes trials after World War II and that of contemporary armed conflicts in divided societies. The former followed an international war in which the Allied powers totally defeated the Axis and imposed terms of unconditional surrender, whereas negotiated settlements have become the preferred solution to internecine conflicts. The former thus reflected the character of war as a whole as a final arbiter of dispute; the war crimes trials effectively imposed the values of the victorious powers on the defeated powers in the context of their having submitted unconditionally. But in contemporary conflicts within divided societies, negotiated settlements produce a different result: the value systems of the parties to the conflict remain intact, and the adversaries agree in principle to some form of compromise in which both remain valid. War crimes proceedings in such cases, the argument goes, can only upset the balance and make the necessary compromise impossible to achieve.

A second concern is that if war crimes investigations lead to indictment and trial of civilian and/or military leaders in either or both parties to a conflict, no leadership may be left to carry out the terms of a negotiated settlement. Another possible outcome of such indictments is renewal of the armed conflict, insofar as such persons remain powerful in their own communities and may decide to make use of the armed force of those communities to protect themselves.

On this view, the alternative to a negotiated end to an armed conflict is to allow the fighting to continue either until one side wins, which may or may not serve the cause of justice, or until both sides are utterly exhausted, in which case the resulting stalemate will perpetuate the fighting, though at a lower level. The former possibility raises a problem of its own for war crimes trials to address atrocities during the armed conflict: that those committed by the winning side are, in practical terms, are likely never to be addressed.

With respect to conflicts in which atrocities are commonplace—that is, those in which one or both of the adversaries engage in warfare against noncombatants in one form or another—ending the fighting as quickly as possible by the most effective means available may seem the best approach to aiding the victims. Yet it is legitimate to ask, as proponents of war crimes proceedings do, whether the interests of these and future potential victims are well served by means that intentionally do not address the injustice of fighting wars by such methods. Even if the effort to set war crimes proceedings in motion has the effect of prolonging the conflict (a contention that is in fact difficult to prove for any particular conflict or for conflict in general), proponents of such proceedings argue that setting them in motion does not ignore the plight of potential victims but, rather, serves them by deterring further atrocities. As to past victims, whose suffering the no-fault position would effectively leave aside as necessary for the purpose of a negotiated settlement, war crimes proceedings would seek to address that suffering by punishing the guilty. In other words, the fundamental arguments for war crimes proceedings follow from the two main functions of such proceedings: both to identify and punish persons guilty of wartime atrocities and to deter future atrocities, both within an ongoing conflict and in other conflicts.

As one whose professional career has focused on the development of restraints on the initiation of war and the conduct of war, and one who, moreover, holds that the deepest moral justification for use of armed force is the service of justice, I clearly belong among the constituency supporting war crimes proceedings. From my perspective, shaped by thinking of morality and war in just war terms, egregious violations of the rights of people caught up in a conflict constitute an injustice that it is immoral not to seek to remedy. Indeed, as I have argued above, such violations justify the interventionary use of military force to stop them and to seek to remedy them; war crimes proceedings serve the same ends. In particular cases, the best way to respond to a pattern of war by atrocity may be to use both measures: I have supported both, for example, in the case of the Bosnian conflict. This is not to argue for a knee-jerk response by these means to every instance of atrocities during a conflict; there must be a pattern of atrocious conduct, and even then, there may be better ways of dealing with it. Within the framework of just war reasoning, the test of last resort needs to be passed before resort to force is finally warranted in moral terms, and it may also be well to think of the institution of war crimes proceedings in this way. Legal sanctions and punishments are tools that serve higher ends; they are not ends in themselves. But in my judgment, demonstrated patterns of atrocious conduct by one or both sides in an armed conflict, as in many contemporary local wars, unambiguously satisfy this concern for caution.

Before the institution of war crimes proceedings, both moral thought within just war tradition and positive international law depended on whether retaliation is justified as a means of responding to atrocities and deterring future ones. The means of retaliation, while they should be robust enough to achieve their ends, were still, preferably, to respect discrimination; that is, they should be attacks against military targets, though noncombatants might be harmed collaterally. The threat of retaliation may be enough to prevent atrocities in the first place; successful retaliation during an armed conflict may prevent a pattern of warfare by atrocity from developing. The danger is that if retaliation fails to prevent recurrence of enemy atrocities, then a pattern of tit for tat may develop, and the conflict may escalate, perhaps with the side originally victimized turning to atrocious means itself. This is the dilemma posed on a much larger scale by nuclear deterrence, a strategy that depends on the threat of retaliation; if deterrence fails, then the resulting nuclear war will bring devastation to both sides.

In Western culture, the development of a consensual *jus in bello* within the framework of just war tradition served also to limit conduct in war, both by establishing a conception of war as a rule-governed activity whereby belligerents guided themselves and by reinforcing retaliation as a proper response to activity that flouted the consensual rules. The coalescence of such rules into international law, first in the form of the law of war/armed conflict and now as a part of international humanitarian law, not only gives concrete form to the idea of war as an activity whose means and targets are not unlimited, but extends that idea in principle across all cultures. The introduction of the concept of war crimes proceedings under international auspices is a response to the definition of the limits to be observed in war and provides a way of dealing with a pattern of atrocious conduct which cannot be attacked by retaliation without leading to escalation and a war without limits on both sides. This, in terms of morality and of international order alike, is an important reason for war crimes proceedings in cases of patterns of atrocity during armed conflicts: to maintain the concept of war as a disciplined activity that must be conducted within certain real limits by a means that ensures justice without resort to the possible injustice of repeated retaliations that themselves turn into atrocities.

Turning the matter around, a conscious decision not to pursue war crimes proceedings under international auspices when there is a pattern of egregious misconduct during an armed conflict undercuts the restraints on warfare set out in the law of armed conflict and human rights law, implying that future warfare by atrocity will also go unpunished. This, to my mind, is the most fundamental problem with the no-fault approach to conflict resolution: it weakens the restraints that help to keep wars from being fought according to the rule that anything goes, and it undermines the protection of human rights by bracketing out of consideration the idea of crimes against humanity. It would be a tragedy for all humankind if the limits on war and the protections against abuses of human rights now in effect in international law were to be diluted in this way.

Finally, a further argument in support of the establishment of international war crimes proceedings in the case of patterns of atrocity during an armed civil conflict is that doing so assists in the setting up of the rule of law, an essential step in the reconstitution of a civil society torn by conflict. Thus war crimes proceedings form part of an overall synthesis of responses to the problem of how to deal with armed conflicts in divided societies, a synthesis that looks beyond the problem of achieving a cease-fire to the long-term, but more fundamental, problem of how the society is to be reconstituted so as to be at peace with itself. Without justice, there can be no peace; in this, the medieval political philosophy based on Augustine remains a source of profound insight into human community.

Morally, then, the case for war crimes proceedings against persons responsible for atrocities during a conflict outweighs the argument for ending the armed stage of the conflict on a no-fault basis. Indeed, the moral case for war crimes proceedings rejects the idea that these are somehow opposed to the achievement of a workable cease-fire; rather, the effort to bring justice vis-à-vis atrocities committed both helps to protect potential victims in the conflict so long as fighting lasts and serves to facilitate a more genuine peace when the fighting ends.

War Fighting and the Goal of Peace

"The utility of fighting limited wars," argues Michael Walzer, ". . . has to do not only with reducing the total amount of suffering, but also with holding open the possibility of peace and the resumption of pre-war activities."[6] Indeed, as Walzer suggests here, these two goals are intimately linked. He continues:

> For if we are (at least formally) indifferent as to which side wins, we must assume that these activities will in fact be resumed and with the same or similar actors. It is important, then, to make sure that victory is also in some sense and for some period of time a settlement among the belligerents. And if that is to be possible, the war must be fought, as [Henry] Sidgwick says, so as to avoid "the danger of provoking reprisals and of causing bitterness that will long outlast" the fighting. (132)

Most moral argument for avoidance of harm to the innocent and for restraint in the destructiveness of means of war centers on the first problem that Walzer identifies here: reducing the suffering caused by war. Examples of powerful and influential contemporary moral reasoning with this focus include the arguments of Paul Ramsey and of Walzer himself examined above in chapter 4. Indeed, the development of the *jus in bello* of just war tradition as a whole, right down through the coalescence of the law of war, has been driven by the same fundamental concern. By contrast, the goal of peace, while recognized as the final aim of a just war, has largely been treated only perfunctorily, if at all, in the context of efforts to limit the harm done by war.

Yet it is important to recognize that the way a war is fought and the purpose at which it aims, including the peace that is sought for the end of the conflict, are not unrelated, whether in practical or in moral terms. The institution of war crimes proceedings, as I have argued in the previous section, implicitly brings the conduct of war and the establishment of a just peace into relation by the effect these proceedings can have on the restoration of the rule of justice and law in a society rent by an armed conflict in which one or both parties have committed crimes of war. War crimes proceedings, of course, have to do with wrong *acts* committed in the course of an armed conflict, not reformation of the attitudes underlying those acts. Restraining the behavior of persons engaged in fighting a war is also the focus of the moral principles of discrimination, or noncombatant immunity, and proportionality. Correspondingly, conceptions of the peace to be sought at the end of a conflict commonly refer to acts and to the structures for action. This is clear in the medieval understanding of the goal of good politics as *tranquillitas ordinis,* the peace that comes from a just ordering of society, as well as in the modern conception of peace as having to do with the establishment and recognition of borders, governments, and patterns of relationships within and among states. It is also clear in the more recent conception of peace as world order. It is obviously acts that Walzer has in mind when, in the passage cited above, he links the way a war is fought to the possibility of an enduring peace in which the parties to the conflict can resume the normal pattern of their lives. Actions and the pattern of actions are his concern elsewhere as well, when he speaks of peace as the goal of war: when he justifies fighting to restore "peace-with-rights" as a response to the violation of those rights that constitutes aggression (51), and when he quotes strategic theorist Basil Liddell Hart that "[t]he object in war is a better state of peace" and then goes on to characterize that better peace as one "more secure than the *status quo ante bellum,* less vulnerable to territorial expansion, safer for ordinary men and women and for their domestic self-determinations" (121–22).

This approach to the concept of peace, linking how a war is fought to the possibility of achieving a genuine peace at war's end, accords well both with a legal approach to conflict such as is found in international law and with moral approaches that assume agreement on the principles of restraint to be observed. From the perspective of these approaches, then, the pressing question is what to do about enforcing the principles in the acts of people fighting a war. A striking feature of contemporary warfare, though, is precisely the lack of agreement on common principles or rules of restraint, deriving from a lack of a sense of community with the enemy that is necessary if war is to be fought in accord with mutually accepted restraints.

It is certainly important, as I stressed when discussing the wrong of warfare against noncombatants and the role of war crimes proceedings in serving justice, to hold fast to an understanding of what is and is not right to do in fighting a war—who may rightly be directly and intentionally targeted for harm and what concerns for proportionality imply for the means employed even against legitimate targets. It is also important to institutionalize this understanding and means for its promulgation and enforcement, which has been the aim of international humanitarian law. But the nature of contemporary warfare means that this may not be enough, either with regard to limiting destruction and suffering during a particular conflict or with regard to the establishment of peace in the aftermath of the fighting.

The American Catholic bishops in their 1993 pastoral letter on war and peace raise this question in the way they formulate the moral content of just war tradition. Not without irony, their description of the just war criteria in their widely read 1983 pastoral letter omitted "the end of peace" from among these criteria, despite the title of the document, *The Challenge of Peace*.[7] The 1993 statement restores this traditional concept, but in an unusual way and in an unusual place. Traditionally, whether a resort to armed force aimed at peace was part of the just war *jus ad bellum*, the part of the tradition providing moral guidance for justified resort to arms. There it was related to another element of the *jus ad bellum*, the concept of right intention, as exemplified in Thomas Aquinas's definition of such intention, citing the following passage from Augustine: "True religion looks upon as peaceful those wars that are waged not for motives of aggrandizement, or cruelty, but with the object of securing peace, of punishing evil-doers, and of uplifting the good."[8] The 1993 statement of the Catholic bishops, while explicitly linking right intention in warfare to the aim of peace, does so in a different way: while the statement's list of moral requirements for just resort to armed force still does not include the end of peace, right intention appears twice, once in its traditional place as a requirement of the *jus ad bellum*, where it is linked to the cause of justice, and once in a new place, as a requirement of the *jus in bello*, where it is described as follows: "Right intention:

Even in the midst of conflict, the aim of political and military leaders must be peace with justice so that acts of vengeance and indiscriminate violence, whether by individuals, military units or governments, are forbidden."[9] In other words, the goal of peace here is explicitly linked to the conduct of war and the intentionality behind it. Defined this way, the link between right intention in the conduct of war and the goal of peace recalls another passage from Augustine cited by Thomas Aquinas: "We do not seek peace in order to be at war, but we go to war that we may have peace. Be peaceful, therefore, in warring, so that you may vanquish those whom you war against, and bring them to the prosperity of peace."[10]

How is it possible to "be peaceful in warring"? For much contemporary thought this is an oxymoron: peace can have nothing to do with the violence of war. Such dichotomization of the two concepts follows both from a pacifistic aversion to all violence as evil in itself and, ironically, from the diametrically opposite position that the conduct of war ought to know no limits except those of necessity. Augustine, though, was thinking differently about war: "What is evil in war? It is not the deaths of some who would soon die anyway. The desire for harming, the cruelty of avenging, an unruly and implacable animosity, the rage of rebellion, the lust of domination and the like—these are the things that are to be blamed in war."[11] In an earlier chapter I cited this passage when arguing that just war tradition is rooted not in a "presumption against war" but, rather, in a presumption against injustice. Now, though, my point is somewhat different: Augustine and the medieval thinkers who followed him thought about violence in terms of the *intention* with which warriors fought. All the examples of what is evil in war—the wish to harm, the desire for revenge, a fundamental and uncontrollable animosity, rebellious rage, a lusting to dominate—are examples of wrong intentions, the kind of intentions whose manifestations in force require that they be countered by uses of force based in right intentions: defense, restoring goods and values wrongly taken away, punishing the evildoers, and thus restoring justice, order, and peace to life in society. The use of armed force, on this conception, is good or bad according to its underlying motivation, the attitude of the heart that informs such use against another person or another people.

There is an enduring lesson here: it is not simply the *acts* of participants in war that may be good or bad, though these are all the law can touch, and moral discourse too has come to focus mainly on acts. Rather, people fighting in war have a more fundamental duty to approach war with a mind-set that keeps them from engaging in cruelty so long as the conflict lasts and helps them to look forward to living peacefully within a peaceful community when the fighting is ended. When medieval thinkers first addressed the conduct of war, they did so by addressing the intentions of warriors, thus following Augustine's lead. Their method, exercised through the sacramental system of the Church, was, after battle, to impose penances on warriors who had done anything "from wrath or hatred or vainglory or passion," even though they had been fighting in a just cause.[12] By the following century this requirement of penance after battle was commonly extended to all soldiers, presumably to guard against unrecognized sin and to rectify it. At roughly the same time, a quite different method of restraining war was also being tried, that of the Peace of God, which sought to do so by listing classes of persons that soldiers were not to harm. This latter approach, which marked the beginning of the ideas of noncombatants and noncombatant immunity and sought to restrain the acts of soldiers fighting in war, rather than to address their underlying intentions, won out, growing in importance and expanding in specificity, even as the requirement of penance for returning soldiers after battle waned and disappeared.

As important as the idea of classes of noncombatants not to be directly and intentionally harmed in war has been for Western—and subsequently international—efforts to restrain war, something important was lost when attention shifted away from the need to have a right intention, not only in the choice to use force, but also in the actual employment of arms against other people. In this regard, the United States Catholic bishops perform a valuable service in their 1993 statement by reintroducing the idea of right intention as a *jus in bello* concept—the need to "be peaceful in warring." What remains lacking, however, is a means to institutionalize this approach to restraint. Within the medieval context, institutionalization was accomplished through the sacramental system. As long as the requirement of penance for returning warriors after combat lasted, it served three important functions: first, it provided a means to reintegrate men of war into both the Church and peaceful society after the war in which they had fought; second, by placing all returning warriors on the same level, regardless of which side they had served during the war, it encouraged general reconciliation of all those who had taken part in the conflict; and third, it preemptively guided the conduct of warriors in future conflicts by reminding them to avoid the attitudes and intentions that would lead them to wrongdoing such as Augustine had identified. Only the last of these was preserved in the approach taken by the Peace of God movement and subsequent developments of the idea of noncombatant immunity. In the terms of Augustine's language, this followed because each example of evil intention was paired with an evil action: wrong desire with the infliction of harm, the seeking of revenge with cruelty, rage with rebellion, uncontrolled lust with the domination of others, and so on. Within a common moral system the acts could stand for the intentions, and avoidance of the acts that followed evil intentions could become the focus. In the cultural economy of the West, fostering good intentions could be left to those institutions concerned with personal morality, while the regulation of war could concentrate on the enforcement of forms of right action. Just war tradition, including not only the work of theorists but military codes of conduct, customary behavior of states during war, and positive international law, developed accordingly.

The nature of contemporary war, though, suggests that more is needed than this approach can provide. To paraphrase Augustine, what is evil in contemporary war is, at basis, the attitudes and motivations that seem characteristically to lead to acts of war that violate the established limits: warfare against noncombatants, warfare by atrocity. Addressing these acts and patterns of action alone, without also addressing the attitudes and motivations underlying them, leaves these attitudes and motives in place to poison efforts at establishing peace. As a result, genuine peace has proved elusive after contemporary conflicts in which the warring parties have not shared—or have repudiated—fundamental moral orientations that maintain a sense of commonality even during armed conflict. To address the problem of restoring peace after such wars, new means must be found to serve the functions served in medieval Western culture by the practice of penance after battle: the constructive reintegration of soldiers into peaceful society after their return from war and the placing of all former enemies and friends on a single level, as partners in a common enterprise of reestablishing a peaceful society. The requirement of penance after battle aimed at helping medieval soldiers confront and deal with their inner guilt for what they had done, whether intentionally or unknowingly, in war; it sought to rectify their wrong attitudes toward the enemy and the intentions and motivations proceeding from these attitudes; and it also sought to help the returning warrior be reconciled to himself, so that he could once more take his place among people of peace. The secondary, but perhaps more important, consequence was the reconciliation of soldiers to one another and to peaceful society and the reconciliation of postwar society itself as a whole. It is such an institutional approach to reconciliation of former enemies that neither the moral tradition of just war nor the legal provisions of international law provides, yet is sorely missed in contemporary armed conflicts. Such an approach must be made up, on contemporary terms and taking account of contemporary cultural contexts, if the establishment of peace is to be more than a distant ideal after bringing contemporary armed conflicts to the stage of cease-fire.

What might such an effort entail? Two potentially useful strategies may be identified: first, active efforts to bring into being conversations and other forms of interaction across existing lines of cultural difference to create a sphere of commonality between potential enemies; second, application of the model of reconstruction of devastated enemy society developed after World War II. Both have limits; neither is a panacea. Yet both address the problem of animosities that may inflame conflict, and both offer promise of replacing such animosities with reconciliation.

The first is actually suggested by Samuel Huntington in the final paragraph of his original "Clash of Civilizations?" article, where he argues that taking seriously the potential for conflict raised by civilizational differences will "require the West to develop a more profound understanding of the basic religious and philosophical assumptions underlying other civilizations and the ways in which people in those civilizations see their interests.

It will require an effort to identify elements of commonality between Western and other civilizations."[13] This is fair enough as far as it goes; and it may even be the case that Western civilization has more resources to undertake such a task than at least some of the other civilizations identified by Huntington. But the problem of contemporary warfare inflamed by cultural differences is not simply or even mainly that of the West in potential confrontation with other cultures; contemporary conflicts involve differences between many pairs of civilizations. The task that Huntington lays out is a global one, involving not only the fostering of greater mutual understanding, but the identification of common interests and values across the cultural or civilizational dividing lines. As I have suggested in chapter 5 above, it should be possible to draw on the resources of any and all cultures to this end, despite their differences.

The second approach focuses on more practical forms of cooperation: mutual assistance across lines of cultural or civilizational difference to build up one another's societies and knit them together cooperatively. The establishment of democracy in post-World War II West Germany and Japan and, indeed, the post–cold war establishment of democratic societies in former Communist dictatorships like Poland, Hungary, and the Czech Republic serve as positive models here. The role of the international community and of the individual states that constitute it is not exhausted by establishing cease-fires or instituting war crimes proceedings; that role also includes a continuing involvement in conflict-torn societies to help them towards a reconstruction of social institutions and the necessary infrastructure needed for a lasting peace.

The limits of each approach, however, can be seen in the fate of Sarajevo, where both cultural integration and cooperation across cultures in the functioning of social life had reached a high level prior to the onset of the Bosnian War. But the war that has brought an end to the sophisticated, well-integrated society of Sarajevo did not begin in that city; rather, it took root and flowered in the far more divided rural areas of Bosnia, where a common life and mutual understanding were less developed or had never existed. So the example of Sarajevo shows how attitudes of distrust and enmity can destroy a peaceful society, even as the prewar city shows what can be accomplished across cultures to defuse potential conflict. Much can be learned from both stages in the recent history of this tragic city.

In common discourse, war and peace are seen as alternative states; in reality, they are often mixed. The ending of armed conflict by a cease-fire or even a peace agreement may prove only temporary unless both parties to the conflict are satisfied by its terms and reach a mutual reconciliation that allows them to remain satisfied; otherwise they may take up arms again, either to seek what they perceive they have been denied or to defend themselves against the former enemy, or both. In contemporary conflicts characterized by warfare against noncombatants or other forms of atrocity, war crimes proceedings represent an important step toward bringing closure to such deeds, by punishing the guilty and reestablishing an element of justice and the rule of law. But to "be peaceful in warring" requires not only that wrong actions and patterns of behavior in war be addressed and remedied; it also requires addressing and reforming the underlying attitudes and motivations of the warring parties. The larger problem of peace after all conflicts is reconciliation of former enemies, including returning soldiers who themselves may have participated in war crimes but will never be tried. War crimes proceedings under international auspices do not hinder peace, as is sometimes argued; rather, they help it to be established on a basis in justice. Yet this is only a beginning in a process that must also include institutional efforts to build mutual understanding and respect across cultural boundaries and to create cooperative forms of living in which each party to the conflict helps to support the other and comes to depend on the other's support in a society defined by mutual and reciprocal cooperation.

Conclusion: Reshaping and Affirming a Consensus on the Purposes and Limits of War

7

At the beginning of this book I called attention to the divergence between the actual character of contemporary warfare and the type of war envisioned and addressed in the main line of recent moral writing on war and peace. In particular, the moral debates of the Vietnam era and the nuclear age continue to cast long shadows over conceptions of morality and military force in the contemporary age, though the shape of war and the prospects for use of armed force today are very different. My purpose throughout the discussions in the above chapters has been to take a step towards remedying this state of affairs by bringing a specific kind of moral analysis, one rooted in the broad tradition of just war in Western culture, to bear on some of the most important and often troubling features of contemporary warfare: the influence on conflict of major cultural differences between belligerent parties, the direct and intentional targeting of noncombatants as a central element in the conduct of war, and the difficulty of reintegrating societies torn by contemporary conflict so as to achieve a genuine and lasting peace. In doing this, I have also addressed two important current debates over the proper shape of national and international responses to contemporary warfare: first, the debate over the justification for military intervention for such diverse purposes as humanitarian relief, responding to threats to international order, stopping abuses of human rights, separating warring parties, and peace-keeping; and second, the debate over internationally sanctioned war crimes proceedings as the proper response to egregious violations of international humanitarian law in the course of a conflict. Throughout the discussions of these issues I have paid particular attention to the close relation between the moral im-plications of just war tradition and the positive provisions of international law for restraining the actions of parties to a con-flict. This close relation reflects, I have argued, the historical connection between positive international law and the moral traditions of the West. Yet I have also argued that the relevant portions of contemporary international law express a broader, more thematic consensus of moral values common to all cul-tures, witnessed by the formal consent of nations across the globe to the relevant treaties, conventions, declarations, and other instruments that define international humanitarian law as it exists today.

By contrast with such issues as these, which must be central in moral reflection on contemporary warfare, the last major debate on morality and war, that of the 1980s, focused on quite different issues: nuclear deterrence, the bilateral superpower re-lationship between the United States and the then Soviet Union, and the possibility of war involving nuclear weapons. The moral arguments put forward in that debate were deeply conditioned by this focus and by analysis reflecting what many moralists believed to be the threat of world-ending holocaust posed by the existence of nuclear weapons. Some contributions to this debate were shaped also by a deep mistrust of the state and all things military, so that in practice, for moralists who held this view, all potential uses of military power by the state were tainted by "militarism." In general terms, the moral debate of the 1980s provided a poor preparation for moral reflection on the most troubling issues of contemporary warfare. Yet this debate served an important purpose in stressing the moral significance of noncombatant immunity from direct, intentional harm and in exploring how to maintain such protection of the innocent in the face of weapons of mass-destructive capability. The contemporary context requires no less that noncombatant immunity be preserved and strengthened, though the threat to noncombatants in contemporary conflicts is typically of a quite different nature.

If one goes back to the previous stage in American moral debate over morality and warfare, that over United States involvement in the war in Vietnam, one encounters a context in which the deep societal divisions generated by that conflict colored the moral analysis and argument directed to it so thoroughly that it is difficult to separate a particular theorist's moral argument about a specific issue pertaining to that war from his or her attitude toward war in general, the war as a whole, or American involvement in it. Taking the moral arguments staked out in this debate and seeking to apply them directly to the case of contemporary war would be mistaken. Indeed, I have deep reservations about some of those arguments and the positions reached from them, notably the tendency to reject all uses of military force on behalf of statecraft as inherently immoral. That I believe that wisdom relevant to contemporary conflict can nonetheless be found in moral analyses and arguments directed to the Vietnam

War is illustrated by the attention I have given to two moral theorists, Paul Ramsey and Michael Walzer, who treated issues raised by this war from essentially opposite positions regarding its overall justice. Yet, as a whole, the moral literature generated by the Vietnam War can hardly be applied directly to the issues raised by contemporary warfare; and this is even more difficult with the moral literature on nuclear deterrence, the superpower relationship, and potential nuclear war. Contemporary armed conflict needs to be assessed morally in its own right, and that has been the purpose of this book.

Because each stage in the moral debate over warfare during the past fifty years reflects the particular concerns of its time, my own thinking about the moral problems raised by contemporary war maintains a deep commitment to a style of analysis and argument that engages just war tradition, a moral tradition formed by a long history of encounter with many different types of war, shaped by the reflection of individuals from many different walks of life, representing a variety of distinct perspectives on the issues at stake. Whereas the moral debates on war as shaped by the context of the conflict in Vietnam or that of the threat of nuclear weapons during the cold war do not translate easily or well to the context of contemporary warfare, a longer historical view helps to set the problems of such warfare and the possibility of its restraint in a more revealing light.

Twentieth-century warfare has often been described as "total war," conflict in which the entire societies of the belligerents are involved, in which their utmost resources are directed to the war effort, and in which both the justifications and the aims of the fighting have an ultimate character. This understanding of war, whose roots reach back considerably earlier, reached a new intensity in the responses to the heavy toll of trench warfare in World War I and the devastation of cities by strategic bombing in World War II. The onset of the age of nuclear weapons, with their capacity for indiscriminate destruction on a global scale, added a new dimension to the idea of "total war" as conflict that would be outside all meaningful human purpose and beyond human control once set in motion. Accordingly, it was often argued during the nuclear debate that the traditional restraints on fighting war—those imposed both by just war tradition and by the law of war—were irrelevant, because of the great destructive power of nuclear weapons, power that made them inherently both disproportionate and indiscriminate. Though contemporary warfare differs greatly in nature and scale from the two world wars and the anticipated nuclear holocaust, clearly contemporary warfare shows the influence of the conception of armed conflict as "total war," especially in the most destructive and morally problematic features of contemporary war: the erasing of a distinction between combatants and noncombatants and the intentional, direct targeting of the latter in what I have called warfare against noncombatants. Once the entire society of the opposing party to a conflict is identified as the enemy who must be fought against, even the most ordinary weapons can be turned into instruments of catastrophic destructiveness.

Yet I have argued strongly both here and in other writings against the argument that traditional restraints no longer have any meaning for warfare in the modern age. This argument has the effect of denying that morality has a place in the conduct of war. A danger in granting it is that it becomes self-fulfilling in the practice of war. Thus I have maintained in this book that there should be a strong national and international response to forms of war conduct that flout the rights of noncombatants, ignore the responsibilities of combatants, and disregard the hard-won international consensus as to the limits of fighting a war. All humanity will lose if regard for these limits disappears.

The particular nature of contemporary warfare leads to the recognition that the problems it raises are in fact not different in kind from those encountered repeatedly in the long pre-modern history of war, problems which the traditional restraints sought to address and remedy. The rules protecting noncombatants, for example, are not some kind of intellectual or legal abstraction remote from the realities of war, but the result of a cumulative response to earlier experience of warfare against noncombatants, and it makes little sense to capitulate to the idea that such warfare is somehow a necessary feature of twentieth-century conflict, "total war." The protection of cities, crops, water supplies, means of production of the necessities of civilian life, and even the cultural heritage of the opposing party in war reflects the realization that observing such protection during the war makes it far easier to return to peace after the war is over, when everyone is a noncombatant. Moreover, the idea at the core of modern-war pacifism, that the scale of modern war necessarily implies the gross and indiscriminate destruction of the enemy's society, even if it were true, hardly applies to the empirical scale of contemporary conflict. The shape of war at the end of the twentieth century has turned out to be not "World War III," a global holocaust extending the model of the two world wars into the age of nuclear weapons, but relatively limited local wars involving types of weapons much like those known a century and more ago. Nor is this kind of war remote from human control; rather, human decisions are immediately and visibly involved in every aspect of its conduct. As a result, it is far from irrelevant to look to traditional ideas of justice and restraint in war and, indeed, historical models of limited war for a renewed moral consensus on the limitation of contemporary war.

When war breaks out between parties to a conflict, it is because efforts to resolve that conflict by means short of resort to arms have failed. Some approaches to the restraint of war focus on keeping conflicts from getting to this stage. In the context of moral discourse about war, this is the approach of pacifism in its various forms: war itself is the problem, and preventing it is the solution. In international law the attempt systematically to reject war is reflected in the effort to outlaw first resort to war that was first given treaty form in the 1928 Pact of Paris and is currently institutionalized in the United Nations Charter. Much diplomacy also focuses on the avoidance of war as the central problem. Such an approach is an important element in an overall effort to restrain war, in that it undoubtedly contributes to keeping some conflicts from reaching the stage of resort to armed force by one or both parties. Yet clearly in the real world wars continue to break out, and once a war has begun, the nature of the problem it poses changes significantly. The trouble with conceiving of resort to armed force as itself the problem that must be solved is that this conception contains no resources for restraining a conflict once it is under way. Indeed, in some circumstances the effort to end an armed conflict may clash with efforts to restrain its conduct; an example is the tension discussed in chapter 6 between war crimes proceedings (which aim at restraining the conduct of war) and no-fault cease-fire efforts (which reflect the conception that the continuation of the war is the problem to be solved).

Another difficulty with the idea that the resort to armed force is the problem and avoiding use of force the solution is that holding consistently to this position means that no resort to military means in face of a conflict is ever right. Yet in the world as it is, there may in fact be values or causes that cannot be defended except by use of military means. This is recognized in the reservation of the right of self-defense against aggressive use of force maintained in international law, as well as in arguments for military intervention in order to protect human rights and provide humanitarian aid to victims of conflicts.

In short, war always poses two somewhat different sorts of moral problems: how to determine when it is justified and how to fight in a justified war. No moral discourse on war is complete without both; international order cannot afford to dispense with either. No effort to prevent the resort to war can remove the need for limits on the conduct of those wars that begin anyway, and no attempt to restrain the conduct of war can remove the need for prevention of resort to war for reasons that do not stand the test of justice. The conception of war as inherently involving totalistic means gives up on the possibility of restraining the fighting of a war; thus the habit of thinking about modern war as "total war" is, I suspect, no small part of the reason for confusion and reticence over what to do about the criminality and excessiveness of many features of the prosecution of contemporary wars. Just war is inherently limited war. Yet, at the same time, even those resorts to force that are strictly limited as to their conduct are unjust if they come about too casually or serve unjustifiable ends. The problem of contemporary wars lies not simply in how they are all too often fought and their effects on the innocent and powerless, but also in the circumstances and choices that give rise to them in the first place.

At the end of the twentieth century, perhaps it is possible finally to give up the conception of all war as inherently total which was nourished by the two world wars and the threat of nuclear war. At the same time, there would be no great advantage in seizing on a paradigm of war like that of the limited but very frequent "sovereigns' wars" of the eighteenth century. Rather, a new consensus is needed in which resort to military force is held to the demands of good statecraft, the service of a just and peaceful international order, and its use is strictly limited by the requirements of a consensually observed international humanitarian law. But for this to be effective, the moral underpinnings must be shared across all the cultures of the globe. Thus in chapter 5 I argued for more thorough exploration of the moral traditions of the world's civilizations, in order to identify and understand the conception of war and its limits to be found in each one. While the efficacy of any cultural moral tradition loses force at the borders of that culture, moral reflection on war can support the development of a strengthened international consensus by energetically exploring avenues for conversation among moral traditions worldwide and by developing those commonly held features that tend toward restraint in the resort to war and the limitation of the conduct of war.

Introduction

1. The inherent immorality of war was argued in several different
   ways during this period, though these different approaches came
   together in the common cause of opposition to the war in Vietnam. One major line of argument proceeded from a principled
   opposition to all violence, derived either from religious convic-
   tions (in the manner of the pacifism of the historic peace
   churches) or from humanistic philosophical reasoning (often itself drawing on religious conceptions, whether Western or Eastern in origin). A second major line of argument that achieved
   some force during this period held, broadly, that the creation of a
   system of world order by means of international law and the
   United Nations had eliminated the right of any state to wage war
   except in self-defense, narrowly defined. War for any other purpose, waged by the state, was now seen as wrong. Often this position was buttressed by a criticism of the United States government
   and, more broadly, of the state system as a whole, as immoral in
   its ends and its acts. The third line of argument, variously called
   "modern war pacifism" and "just war pacifism," proceeded from a
   judgment that the inherent destructiveness of modern war has
   made it impossible for belligerents to satisfy the moral require-

ments for just conduct in war, discrimination or noncombatant immunity and proportionality of means. Since modern war cannot be fought morally, this argument held, then there can be no morally justifiable war.

The first two lines of argument gave contemporary expression to two much older traditions of opposition to war; see further my description of these traditions in *The Quest for Peace* (Princeton, N.J., and Guildford, Surrey: Princeton University Press, 1987), xi–xvi and chaps. 2–5, *passim*. The third made use of the principles of the *jus in bello* of just war tradition, that part of the tradition bearing on moral conduct in war, but made them do a duty reserved in just war tradition for another set of principles, those of the *jus ad bellum*, which establish when it is justified to undertake war. To illustrate the difference, consider the classic statement of the *jus ad bellum* summarized by Thomas Aquinas (*Summa Theologica* [New York: Benziger Brothers, Inc., 1947] II/II, Q. 40, A. 1): "In order for a war to be just, three things are necessary": viz., sovereign authority, just cause (the righting of injustice), and right intention (not to dominate but to seek justice and peace). Writing near the beginning of United States intervention in Vietnam, theologian Paul Ramsey exemplified the application of these criteria to that context, concluding that the military intervention was just (Ramsey, *The Just War* [New York: Charles Scribner's Sons, 1968], chap. 2); writing toward the end of that same conflict, Michael Walzer drew on the same criteria to conclude that the United States entry into the war had never been just (Walzer, *Just and Unjust Wars* [New York: Basic Books, 1977], 97–101). It is quite different to argue that the justice of undertaking any war in the first place depends on whether it is fought justly. In the case of the war in Vietnam, opponents of the war could draw on close and vivid news accounts showing harm to Vietnamese civilians to argue that this war was being fought unjustly and that therefore it was unjust for the United States to be engaged in the war. Subsequent to the Vietnam era, the same reasoning was carried over to argue against all war in the age of nuclear weapons, whose destructiveness, it was argued, is inherently indiscriminate and disproportionate.

In the context of this book this third line of argument against contemporary war is the most important, and I return to it in various contexts in what follows. My own position is that this argument proceeds from a mistake in judgment and a mistake in logic. The mistake in judgment is to assume that no limits on the conduct of warfare can work any more; my argument in this book is that not only can they work—i.e., the possibility of war being a moral enterprise still exists—but that they must be made to work so as to limit the very kinds of harm to noncombatants and to entire societies that have become commonplace in contemporary armed conflicts. The mistake in logic is really a matter of the meaning of just war reasoning: I hold that the traditional concerns of the *jus ad bellum* remain prior. There continues to be a place for the use of military force as an instrument of justice in the service of peace and order within the framework of the practice of statecraft. Of course, such use of force should itself proceed justly—i.e., it should be neither indiscriminate nor disproportionate. But these concerns simply do not enter the picture, I maintain, until the prior concerns of justice, peace, and order (or just cause, right intention, and sovereign authority) have been satisfied.

2. Thus important representatives of the main-line Protestant churches came to take the position earlier limited to the historic peace churches, that war is incompatible with Christian principles; see, e.g., the United Methodist bishops' pastoral statement *In Defense of Creation* (Nashville, Tenn.: Graded Press, 1986), 20. Similarly, the United States Catholic bishops had earlier made their own the claim that "Catholic teaching begins in every case with a presumption against war" (National Conference of Catholic Bishops, *The Challenge of Peace* [Washington, D.C.: United States Catholic Conference, 1983], iii).

3. I have discussed this position in n. 1 in connection with opposition to the Vietnam War and nuclear weapons, but in fact its origins can be traced back more than a century, to a position document presented to Vatican Council I in 1870 reflecting the destructiveness of then-contemporary warfare, denounced as "hideous massacres" which the Catholic Church ought not to regard as just (cited from John Eppstein, *The Catholic Tradition of the Law of Nations* [Washington, D.C.: Catholic Association for International Peace, 1935], 132). One may read the history of such criticism of modern warfare as a story of the development of war as an inherently immoral spasm of uncontrollable destructiveness; but one may also read this same story quite differently: as evidence of the realization that formal restraints on the conduct of war should be defined and adopted. The first steps toward a positive law of war came out of precisely the same period as the Vatican I document above and characteristically cited the need to

alleviate the destructive effects of war; see, e.g., Adam Roberts and Richard Guelff, eds., *Documents on the Laws of War*, 2d ed. (Oxford: Clarendon Press, 1989), 30 (The St. Petersburg Declaration of 1868) and 45 (1907 Hague Convention IV). So the growth of destructive means of war does not mean that war must necessarily be "hideous massacres"; rather, it means that responsible statecraft requires that steps be taken to establish, respect, and maintain limits on the means of war actually used.

4. British strategic analyst John Garnett identifies four reference points for the idea of limited war: limitation to a relatively small area of conflict, limited objectives, limited means, and some restraint or choice in the selection of targets for attack (John Baylis, Ken Booth, John Garnett, and Phil Williams, *Contemporary Strategy* [New York: Holmes and Meier Publishers, 1975], 121–24). Limited war defined in these ways is not, of course, automatically moral warfare: the objectives might be unjust (e.g., total elimination or subjugation of the enemy population), or the targets chosen might be limited but involve indiscriminate or disproportionate destruction (e.g., the case of the siege of Srebrenica discussed below in chap. 4). It is in these two areas that contemporary warfare poses the greatest challenges to ideas of restraint, whether expressed in moral argument or in international law.

Chapter 1: Politics, Power, and the International Order

1. These forms of war were my focus in *Can Modern War Be Just?* (New Haven, Conn., and London: Yale University Press, 1984). See especially chap. 2 of that book.

2. See, e.g., the essays collected in Alberto R. Coll, James S. Ord, and Stephen A. Rose, *Legal and Moral Restraints on Low-Intensity Conflict* (Newport, R.I.: Naval War College, 1995).

3. See Introduction, n. 2, above.

4. National Conference of Catholic Bishops, *Challenge of Peace,* 3.

5. Ibid., iii.

6. National Conference of Catholic Bishops, *The Harvest of Justice Is Sown in Peace* (Washington, D.C.: United States Catholic Conference, 1993), 2, 9–12.

7. As conveyed, for example, in the following statement: "[I]mportant in the age of modern warfare is the recognition that the justi-

fiable reasons for the use of force have been restricted to instances of self-defense or defense of others under attack" (National Conference of Catholic Bishops, *The Challenge of Peace*, 67).

8. National Conference of Catholic Bishops, *Harvest of Justice*, 16.

9. For an overview of these developments see Brian Hall, "Blue Helmets, Empty Guns," *New York Times Magazine*, 2 Jan. 1994: 18–25, 30, 38, 41, 43.

10. There were two forms of UNOSOM, UNOSOM I and UNOSOM II, the latter created after the withdrawal of American troops. On the American intervention and UNOSOM (I and II) see further Don Oberdorfer, "The Road to Somalia," *Washington Post National Weekly Edition*, 14–20 Dec. 1992: 6–7; John R. Bolton, "Somalia and the Problems of Doing Good: A Perspective from the State Department," and Alberto R. Coll, "Somalia and the Problems of Doing Good: A Perspective from the Defense Department," in Elliott Abrams, ed., *Close Calls* (Washington, D.C.: Ethics and Public Policy Center, 1998), 145–60, 161–82 resp.

11. See, e.g., the argument in National Conference of Catholic Bishops, *Harvest of Justice*, 8.

12. On this movement and its ideals see further Johnson, *Quest for Peace*, chap. 4.

13. Walzer, *Just and Unjust Wars*, xiv.

14. Paul Ramsey, *War and the Christian Conscience* (Durham, N.C.: Duke University Press, 1961), chap. 2; *idem, Just War*, chap. 6.

15. Stanley Hoffmann, *Duties Beyond Borders* (Syracuse, N.Y.: Syracuse University Press, 1981), 46, 50, 55–85.

16. For fuller development of this argument see James Turner Johnson, "Historical Roots and Sources of the Just War Tradition," in John Kelsay and James Turner Johnson, eds., *Just War and Jihad* (New York; Westport, Conn.; and London: Greenwood Press, 1991), chap 1.

17. See further James Turner Johnson, "Just War Thinking and Its Contemporary Application: The Moral Significance of the Weinberger Doctrine," in Alan Ned Sabrosky and Robert L. Sloane, eds., *The Recourse to War: An Appraisal of the "Weinberger Doctrine"* (Carlisle Barracks, Pa.: Strategic Studies Institute, U.S. Army War College, 1988), chap. 5; and James Turner Johnson and

George Weigel, *Just War and the Gulf War* (Washington, D.C.: Ethics and Public Policy Center, 1991), Part One.

18. James F. Childress, *Moral Responsibility in Conflicts* (Baton Rouge, La., and London: Louisiana State University Press, 1982), 63–94.

19. National Conference of Catholic Bishops, *Challenge of Peace*, 26–8.

20. See above, n. 15.

21. See, e.g., Ramsey, *Just War*, chap. 11; *idem*, "A Political Ethics Context for Strategic Thinking," in Morton A. Kaplan, ed., *Strategic Thinking and Its Moral Implications* (Chicago: University of Chicago Press, 1973), 101–47, at 124–25; and *idem, Speak Up for Just War or Pacifism* (University Park, Pa.: Pennsylvania State University Press, 1988), 197.

22. Walzer, *Just and Unjust Wars*, Parts Two and Three.

23. William V. O'Brien, "Just War Doctrine's Complementary Role in the International Law of War," in Coll et al., eds., *Legal and Moral Constraints*, chap. 7.

24. On this development see further James Turner Johnson, *Just War Tradition and the Restraint of War* (Princeton, N.J., and Guildford, Surrey: Princeton University Press, 1981), 150–65.

25. Thomas Aquinas's description of the necessary authority for just war is typical; see Aquinas, *Summa Theologica*, II/II, Q. 40, A. 1.

26. See further the discussion in Coll et al., *Legal and Moral Constraints*, 43–144.

27. Augustine, *Contra Faustum*, 22.74, cited from Aquinas, *Summa Theologica*, II/II, Q. 40, A. 1.

28. Augustine, *Quaestionum in Heptateuchum*, Q. x, *Super Josue*, and *Letter to Count Boniface*, 189, both cited here from ibid.

29. For further discussion see Bernard J. Verkamp, "Moral Treatment of Returning Warriors in the Early Middle Ages," *Journal of Religious Ethics* 16, no. 2 (Fall 1988): 223–49.

30. Ramsey, *Just War*, 405. In my judgment, as already suggested in the Introduction, a worse form of *jus contra bellum* results from using the *jus in bello* categories of discrimination and proportionality as if they were able by themselves to determine the justice or injustice of a war.

31. National Conference of Catholic Bishops, *Challenge of Peace*, 22, 26, 27.

32. See, e.g., the discussion of recent Catholic just war thinking in J. Bryan Hehir, "Just War Theory in a Post–Cold War World," *Journal of Religious Ethics* 20, no. 2 (Fall 1992): 237–57.

33. See further my argument on the "presumption against war" idea in James Turner Johnson, "Just War: The Broken Tradition," *National Interest*, no. 45 (Fall 1996): 27–36.

34. See further Johnson, *Just War Tradition*, 124–50.

35. See further James Turner Johnson, *Ideology, Reason, and the Limitation of War* (Princeton, N.J.: Princeton University Press, 1975), 214–32.

36. See further Johnson, *Just War Tradition*, 204–19.

37. See further O'Brien, "Just War Doctrine's Complementary Role."

Chapter 2: Conditions for Just Resort to Armed Force

1. Thomas Aquinas, *Summa Theologica*, II/II, Q. 40, A. 1.

2. Defining right intention positively as the aim of peace, Augustine wrote: "We do not seek peace in order to be at war, but we go to war that we may have peace. Be peaceful, therefore, in warring, so that you may vanquish those whom you war against, and bring them to the prosperity of peace" (*Letter to Count Boniface*). See further the discussion of right intention above, chap. 1, pp. 32–34, and n. 31.

3. See further my examination of this period in the development of just war tradition in Johnson, *Ideology, Reason, and the Limitation of War*, chap. 1.

4. This position is defined in Aquinas, *Summa Theologica*, II/II, Q. 40; the core ideas of just cause, proper authority, and right intention are treated in Article 1 of this Question. All the references in the following discussion are to this locus.

5. Further on Gratian and his successors see Johnson, *Ideology, Reason, and the Limitation of War*, 35–53, and Frederick H. Russell, *The Just War in the Middle Ages* (Cambridge: Cambridge University Press, 1975), chaps. 3–5; on Vitoria and Suarez see Johnson, *Ideology, Reason, and the Limitation of War*, 150–71, 178–95, 204–206.

6. A prominent example of this is National Conference of Catholic Bishops, *Challenge of Peace*, 28, which in listing the criteria of the *jus ad bellum* puts just cause first, competent authority second.

7. Further on the canonists' treatment of authority to wage just war see Russell, *Just War in the Middle Ages*, chaps. 4–5; on the relation of this just war requirement to the social tensions within medieval society see Philippe Contamine, *War in the Middle Ages* (Oxford: Basil Blackwell, 1984), 270–84. Further on Thomas Aquinas on sovereignty, see Thomas Aquinas, *On Princely Government*, in A. P. d'Entrèves, ed., *Aquinas, Selected Political Writings* (New York, Barnes & Noble, Inc., 1959), 3–83.

8. Walzer, *Just and Unjust Wars*, 51ff.

9. Alfred Vanderpol, *La Doctrine scolastique du droit de guerre* (Paris: A. Pedone, 1919), 250.

10. See above, chap. 1, n. 18.

11. Hugo Grotius, *The Law of War and Peace* (Roslyn, N.Y.: Walter J. Black, Inc., 1949), book I, chap. 3, sec. 7.

12. Ibid., chap. 3, sec. 6.

13. Ibid., chap. 4, sec. 2.

14. Ibid., book III, chap. 3. In actuality, at the time Grotius wrote, it was far from easy to distinguish the private interests of a sovereign from the public interests of his state in the exercise of "sovereign power," especially in time of war, when the sovereign's personal resources would be deeply committed and the outcome of the war would mean an increase or diminution of his wealth and power—perhaps even the loss of his throne. But the history of Dutch resistance to Spanish rule, which continued as one of the causes at stake in the origins of the Thirty Years' War, made Grotius sensitive to the claim that Spanish rule violated the ancient rights and privileges of the Dutch people and thus rendered that rule void. The right of sovereignty, therefore, rested with the Dutch and the state they constituted, and not with the faraway king who claimed the right to govern. As the modern period developed, this latter conception of sovereignty and its roots gradually became more established and ultimately became institutionalized in international law.

15. Ibid., chap. 3, sec. 5.

16. Ibid., book II, chap. 1.

17. Ibid., chap. 1, sec. 5.

18. Geoffrey Best, *Humanity in Warfare* (New York: Columbia University Press, 1980), 85.

236

19. Carl von Clausewitz, *On War*, ed. and trans. Michael Howard and Peter Paret (Princeton, N.J.: Princeton University Press, 1976), 367.

20. For texts see Dietrich Schindler and Jiri Toman, eds., *The Laws of Armed Conflicts* (Leiden: A. W. Sijthoff; Geneva: Henri Dunant Institute, 1973), 3–23, 199–210.

21. For examples of a range of such positions see the essays collected in Ronald H. Stone and Dana Wilbanks, eds., *The Peacemaking Struggle: Militarism and Resistance* (Lanham, Md.: University Press of America, 1985).

22. Cited from Eppstein, *Catholic Tradition of the Law of Nations*, 132. See Introduction, n. 3, above.

23. See, e.g., John Courtney Murray, *Morality and Modern War* (New York: Council on Religion and International Affairs, 1959), 11; Pope Paul VI, *Never Again War* (New York: United Nations Office of Public Information, 1965), 37–39; Hehir, "Just War Theory," 250; Johnson, "Just War," 30–33.

24. On the right of states to use force, see United Nations Charter, Articles 2 and 51; on internationally mandated use of force against threats to international peace and order, see the United Nations Charter, Chap. VII.

25. Pope John XXIII, *Pacem in Terris* (Glen Rock, N.J.: Paulist Press, 1963), par. 127.

26. See further my discussion in Johnson and Weigel, *Just War and the Gulf War*, 21–24.

Chapter 3: The Question of Intervention

1. Ramsey, *Just War*, 19–41.

2. Walzer, *Just and Unjust Wars*, 86–108.

3. National Conference of Catholic Bishops, *Harvest of Justice*, 15–16.

4. Augustine, *The City of God*, 19.7; cited from Whitney J. Oates, ed., *Basic Writings of St. Augustine* (New York: Random House, 1948), 1:481–82.

5. Augustine, *Questions on the Heptateuch*, q. x.

6. See the discussion of just cause in Thomas Aquinas's *Summa Theologica* in chap. 2 above; compare the canonist Gratian, *Decretum*, Part II, Causa XXIII, Question II, Canon II.

7. Ambrose, *On the Duties of the Clergy*, 1.36.179; cited from Philip

Schaff and Henry Wace, eds., *A Select Library of Nicene and Post-Nicene Fathers of the Christian Church,* 2d ser. vol. 10, *St. Ambrose* (Grand Rapids, Mich.: Wm. B. Eerdmans Publishing Company, 1955), 30.

8. Ramsey, *Just War,* 20.

9. Ibid., 22–23, 25–27; in what follows, page references are given in the text in parentheses.

10. Ibid., 27–33, for these terms and the following quotations explaining them.

11. Cf. Walzer, *Just and Unjust Wars,* 90.

12. Ramsey, *Just War,* 33.

13. Indeed, this is one element in Michael Walzer's argument against the justice of United States' intervention in Vietnam; see Walzer, *Just and Unjust Wars,* 97–101.

14. Ramsey, *Just War,* 33.

15. Walzer, *Just and Unjust Wars,* 61–62; in what follows, page references are given in the text in parentheses.

16. National Conference of Catholic Bishops, *Challenge of Peace;* in what follows, page references are given in the text in parentheses.

17. See the discussion of the "presumption against war" in chap. 1 above.

18. National Conference of Catholic Bishops, *Harvest of Justice;* in what follows, page references are given in the text in parentheses.

19. *Origins* 23, no. 2 (May 1993), 22–23.

20. Useful compilations of documents defining the law of war include Leon Friedman, ed., *The Law of War: A Documentary History,* 2 vols. (New York: Random House, 1972); Schindler and Toman, eds., *Laws of Armed Conflicts;* and Roberts and Guelff, eds., *Documents on the Laws of War.*

21. Roberts and Guelff, eds., *Documents on the Laws of War,* 169–337.

22. Geneva Protocol Additional to the Geneva Conventions of 13 August 1949 and Relating to the Protection of Victims of Non-International Armed Conflicts (Protocol II), 12 Dec. 1977. UN doc. A/32/144 (1977). Roberts and Guelff, eds., *Documents on the Laws of War,* 447–68.

23. Myres S. McDougal and Florentino P. Feliciano, *Law and*

Minimum World Public Order (New Haven, Conn., and London: Yale University Press, 1961), 289–90.

24. On the concept of territorial integrity and the inviolability of borders in international law see further ibid., 177, 179–80, 200, 225, 227–28, 259, 274, 528.

25. See the account by Jan Willem Honig and Norbert Both, *Srebrenica: Record of a War Crime* (New York: Penguin Books, 1997), 3–26.

Chapter 4: War Against Noncombatants

1. In this discussion I employ the terms "civilian" and "soldier" somewhat interchangeably with "noncombatant" and "combatant"; properly, there is a difference. A soldier (or sailor, airman, or marine) is someone who wears a uniform or other distinguishing visible marks and participates in warfare as a member of a unit that is part of a larger institution governed by some form of military discipline enforced through a hierarchical chain of command. (In this definition I include people who fight under such names as guerillas, partisans, or auxiliaries, provided they meet the standard tests imposed by international law; see Hague Convention IV [1907], Annex, Section I, Chapter I, Article I: Roberts and Guelff, eds., *Documents on the Laws of War*, 48.) Such a person may have duties that make him (or her) not a combatant; examples in the American military include medical and religious personnel (doctors, nurses, corpsmen, and chaplains and their staffs). Others (for example, cooks, transport personnel, clerks) are formally combatants, though their normal duties do not involve fighting. Other soldiers may have been combatants in the fullest sense but have been made noncombatants by being wounded or otherwise incapacitated or by being taken prisoner. Civilians, by contrast, are persons not engaged in formal military service, and they are normally noncombatants; they may become combatants, though, by engaging in activities through which they directly participate in fighting the war. (They may or may not actually take up arms; civilians cease to be noncombatants by, for example, digging trenches or involvement in military transport.) The terms "soldier" and "civilian" refer to an individual's *status* in society; the terms "combatant" and "noncombatant," on the other hand, refer to an individual's *function* with regard to the war in question. The latter is the more critical distinction for moral analysis, and it has become so in the legal context as well. Neverthe-

less, common usage imposes a burden of proof: a soldier's normal function is to fight, and a noncombatant soldier must be specially defined and wear distinguishing marks; while for a civilian to be treated as a combatant, there must be a special justification for denying his or her normal noncombatancy. It is in this sense of the common usage that I employ these two sets of terms alternatively above and elsewhere in this chapter, though my central concern throughout is with the issue of combatancy versus noncombatancy—that is, with a person's or a group's function with regard to the actual fighting taking place in a particular armed conflict.

2. Desiderius Erasmus, *Bellum Erasmi* (London: Thomas Berthelet, 1533), 4.

3. Lester K. Born, *The Education of a Christian Prince by Desiderius Erasmus* (New York: Octagon Books, 1965), 265–66.

4. Thomas Churchyard, *A Generall Rehearsall of Warres* (London: Edward White, 1579), sig. Q ii.

5. Important examples include Pierino Belli, *De Re Militari et Bello Tractatus* (1563) (Oxford: Clarendon Press; London: Humphrey Milford, 1936), and Balthasar Ayala, *De Jure et Officis Bellicis et Disciplini Militari,* 3 vols. (Duaci: Ioannes Bogardi, 1582); later examples of such works include *The Swedish Discipline* (London: John Dawson for Nathaniel Butter and Nicholas Bourne, 1632) of Swedish King Gustavus Adolphus and the *Lawes and Ordinances of Warre* (Newcastle: Robert Barker, 1639) promulgated by Charles I of England.

6. See Francisco de Vitoria (Franciscus de Victoria), *De Indis et De Jure Belli Relectiones* (Washington, D.C.: Carnegie Institute, 1917); Francisco Suarez, *Selections from Three Works of Francisco Suarez, S.J.* (Oxford: Clarendon Press; London: Humphrey Milford, 1944); Alberico Gentili, *De Jure Belli* (Oxford: Clarendon Press, 1964); and Hugo Grotius, *De Jure Belli ac Pacis Libri Tres* (Oxford: Clarendon Press; London: Humphrey Milford, 1925). On these four theorists and their contexts see further LeRoy B. Walters, "Five Classic Just-War Theories" (Ph.D. diss., Yale University, 1971), 218–61.

7. Grotius, *De Jure Belli ac Pacis,* book II, chap. 1 and chap. 22, secs. 14–15; Vitoria, *De Jure Belli,* sec. 10.

8. See James A. Aho, *Religious Mythology and the Art of War* (West-

port, Conn.: Greenwood Press, 1981), 21–141; John Kelsay, *Islam and War* (Louisville, Ky.: Westminster/John Knox Press, 1993), 57–76.

9. For use of this term see McDougal and Feliciano, *Law and Minimum World Public Order,* 43, and Tom J. Farer, *The Laws of War 25 Years after Nuremberg, International Conciliation,* no. 583 (May 1971), 16.

10. *The Pastoral Constitution on the Church in the Modern World,* par. 80, cited from Walter J. Abbott, S.J., ed., *The Documents of Vatican II* (New York: Guild Press, America Press, Association Press, 1966).

11. National Conference of Catholic Bishops, *Challenge of Peace,* 33.

12. Ibid.

13. Ibid., 34.

14. National Conference of Catholic Bishops, *Harvest of Justice,* 6.

15. Ibid.

16. Ibid., 16.

17. Ramsey, *Just War,* 143–44.

18. Ibid., 145.

19. Ramsey, *War and the Christian Conscience,* 144.

20. Ramsey, *Just War,* 428–29.

21. Ramsey, *War and the Christian Conscience,* 47.

22. Ibid., 273.

23. Walzer, *Just and Unjust Wars,* 35; in what follows, page references are given in the text in parentheses.

24. In this discussion Walzer defines the rule of double effect, as traditionally understood, to require four conditions:

1. The act is good in itself or at least indifferent, which means, for our purposes, that it is a legitimate act of war.

2. The direct effect is morally acceptable—the destruction of military supplies, for example, or the killing of enemy soldiers.

3. The intention of the actor is good—that is, he aims only at the acceptable effect; the evil effect is not one of his ends, nor is it a means to his ends.

4. The good effect is sufficiently good to compensate for allowing the evil effect; it must be justifiable under Sidgwick's proportionality rule.

The requirement of "double intention" changes the third of these conditions to the following:

> 3. The intention of the actor is good—that is, he aims narrowly at the acceptable effect; the evil effect is not one of his ends, nor a means to his ends, and, aware of the evil involved, he seeks to minimize it, accepting costs to himself.

25. See further Johnson, *Just War Tradition*, 131–50.

26. See further Johnson, *Ideology, Reason, and the Limitation of War*, 234–40, 246–53.

27. On the medieval restraints see further Johnson, *Just War Tradition*, 124–27, 128–30. On avoiding targets that serve human needs and/or values see Hague Convention IV (1907), Annex, Section II, Article 27; Hague Convention IX (1907), Article 5; 1923 Hague Rules of Aerial Warfare, Article 25; 1954 Hague Convention and Protocol for the Protection of Cultural Property in the Event of Armed Conflict; all in Roberts and Guelff, eds., *Documents on the Laws of War*, 53, 96, 127, 339–70.

28. The relevant documents are collected in Roberts and Guelff, eds., *Documents on the Laws of War*.

29. Hague Convention IV (1907), Annex, Article 22, in ibid., 52.

30. On the idea of crimes against humanity see Roberts and Guelff, eds., *Documents on the Laws of War*, 154–57; on the idea of genocide see ibid., 157–68.

31. In this summary I follow the accounts published in the *New York Times* and the *Washington Post* on the development of this armed conflict through the period indicated.

32. *Washington Post National Weekly Edition*, 16 June 1997: 16.

33. Walzer, *Just and Unjust Wars*, chap. 10.

34. Vitoria, *De Jure Belli*, sec. 37.

35. See Antoine Henri Baron de Jomini, *The Art of War* (Westport, Conn.: Greenwood Press, n.d.; repr. of original publication, Philadelphia: J. B. Lippincott and Co., 1862), 102, 133–40, 344–48; and Clausewitz, *On War*, 393–415, 551–55, and *passim*.

36. See the documents indicated in n. 27 above.

37. Reports indicate that these actions too included elements of warfare directly and intentionally targeting noncombatants. See the

coverage in *New York Times*, 3 July–3 Aug. 1995; see also Honig and Both, *Srebrenica*, 3–67.

38. Walzer, *Just and Unjust Wars*, 161.

39. Ibid., 162.

40. Ibid., 168. A similar prescription for carrying out sieges was set out by the early nineteenth-century military theorist Jomini, who strongly influenced the tactics of many European armies during much of the nineteenth century and provided the standard text for the American army prior to the Civil War. See Jomini, *Art of War*, 102–40, 344–48. For an example of a conscious operationalizing of this conception during the American Civil War see Stephen E. Ambrose, *Halleck: Lincoln's Chief of Staff* (Baton Rouge, La.: Louisiana State University Press, 1962), chap. 4.

41. In describing these possibilities, I depart from the specific terms of Walzer's analysis, though I agree with him on the general issues at stake. For his description of the possibilities see *Just and Unjust Wars*, 169.

42. This summarizes the account given in the *New York Times*, 13–23 July 1995.

43. *New York Times*, 28 June 1995.

44. For fuller discussion of this topic see my chapter, "War for Cities and Noncombatant Immunity in the Bosnian Conflict," in G. Scott Davis, ed., *Religion and Justice in the War over Bosnia* (New York and London: Routledge, 1996), 63–90.

45. Vitoria, *De Jure Belli*, sec. 10.

46. Emmerich de Vattel, *The Law of Nations; or, Principles of the Law of Nature* (London: n.n., 1740), sec. 145; emphasis added.

47. "Letter from Gen. Halleck to Gen. Rosecrans on the Treatment of Disloyal Persons within our Lines. Washington, Sunday, March 15, [1863]"; number LI 176 in the Francis Lieber collection of the Huntington Library, San Marino, Calif. See further my discussion in Johnson, *Just War Tradition*, 313.

48. 1925 Geneva Protocol; in Roberts and Guelff, eds., *Documents on the Laws of War*, 137–46.

49. 1981 United Nations Convention; ibid., 471–89.

50. Augustine, *Letter to Count Boniface*.

Chapter 5: Conflicts Inflamed by Cultural Differences

1. Barry Rubin, "Religion and International Affairs," in Douglas Johnston and Cynthia Sampson, eds., *Religion: The Missing Dimension in Statecraft* (New York and Oxford: Oxford University Press, 1994), chap. 3, at 20.

2. Ibid., 33.

3. Quincy Wright, *A Study of War*, 2 vols. (Chicago: University of Chicago Press, 1942).

4. Ibid., 2: 681.

5. See n. 1 above; see also David Little, *Ukraine: The Legacy of Intolerance* (Washington, D.C.: United States Institute of Peace Press, 1991); *idem, Sri Lanka: The Invention of Enmity* (Washington, D.C.: United States Institute of Peace Press, 1994) and David Little, John Kelsay, and Abdulaziz Sachedina, *Human Rights and the Conflict of Cultures* (Columbia, S.C.: University of South Carolina Press, 1988).

6. See Samuel P. Huntington, "The Clash of Civilizations?," *Foreign Affairs* 72, no. 3 (Summer 1993): 22–49. In what follows, page references are given in the text in parentheses. Huntington employs the term "civilization" for "the highest cultural grouping of people and the broadest level of cultural identity people have short of that which distinguishes humans from other species" (24). But in standard usage the term "culture" is employed for such groupings as well as for lower levels of groupings of people and cultural identity. In discussing Huntington's thesis directly I use his term "civilization"; otherwise I use the term "culture."

7. Samuel P. Huntington et al., *The Clash of Civilizations? The Debate: A Foreign Affairs Reader* (New York: Council on Foreign Relations, 1993).

8. Cf. Johnston and Sampson, eds., *Religion*, 6–7, 37–282.

9. Huntington provides a similar list of elements that make up civilizations, distinguishing "objective elements" (language, history, religion, customs, and institutions) from "the subjective self-identification of people." See "Clash of Civilizations?," 24. As will be clear from my discussion, I do not agree with this distinction. Especially when thinking about the relation of culture to conflict, what matters most is how the elements that Huntington regards as objective are interpreted subjectively for the purpose of defin-

ing identity. In any case, history and religion in particular are hardly objective realities.

10. Huntington's thesis is of this sort; see also the works cited in n. 1 and 5 above.

11. For examination of this comparison between Augustine and the early Islamic jurists on the question of the relation of war to religion see James Turner Johnson, *The Holy War Idea in Western and Islamic Traditions* (University Park, Pa.: Pennsylvania State University Press, 1997), chaps. 3–4.

12. For fuller treatment of the themes discussed here see Ann K. S. Lambton, *State and Government in Medieval Islam* (Oxford: Oxford University Press, 1981), chap. 2; Majid Khadduri, *The Islamic Law of Nations: Shaybani's Siyar* (Baltimore, Md.: Johns Hopkins Press, 1966), 1–22; for a comparative discussion of the juristic norm and historical practice see James P. Piscatori, *Islam in a World of Nation-States* (Cambridge: Cambridge University Press, 1986), chap. 3.

13. See further Michael Bonner, *Aristocratic Violence and Holy War* (New Haven, Conn.: American Oriental Society, 1996), 101–104.

14. For a chronology including this development see Piscatori, *Islam in a World of Nation-States*, 151–58.

15. See further Rudolph Peters, *Islam and Colonialism* (The Hague: Mouton, 1979), 110–11, and Ann Elizabeth Mayer, "War and Peace in the Islamic Tradition and International Law," in Kelsay and Johnson, eds., *Just War and Jihad*, chap. 8, at 202–206.

16. Cf. the rhetoric of Saddam Hussein during the Gulf War, cited by Kelsay in *Islam and War*, 13–14, and the language of the 1979 Iranian Constitution, cited by Mayer in Kelsay and Johnson, *Just War and Jihad*, 206.

17. Douglas Porch nicely characterizes how this reasoning can be translated into the political assumptions of individual Muslims, describing the attitude of the inhabitants of the Tuat oasis in Western Sahara toward their particular sovereign, the Sultan of Morocco, about 1900: "The important thing was to be included in the Dar al Islam—the House of Islam—of which, in the northwest corner of Africa, [the Sultan] was head." See Douglas Porch, *The Conquest of Morocco* (New York: Alfred A. Knopf, 1983), 212.

18. Georg Schwarzenberger, *The Frontiers of International Law* (London: Stevens and Sons, 1962), chap. 1.

19. See Georg Schwarzenberger, *A Manual of International Law*, 5th ed. (London: Stevens and Sons, 1967), 197–99.

20. McDougal and Feliciano, *Law and Minimum World Public Order*, 72.

21. Further on the perpetual peace theories and these alternative structures of international order see Johnson, *Quest for Peace*, 176–98.

22. Robin Wright, *Sacred Rage: The Crusade of Modern Islam* (New York: Linden Press/Simon & Schuster, 1985), 55.

23. Khadduri, *Islamic Law of Nations*, 56–57. For a detailed discussion of Shaybani's life, his important role in the development of Islamic law, and the contribution of his *Siyar* see ibid., 22–57.

24. Ibid., and Majid Khadduri, *War and Peace in the Law of Islam* (Baltimore, Md., and London: Johns Hopkins Press, 1955).

25. John Kelsay, "Islam and the Distinction between Combatants and Noncombatants," in James Turner Johnson and John Kelsay, *Cross, Crescent, and Sword* (New York; Westport, Conn., and London: Greenwood Press, 1990), chap. 9; cf. Kelsay, *Islam and War*, chap. 4.

26. Johnson, *Holy War Idea*, chap. 5.

27. See further Moulavi Cherágh Ali, *A Critical Exposition of the Popular "Jihad"* (Karachi, Pakistan: Karimsons, 1977), 166–67.

28. Shaybani, *Siyar*, sec. 1, in Khadduri, *Islamic Law of Nations*, 76; cf. Kelsay, "Islam and the Distinction between Combatants and Noncombatants," 198.

29. Shaybani, *Siyar*, secs. 28–30, in Khadduri, *Islamic Law of Nations*, 87, 91–92; cf. Kelsay, "Islam and the Distinction between Combatants and Noncombatants," 199.

30. Shaybani, *Siyar*, secs. 110–11, in Khadduri, *Islamic Law of Nations*, 101.

31. Shaybani, *Siyar*, secs. 112–23, in Khadduri, *Islamic Law of Nations*, 101–102.

32. Khadduri, *Islamic Law of Nations*, 104.

33. On these Western lists see further Johnson, *Just War Tradition*, 131–50.

34. See further Kelsay, "Islam and the Distinction between Combatants and Noncombatants," 199–200.

35. Grotius, *The Law of War and Peace,* book III, chaps. 4–7, 11–14.

36. The language is Huntington's in "Clash of Civilizations?," 25.

37. Ibid., 49.

38. E.g., Johnson, *Holy War Idea,* chap. 5.

Chapter 6: War Crimes and Reconciliation after Conflict

1. For particulars, including the legal basis for the war crimes tribunal, its competence, and its scope, see United Nations, "Report of the Secretary-General pursuant to Paragraph 2 of Security Council Resolution 808 (1993), including the Statute of the Tribunal," U.N. doc. no. s/25704 & Add. 1 (1993). The statute gives the tribunal competence "to prosecute persons responsible for serious violations of international humanitarian law committed in the territory of the former Yugoslavia since 1991" and specifically details four areas of violations to be addressed: "grave breaches of the Geneva Conventions of 1949," "violations of the laws or customs of war," "genocide," and "crimes against humanity" (Articles 1–5 of the statute).

2. The language establishing the Rwandan tribunal and defining its powers is intentionally broad, mirroring that of the statute of the tribunal for former Yugoslavia, and gives the tribunal competence to prosecute all "persons responsible for serious violations of international humanitarian law" in Rwanda and neighboring territories. Yet the tribunal was established at the request of the Tutsi-dominated government of Rwanda and has jurisdiction only over crimes committed between 1 January and 31 December 1994, the period of the Hutu massacre of Tutsis and mixed-blood Rwandans. See United Nations, "Security Council Resolution 955 (1994) and Annex," U.N. doc. S/RES/955 (1994).

3. Cf. "Searching in Vain for Rwanda's Moral High Ground," *New York Times,* Sunday, 21 Dec. 1997, "The Week in Review," 3.

4. A detailed examination of issues relating to the establishment of the first of these tribunals, that for former Yugoslavia, is provided in *Criminal Law Forum* 5, nos. 2–3 (1994): 223–714. This study includes as appendices the statutes for the tribunals in both former Yugoslavia and Rwanda, as well as other relevant United Nations documents.

5. The discussion which follows summarizes a complex, extensive history of developments. On the positive law of armed conflicts

247

and its development see Roberts and Guelff, eds., *Documents on the Laws of War;* Schindler and Toman, eds., *Laws of Armed Conflict;* and Friedman, ed., *Law of War.* On the historical and thematic relationship between the international law of war and just war tradition see James Brown Scott, *The Spanish Origin of International Law,* Part I, *Francisco de Vitoria and His Law of Nations* (Oxford: Clarendon Press; London: Humphrey Milford, 1934).

6. Walzer, *Just and Unjust Wars,* 132; in what follows, page references will be given in the text in parentheses.

7. National Conference of Catholic Bishops, *Challenge of Peace,* 28–31.

8. Aquinas, *Summa Theologica,* II/II, Q. 40, A. 1.

9. National Conference of Catholic Bishops, *Harvest of Justice,* 5–6.

10. Aquinas, *Summa Theologica,* II/II, Q. 40, A. 1.

11. Augustine, *Contra Faustum,* 22.74.

12. This language is that employed by a council of bishops after the Battle of Fontenay in 841, cited from Verkamp, "Moral Treatment of Returning Warriors in the Early Middle Ages," 231.

13. Huntington, "Clash of Civilizations?," 49.

Abbott, Walter J., S.J., ed. *The Documents of Vatican II*. New York: Guild Press, America Press, Association Press, 1966.

Abrams, Elliott, ed. *Close Calls*. Washington, D.C.: Ethics and Public Policy Center, 1998.

Aho, James A. *Religious Mythology and the Art of War*. Westport, Conn.: Greenwood Press, 1981.

Ali, Moulavi Cherágh. *A Critical Exposition of the Popular "Jihad"*. Karachi, Pakistan: Karimsons, 1977.

Ambrose, Saint. *On the Duties of the Clergy*. In Philip Schaff and Henry Wace, eds., *A Select Library of Nicene and Post-Nicene Fathers of the Christian Church*, 2d ser., vol. 10, *St. Ambrose*, 1–89. Grand Rapids, Mich.: Wm. B. Eerdmans Publishing Company, 1955.

Ambrose, Stephen E. *Halleck: Lincoln's Chief of Staff*. Baton Rouge, La.: Louisiana State University Press, 1962.

Aquinas, Thomas, Saint. *On Princely Government*. In A. P. d'Entrèves, ed., *Aquinas: Selected Political Writings*, 3–83. New York: Barnes & Noble, Inc., 1959.

——. *Summa Theologica*, vol. 2. New York: Benziger Brothers, Inc., 1947.

stine, Saint. *The City of God*. In Whitney J. Oates, ed., *Basic Writ-St. Augustine* (New York: Random House, 1948), vol. 1.

———. *Quaestionum in Heptateuchum Libri VII*. *Corpus Christianorum, Series Latina*, vol. 33, *Aurelii Augustini Opera*, pt. 5, 1–377. Turnholti: Typographi Brepols Editores Pontificii, 1958.

———. *Reply to Faustus the Manichaean* (*Contra Faustum Manichaeum*). In Philip Schaff, ed., *A Select Library of the Nicene and Post-Nicene Fathers of the Christian Church*, vol. 4, 155–345. Buffalo, N.Y.: Christian Literature Company, 1887.

———. *Saint Augustine: Letters*. In Roy Joseph Defarri et al., eds., *The Fathers of the Church*, vol. 4. New York: Fathers of the Church, Inc., 1955.

Ayala, Balthasar. *De Jure et Officis Bellicis et Disciplini Militari*. 3 vols. Duaci: Ioannes Bogardi, 1582.

Baylis, John; Booth, Ken; Garnett, John; and Williams, Phil. *Contemporary Strategy*. New York: Holmes and Meier Publishers, 1975.

Belli, Pierino. *De Re Militari et Bello Tractatus*. Oxford: Clarendon Press; London: Humphrey Milford, 1936.

Best, Geoffrey. *Humanity in Warfare*. New York: Columbia University Press, 1980.

Bonner, Michael. *Aristocratic Violence and Holy War*. New Haven, Conn.: American Oriental Society, 1996.

Born, Lester K. *The Education of a Christian Prince by Desiderius Erasmus*. New York: Octagon Books, 1965.

Charles I, King of England. *Lawes and Ordinances of Warre*. Newcastle: Robert Barker, 1639.

Childress, James F. *Moral Responsibility in Conflicts*. Baton Rouge, La., and London: Louisiana State University Press, 1982.

Churchyard, Thomas. *A Generall Rehearsall of Warres*. London: Edward White, 1579.

Clausewitz, Carl von. *On War*. Ed. and trans. by Michael Howard and Peter Paret. Princeton, N.J.: Princeton University Press, 1976.

Coll, Alberto R.; Ord, James S.; and Rose, Stephen A. *Legal and Moral Restraints on Low-Intensity Conflict*. Newport, R.I.: Naval War College, 1995.

Contamine, Philippe. *War in the Middle Ages*. Oxford: Basil Blackwell, 1984.

Criminal Law Forum 5, nos. 2–3 (1994).

Davis, G. Scott, ed. *Religion and Justice in the War over Bosnia.* New York and London: Routledge, 1996.

Eppstein, John. *The Catholic Tradition of the Law of Nations.* Washington, D.C.: Catholic Association for International Peace, 1935.

Erasmus, Desiderius. *Bellum Erasmi.* London: Thomas Berthelet, 1533.

Farer, Tom J. *The Laws of War 25 Years after Nuremberg. International Conciliation,* no. 583 (May 1971).

Friedman, Leon, ed. *The Law of War: A Documentary History.* 2 vols. New York: Random House, 1972.

Gentili, Alberico. *De Jure Belli.* Oxford: Clarendon Press, 1964.

Gratian. *Decretum.* In *Corpus Juris Canonici Gregorii XIII.* 2 vols. Graz: Akademische druck-u. Verlagsanstalt, 1955.

Grotius, Hugo. *De Jure Belli ac Pacis Libri Tres.* Oxford: Clarendon Press; London: Humphrey Milford, 1925.

———. *The Law of War and Peace.* Roslyn, N.Y.: Walter J. Black, Inc., 1949.

Hall, Brian. "Blue Helmets, Empty Guns." *New York Times Magazine,* 2 Jan. 1994, 18–25, 30, 38, 41, 43.

Halleck, Henry Wager. "Letter from Gen. Halleck to Gen. Rosecrans on the treatment of disloyal persons within our lines. Washington, Sunday, March 15, [1863]." Number LI 176 in the Francis Lieber Collection of the Huntington Library, San Marino, Calif.

Hehir, J. Bryan. "Just War Theory in a Post–Cold War World." *Journal of Religious Ethics* 20, no. 2 (Fall 1992): 237–57.

Hoffmann, Stanley. *Duties Beyond Borders.* Syracuse, N.Y.: Syracuse University Press, 1981.

Honig, Jan Willem, and Both, Norbert. *Srebrenica: Record of a War Crime.* New York: Penguin Books, 1997.

Huntington, Samuel P. "The Clash of Civilizations?" *Foreign Affairs* 72, no. 3 (Summer 1993): 22–49.

Huntington, Samuel P., et al. *The Clash of Civilizations? The Debate: A Foreign Affairs Reader.* N.Y.: Council on Foreign Relations, 1993.

John XXIII, Pope. *Pacem in Terris.* Glen Rock, N.J.: Paulist Press, 1963.

Johnson, James Turner, *Can Modern War Be Just?* New Haven, Conn., and London: Yale University Press, 1984.

————. *The Holy War Idea in Western and Islamic Traditions.* University Park, Pa.: Pennsylvania State University Press, 1997.

————. *Ideology, Reason, and the Limitation of War.* Princeton, N.J.: Princeton University Press, 1975.

————. *Just War Tradition and the Restraint of War.* Princeton, N.J., and Guildford, Surrey: Princeton University Press, 1981.

————. "Just War: The Broken Tradition," *National Interest,* no. 45 (Fall 1996): 27–36.

————. *The Quest for Peace.* Princeton, N.J., and Guildford, Surrey: Princeton University Press, 1981.

Johnson, James Turner, and Kelsay, John. *Cross, Crescent, and Sword.* New York; Westport, Conn.; and London: Greenwood Press, 1990.

Johnson, James Turner, and Weigel, George. *Just War and the Gulf War.* Washington, D.C.: Ethics and Public Policy Center, 1991.

Johnston, Douglas, and Sampson, Cynthia, eds. *Religion: The Missing Dimension in Statecraft.* New York and Oxford: Oxford University Press, 1994.

Jomini, Antoine Henri Baron de. *The Art of War.* Westport, Conn.: Greenwood Press, n.d.; repr. of original publication, Philadelphia: J. B. Lippincott & Co., 1862.

Kelsay, John. *Islam and War.* Louisville, Ky.: Westminster/John Knox Press, 1993.

Kelsay, John, and Johnson, James Turner, eds. *Just War and Jihad.* New York; Westport, Conn.; and London: Greenwood Press, 1991.

Khadduri, Majid. *The Islamic Law of Nations: Shaybani's Siyar.* Baltimore, Md.: Johns Hopkins Press, 1966.

————. *War and Peace in the Law of Islam.* Baltimore, Md., and London: Johns Hopkins Press, 1955.

Lambton, Ann K. S. *State and Government in Medieval Islam.* Oxford: Oxford University Press, 1981.

Little, David. *Sri Lanka: The Invention of Enmity.* Washington, D.C.: United States Institute of Peace Press, 1994.

————. *Ukraine: The Legacy of Intolerance.* Washington, D.C.: United States Institute of Peace Press, 1991.

Little, David; Kelsay, John; and Sachedina, Abdulaziz. *Human Rights and the Conflict of Cultures*. Columbia, S.C.: University of South Carolina Press, 1988.

McDougal, Myres S., and Feliciano, Florentino P. *Law and Minimum World Public Order*. New Haven, Conn., and London: Yale University Press, 1961.

Murray, John Courtney. *Morality and Modern War*. N.Y.: Council on Religion and International Affairs, 1959.

National Conference of Catholic Bishops. *The Challenge of Peace.* Washington, D.C.: United States Catholic Conference, 1983.

——. *The Harvest of Justice Is Sown in Peace*. Washington, D.C.: United States Catholic Conference, 1993. Also in *Origins: CNS Documentary Service* 23, no. 26 (9 Dec. 1993), 449, 451–64.

Oberdorfer, Don. "The Road to Somalia." *Washington Post National Weekly Edition,* 14–20 Dec. 1992, 6–7.

Paul VI, Pope. *Never Again War*. N.Y.: United Nations Office of Public Information, 1965.

Peters, Rudolph. *Islam and Colonialism*. The Hague: Mouton, 1979.

Piscatori, James P. *Islam in a World of Nation-States*. Cambridge: Cambridge University Press, 1986.

Porch, Douglas. *The Conquest of Morocco*. N.Y.: Alfred A. Knopf, 1983.

Ramsey, Paul. *The Just War: Force and Political Responsibility*. N.Y.: Charles Scribner's Sons, 1968.

——. "A Political Ethics Context for Strategic Thinking." In Morton A. Kaplan, ed., *Strategic Thinking and Its Moral Implications,* 101–47. Chicago: University of Chicago Press, 1973.

——. *Speak Up for Just War or Pacifism*. University Park, Pa.: Pennsylvania State University Press, 1988.

——. *War and the Christian Conscience*. Durham, N.C.: Duke University Press, 1961.

Roberts, Adam, and Guelff, Richard, eds. *Documents on the Laws of War,* 2d ed. Oxford: Clarendon Press, 1989.

Russell, Frederick H. *The Just War in the Middle Ages*. Cambridge: Cambridge University Press, 1975.

Sabrosky, Alan Ned, and Sloane, Robert L., eds. *The Recourse to War:*

An Appraisal of the "Weinberger Doctrine." Carlisle Barracks, Pa.: Strategic Studies Institute, U.S. Army War College, 1988.

Schindler, Dietrich, and Toman, Jiri, eds. *The Laws of Armed Conflicts.* Leiden: A. W. Sijthoff; Geneva: Henri Dunant Institute, 1973.

Schwarzenberger, Georg. *The Frontiers of International Law.* London: Stevens and Sons, 1962.

——. *A Manual of International Law,* 5th ed. London: Stevens and Sons, 1967.

Scott, James Brown. *The Spanish Origin of International Law,* Part I, *Francisco de Vitoria and His Law of Nations.* Oxford: Clarendon Press; London: Humphrey Milford, 1934.

Stone, Ronald H., and Wilbanks, Dana, eds. *The Peacemaking Struggle: Militarism and Resistance.* Lanham, Md.: University Press of America, 1985.

Suarez, Francisco. *Selections from Three Works of Francisco Suarez, S.J.* Oxford: Clarendon Press; London: Humphrey Milford, 1944.

The Swedish Discipline. London: John Dawson for Nathaniel Butter and Nicholas Bourne, 1632.

United Methodist Bishops. *In Defense of Creation.* Nashville, Tenn.: Graded Press, 1986.

United Nations. "Report of the Secretary-General pursuant to Paragraph 2 of Security Council Resolution 808 (1993), including the Statute of the Tribunal." U.N. doc. no. s/25704 & add. 1 (1993).

——. "Security Council Resolution 955 (1994) and Annex." U.N. doc. no. S/RES/955 (1994).

Vanderpol, Alfred. *La Doctrine scolastique du droit de guerre.* Paris: A. Pedone, 1919.

Vattel, Emmerich de. *The Law of Nations; or, Principles of the Law of Nature.* London: n.n., 1740.

Verkamp, Bernard J. "Moral Treatment of Returning Warriors in the Early Middle Ages." *Journal of Religious Ethics* 16, no. 2 (Fall 1988): 223–49.

Vitoria, Francisco de (Franciscus de Victoria). *De Indis et De Jure Belli Relectiones.* Washington, D.C.: Carnegie Institute, 1917.

Walters, LeRoy B. "Five Classic Just-War Theories." Ph.D. dissertation, Yale University, 1971.

Walzer, Michael. *Just and Unjust Wars.* N.Y.: Basic Books, 1977.

Wright, Quincy. *A Study of War.* 2 vols. Chicago: University of Chicago Press, 1942.

Wright, Robin. *Sacred Rage: The Crusade of Modern Islam.* N.Y.: Linden Press/Simon & Schuster, 1985.

Aquinas, Thomas, 41–42, 44–50, 210
Augustine, 16–17, 42, 44, 45, 47–49, 75–76, 174, 210–12

Bosnia, conflict in, 62–63, 95, 124, 135, 142–52, 192–93, 196, 198, 199

"clash of civilizations" hypothesis, 164–65, 188–89, 215–16
combatant–noncombatant distinction, 6, 120, 125, 129–30, 131–32, 152–57, 184–85, 239–40
compétence de guerre, 54, 56
contemporary warfare: characteristics of, 3–4; moral problems of, 4–7
cultural difference as cause for war, 154–56, 159–90, 215–16

discrimination, principle of, 18–19, 36–38, 126–28, 129–31, 132–33, 152. See also *jus in bello*
double effect, rule of, 130, 132–33, 140–41, 184, 241–42

end of peace, criterion of, 27

Geneva Conventions. *See* international humanitarian law; law of armed conflicts
genocide, 120, 135, 193, 198

Gratian, canonist, 45
Grotius, Hugo, 52–54

human rights, 13, 89, 92–93, 95, 100–01, 105, 128, 131, 198

international humanitarian law, 97, 100–01, 113, 197–98, 201, 205
international law, 52, 58–65, 68–69, 78–79, 96–101, 103–09, 134–35. *See also* international humanitarian law; law of armed conflicts
intervention, 2, 7, 13, 71–118; humanitarian, 89–91, 92–95, 108–09, 112
Islamic tradition and war, 168–86

jihad, 173, 180, 181, 182–86
jus ad bellum, 27–36, 41–70, 112–13, 210, 230
jus in bello, 18, 36–38, 113–14, 130, 181, 185, 205, 209, 230
just cause, criterion of, 27, 28–31, 41–43, 69, 230
just war, idea of, 18, 19–22, 123, 152, 156–57. See also *jus ad bellum; jus in bello;* just war tradition
just war tradition: thematic content of, 27–38; development of, 22–27
justice, goal of, 13, 78–81, 91, 124, 158, 191–218, 230–31

law of armed conflicts, 7, 96–99, 134–35, 152, 156–57, 197–98, 205
Lieber, Francis, 56
low-intensity conflict, 11

moral debate on war, stages in, 1–2

national interest, 19–21, 56, 66–69
NATO, 14, 17, 63–65, 67, 177
noncombatant immunity. *See* discrimination; noncombatants, protection of
noncombatants: protection of, 36–38, 125–35, 185; warfare against, 119–58, 203
nuclear weapons, moral debate over, 1–3, 10–11

pacifism, 56–57, 229
peace, goal of, 13, 49–50, 91, 158, 171, 174, 191–218. *See also* end of peace, criterion of
"presumption against war," 12, 35, 57, 231, 235
proportionality of ends, criterion of, 27
proportionality of means, principle of, 18–19, 36–38, 126–28, 130–31, 152. See also *jus in bello*

Ramsey, Paul, 21, 76–81, 88, 129–31
realism, political, 19–22, 160, 161–63, 178, 186–87
religion in relation to conflict, 159, 161, 163, 167–86, 210
right authority, criterion of, 27–28, 31–32, 41–43, 53–54, 61, 68–69, 230
right intention, criterion of, 27–28, 32–34, 41–43, 69, 81, 210–14, 230
Rwanda–Zaire, conflict in, 124, 135–42, 193, 196, 198, 199

self-determination, 104–05
sovereignty, 48, 53–54, 61, 93–95, 103–06, 236

terrorism, 3, 10

United Methodist bishops, position of, 11–12
United Nations, 13–15, 17, 58–66, 68–69, 72–73, 102, 149, 176, 198, 199
United States Catholic bishops, position of, 11–12, 91–96, 127–28, 210–11
utopianism, 15, 21, 60

Vietnam War, moral debate over, 8–10, 76–91
"vindicative justice," 48, 90

Walzer, Michael, 18–19, 21, 81–91, 131–33, 143, 146–47, 207–09
war crimes, 135, 191–218
world order, goal of, 15–16, 20, 105–06

Yugoslavia, former. *See* Bosnia